A TREASURY OF NEW TESTAMENT SYNONYMS

by Stewart Custer

Stewart Custer
I Cor. 2:13

BOB JONES UNIVERSITY PRESS, INC.
GREENVILLE, SOUTH CAROLINA 29614

A Treasury of New Testament Synonyms
by Stewart Custer

© Bob Jones University Press, Inc. 1975
Greenville, South Carolina 29614
ISBN 0-89084-025-3

All rights reserved. No part of this book may be reproduced in any form or by any means without permission in writing from the publisher.

Printed in the United States of America

This volume
is dedicated to my
wife,
whose help
and encouragement
have been
an enormous
benefit.

List of Abbreviations

The following abbreviations appear in the footnotes. With the exception of the *Oxyrhynchus Papyri,* these works are cited from either Liddell and Scott, *A Greek-English Lexicon,* or Moulton and Milligan, *The Vocabulary of the Greek Testament,* and are therefore not included in the Bibliography.

Lysias. Lysias Orator (A.D. 411). Cited in Liddell and Scott, *A Greek-English Lexicon,* p. 104.

OGIS. Orientis Graeci Inscriptiones Selectae. Ed. W. Dittenberger. 2 vols. Leipzig, 1903–05.

P. Par. Paris Papyri. Published in *Notices et Extraits,* XVIII, ii. Ed. Brunet de Presle. Paris, 1865.

P. Fay. Fayum Towns and Their Papyri. Ed. B. P. Grenfell, A. S. Hunt, and D. G. Hogarth. London, 1900.

P. Flor. Papiri Fiorentini. Ed. G. Vitelli and D. Comparetti. Milan, 1906–15.

P. Grenf. An Alexandrian Erotic Fragment, and Other Greek Papyri, Chiefly Ptolemaic. Ed. B. P. Grenfell. Oxford, 1896.

P. Hib. The Hibeh Papyri, I. Ed. B. P. Grenfell and A. S. Hunt. London, 1906.

P. Lond. Greek Papyri in the British Museum. Ed. F. G. Kenyon and H. I. Bell. 5 vols. London, 1893–1917.

P. Magd. Papyrus de Magdola. Ed. J. Lesquier. Paris, 1912.

P. Oxy. The Oxyrhynchus Papyri. Ed. B. P. Grenfell, A. S. Hunt, and H. I. Bell. 17 vols. London, 1898–1927.

P. Petr. The Flinders Petrie Papyri. Published in the Proceedings of the Royal Irish Academy. Ed. J. P. Mahaffy and J. G. Smyly. Dublin, 1891–94.

Priene. Die Inschriften von Priene. Ed. H. von Gaertringen. Berlin, 1906.

P. Ryl. Catalogue of the Greek Papyri in the John Rylands Library, Manchester. Ed. A. S. Hunt, J. de M. Johnson, and V. Martin. 2 vols. Manchester, 1911–15.

P. Tebt. The Tebtunis Papyri. Ed. B. P. Grenfell, A. S. Hunt, J. G. Smyly, and E. J. Goodspeed. 2 vols. London, 1902–07.

Syll. Sylloge Inscriptionum Graecarum. Ed. W. Dittenberger. 3 vols. Leipzig, 1915–24.

Preface

The pastor or Bible teacher who seriously tries to present the teaching of the New Testament is often confronted by words that are confusingly similar in meaning. Sometimes the theological meaning of a passage will be influenced by the connotation of these words. In every case the conservative doctrine of inspiration implies that a specific word was used for a specific purpose and should not be interchanged with a similar word that may have a different connotation.

There has been no major work in English on New Testament synonyms since Archbishop Trench's *Synonyms of the New Testament* in 1854 (the ninth edition of 1880 is the one which has received worldwide dissemination). The popular bibliographic studies will often say that Trench's work on synonyms "is antiquated" (Danker, *Multipurpose Tools for Bible Study*, p. 130) or "needs to be supplemented by modern work" (Union Theological Seminary, "Essential Books for a Pastor's Study," p. 31). Vast amounts of papyri and other sources have been discovered since then, and many improved lexicons have also appeared. Trench himself listed many groups of synonyms in his introduction that he could not treat and strongly urged others to continue the study (a number of which have been treated in the present work). Although Trench was influential in starting the Oxford *New English Dictionary* and in promoting the revised translation of the New Testament, it is strange that no one has heeded his plea for continuing his investigation of synonyms.

We have never had in English the equivalent of the classic German work by Schmidt, *Synonymik der Griechischen Sprache,* in four volumes, 1876, 1878, 1879, 1886. Thayer in his *Greek-English Lexicon,* 1886, does make a systematic attempt to differentiate synonyms in the separate vocabulary entries. There is also a small supplement in Berry's *Greek-English Lexicon,* 1897, pages 117–137, that briefly discusses a few synonyms. In a more popular vein, Wuest has a few studies that deal with this topic: *Studies in the Vocabulary of the Greek New Testament,* 1945, and *The Practical Use of the Greek New Testament,* 1946, pp. 72–83.

The standard sets of word studies by M. R. Vincent, 1887, and A. T. Robertson, 1930, sometimes provide good material. Some help may be found in Barclay, *New Testament Wordbook,* 1956, and *More New Testa-*

ment Words, 1958, and in Leete, *New Testament Windows,* 1939. In addition there are some very valuable studies in synonyms and related words in the major commentaries: Westcott, *Epistle to the Hebrews,* 1889, pp. 230–233; Hort, *First Epistle of St. Peter I:1–II:17,* 1898, pp. 154–156; Milligan, *St. Paul's Epistles to the Thessalonians,* 1908, pp. 145–151, and numerous others. The modern lexicons by Moulton and Milligan and by Arndt and Gingrich are powerful tools in any study of this nature.

It is obvious, however, that a fresh study of synonyms is long overdue. The present study has utilized the new sources of material in order to determine the limits within which certain synonyms are equivalent and outside of which they are not. It has largely avoided the words included in Trench, for in most cases his work is adequate, even though it needs revision. It has been necessary, however, to rework some of his groups of synonyms *(I anoint, time)* which have received considerable attention in recent years.

For the benefit of the student who is new to such Greek studies, each group of words begins with the lexical definitions of the words found in Arndt and Gingrich, amplified when necessary by distinctions given in Liddell and Scott and in Thayer. Not all possible meanings are given, but only those which contribute to the comparison of words in that group. These words are then traced through classical Greek, the papyri, the Septuagint, the New Testament, and occasionally the writings of the apostolic fathers and later theological writers. The meanings these synonyms can convey are illustrated from as many of these sources as possible. In addition to the lexicons mentioned, such works as Moulton and Milligan's *Vocabulary of the Greek New Testament,* Kittel's *Theological Dictionary,* and Cremer's *Biblico-Theological Lexicon* have been freely consulted. For this reason the meanings given in the summary at the end of each group should not be considered arbitrary; they appear in the standard reference works, and in the body of the following word studies they are illustrated again and again. Sometimes the survey of the literature using a word within a group of synonyms has led to conclusions concerning their connotations not found in any lexicon. Such conclusions the reader is encouraged to verify for himself.

The reader's convenience has been regarded throughout. A concise synonymy appears at the end of the discussion of each group of words. The examples cited from the literary sources include enough English translation to enable the student to grasp the sense of the passage, along with only enough Greek for unpedantic illustration. An Index of Greek Words will speed the locating of particular words included in the discussions of synonyms. Abbreviations of works frequently cited in the footnotes appear in

PREFACE

the List of Abbreviations. Full bibliographical information for cited works not included in the List of Abbreviations may be found in the Bibliography. (The standard Greek lexicons are referred to by the authors' last names only.)

Special thanks is due to Dr. Marshall Neal, Dr. Daniel Krusich, and Dr. Charles Smith for their many valuable criticisms and suggestions. Equally helpful were the recommendations of Dr. Ronald Horton concerning difficult English phraseology and logical consistency. Miss Margaret Bald, head librarian of Bob Jones University, and Dr. Robert Cinnamond Tucker, head librarian of Furman University, were especially kind in supplying the large number of technical books necessary for this work.

Contents

xiii Introduction

Substantives

1	BURDEN	βάρος, φορτίον, ὄγκος
5	DEVIL	διάβολος, δαίμων, δαιμόνιον
9	GLORY	δόξα, ἔπαινος, τιμή
14	GOOD	ἀγαθός, καλός
20	GUARDIAN	ἐπίτροπος, οἰκονόμος
24	POSSESSIONS	κτήματα, ὑπάρξεις
27	POWER	βία, δύναμις, κράτος, ἰσχύς, ἐξουσία, ἐνέργεια
34	RAIN	ὑετός, βροχή, ὄμβρος
37	REMEMBRANCE	ἀνάμνησις, ὑπόμνησις
40	REST	ἀνάπαυσις, κατάπαυσις
43	RIGHTEOUSNESS	δικαίωμα, δικαίωσις, δικαιοσύνη
49	RIVER	ποταμός, χείμαρρος
52	SON OF GOD	υἱὸς θεοῦ, παῖς θεοῦ
56	SOUL	καρδία, νοῦς, πνεῦμα, ψυχή
62	STRANGER	ξένος, πάροικος, παρεπίδημος
66	STRIFE	ἔρις, ἐριθεία
69	SWORD	μάχαιρα, ῥομφαία
72	TRICKERY	κυβεία, μεθοδεία, πανουργία
75	WELL	φρέαρ, πηγή
78	WORD	λόγος, ῥῆμα

Verbs

83	I ANOINT	ἀλείφω, χρίω
86	I ANSWER	ἀποκρίνομαι, ὑπολαμβάνω
89	I COMPLETE	καταρτίζω, τελειόω
93	I DECEIVE	ἀπατάω, παραλογίζομαι, πλανάω
97	I ESTABLISH	βεβαιόω, θεμελιόω, ῥιζόομαι, στηρίζω
102	I FILL	πληρόω, πίμπλημι
106	I KNOW	γινώσκω, οἶδα, ἐπίσταμαι
113	I SEND	πέμπω, ἀποστέλλω
117	I STRUGGLE	ἀγωνίζομαι, κοπιάω
121	I TEACH	διδάσκω, νουθετέω, σωφρονίζω
124	I THINK ABOUT	φροντίζω, μεριμνάω

A TREASURY OF NEW TESTAMENT SYNONYMS

127   I WATCH τηρέω, φυλάσσω, φρουρέω, γρηγορέω, ἀγρυπνέω, νήφω

135   Bibliography

142   Index of Greek Words

Introduction

The Greek language, being one of the most precise in the world, lent itself easily to fine distinctions between words. In ancient Greece the philosophers loved to differentiate between close synonyms. The revelation communicated in the New Testament, however, raised the study of synonyms to the highest importance, for the doctrinal content of the New Testament is not the word of man but the Word of the Living God. Since the meaning of some of these synonyms is basic to both New Testament exegesis and New Testament theology, no interpretation in either field dare ignore the shades of meaning in important words. It is crucial to determine as carefully as possible the exact meaning of words which might be confused but should be distinguished.

I. CHARACTERISTICS OF SYNONYMS

A synonym is, of course, one of two or more words with similar meaning. The word comes from the Greek συνώνυμος, which means "having the same name" and, hence, "definition." It is very rare to find words perfectly identical in meaning, but it is common to find words which are close enough in meaning so as to be confusing in certain contexts. Although some words are interchangeable in most contexts, there is almost always a difference in connotation. The words *house* and *home,* for example, are synonyms but differ in connotation; *mansion, cottage,* and *duplex,* though mutually exclusive, may each be used as equivalent to *house* or *home* in some contexts. Two synonyms may have a wide area in which they can be used interchangeably and one area in which they cannot (ξένος, πάροικος). Sometimes one word will have a very wide latitude of meaning and the other will be more limited (λόγος, ῥῆμα). The reason may be that one word is a general term and the other is a specific term (ποταμός, χείμαρρος). On the other hand, two synonyms may have one area in which they are interchangeable and a wider area in which they are not (υἱὸς θεοῦ, παῖς θεοῦ). There may be a slight distinction between two words which is always observed (ἀνάμνησις, ὑπόμνησις). At times the types of grammatical endings will provide distinctions (δικαίωμα, δικαίωσις, δικαιοσύνη).

An outstanding characteristic of all language is the change that it undergoes over the centuries, and Greek is no exception. Although many synonyms did preserve their early meaning for many centuries in the *Koine* period, it remains true that two synonyms may be distinguished in one period of time and not in other periods. An obvious example is the difference between the strict distinctions observed in classical usage and the much looser use of the same words in *Koine* Greek (κτήματα, ὑπάρξεις). In some instances the New Testament revelation modified the meaning of a whole group of synonyms; for example after the New Testament teaching on "righteousness" and "justification," the words on the δίκαιος stem could never be the same.

One fact that complicates the study of synonyms is that the same word may have many different meanings (λόγος). It is also a common axiom that different authors use words in characteristically different senses. Thus the context must finally govern the meaning of a word in any single passage. Only by examining many different authors from various periods can the investigator perceive the true meaning of a word. Of course, some words are used in a vague sense, and hence scholars may well debate their real meaning.

II. THEOLOGICAL INTERPRETATIONS OF SYNONYMS

The widest possible reading is not too great a preparation for this kind of word study. Archbishop Trench's vast reading led him to write concerning one pair of words, "ἀλείφειν is the mundane and profane, χρίειν the sacred and religious, word." (*Synonyms,* pp. 136–37). Further investigation, however, proved that such a distinction was not absolute (Moulton and Milligan, p. 21). Even though great care is exercised in the treatment of words, later discoveries may modify our understanding of the meaning they bear.

Certain synonyms are veritable battlegrounds for important theological interpretations. A classic example of this is the continuing debate on the words for "time." When Trench treated these words, he said, "Χρόνος is time, contemplated simply as such . . . . Καιρός . . . is time as it brings forth its several births, . . . the critical epoch-making periods fore-ordained of God" (*Synonyms,* pp. 210–11). John Marsh amplified this by saying, "It is interesting that the Old Testament has no means for expressing abstractly the distinction between chronological and realistic time. . . . The New Testament can reproduce our modern distinction. 'Chronos' is its word for chronological time, and the word 'kairos,' which has been given a new currency by the writings of Professor Tillich, stands for realistic time" (*The Fulness of Time,* p. 20). By "realistic time" he means time identified by its content, such as the "time" of the advent of Christ.

INTRODUCTION

James Barr, however, flatly contradicts Marsh's distinctions by citing Mark 1:15 and Galatians 4:4 to show that such distinctions were not, in fact, observed in the New Testament (*Biblical Words for Time,* pp. 22ff).

Oscar Cullmann, discussing καιρός, said, "The characteristic thing about *kairos* is that it has to do with a definite *point of time* which has a fixed content. . . . The relation of the redemptive history to general history finds its confirmation in this central New Testament time concept of the *kairos*" (*Christ and Time,* pp. 39ff). Barr contradicts Cullmann as well and warns of the dangers of vague terminology such as the "*kairos* concept" and also warns against the practice of transliterating a word without the discipline of translating the proper meaning for the context (pp. 51ff). It is true that when one speaks of a "*kairos* concept," it does imply that there is only one meaning to that term. If καιρός really has only one meaning, well and good, but it is Barr's contention that it does not (p. 38; see Mark 10:30 and Eph. 2:12 in which the proper translation for καιρός is simple "time"). The importance of the study of these synonyms for the theological interpretation of these words is obvious.

In his conclusion Barr gives some very wholesome warnings against the common practice of drawing up a list of synonyms and then claiming that such a list constitutes the "Biblical teaching" on a certain doctrine (pp. 155ff). This practice is misleading because the Biblical teaching on a doctrine is the actual propositional statements in the Bible on that doctrine, not just a list of vocabulary words. These words, of course, influence the theologian's understanding of the Biblical statements, but they are not in themselves the "Biblical doctrine."

Several other groups of synonyms should receive the same attention and sifting which the words for "time" have received. In particular, the words for "righteousness" and "soul" obviously deserve much more careful study then they have yet received. But many of the "common" words such as "I know," "I teach," or "I establish" will also advance our understanding of the Word of God if scholars will only subject them to diligent investigation and discussion. It is the author's hope that the present word studies will provide an impetus toward a thorough investigation of many of these groups of synonyms by other students of the Word.

III. PRINCIPLES OF SYNONYMITY

Context. The final determinant in the meaning of a word is its context. The investigator's preconceived ideas on the meaning of a word must be set aside in favor of a candid appraisal of its use in the context. Unless the context is given its full weight in each occurrence of the word, no conclusions will be valid.

A TREASURY OF NEW TESTAMENT SYNONYMS

Breadth of study. In a sense the requisite breadth includes the whole of Greek literature. To arrive at valid conclusions it is necessary to trace the words throughout Classical and *Koine* Greek. The greater the area overlooked, the greater the possibility of error in meaning.

Source in classical Greek. No investigator can afford to overlook the fountainhead of meaning in the early uses of the words, any more than he can afford to ignore the etymology of the words. Sometimes the classical meaning stays with a word throughout its history; certainly it is vital toward understanding the derived meanings of a word.

Distinctive Biblical use. The investigator must not assume that the classical meaning is automatically the Biblical meaning, but he must carefully survey the Biblical usage to see if the Biblical revelation has modified the meaning of the words. The Biblical meaning must not be cut off from the classical—or, for that matter, from the wider extra-Biblical—usage, but neither must it be considered as cast in the same iron-clad mold.

Accurate translation. Vague terminology or transliteration is no substitute for the discipline of a precise translation that fits the context and brings out the full meaning of the word. If such a translation cannot be fully attained, at least it should always be the goal.

This work is now sent forth with the prayer that the Holy Spirit of God will use it to stir up others to dedicated and reverent study of the meaning of His holy Word.

Substantives

1. Burden: βάρος, φορτίον, ὄγκος

The term βάρος means *burden* or *weight;* φορτίον *load, burden, pack,* or *cargo,* ὄγκος *encumbrance, bulk,* or even *trouble.*

βάρος

In classical Greek βάρος is commonly used in the sense of a "weight" (Herodotus 2.73). When the messenger in Sophocles' *Antigone* sees the silent grief of Eurydice, he says, "Where there is too great silence, there is a heavy *weight.*" που σιγῆς βάρος (line 1256). The silence was an ominous and dangerous "weight" which foreshadowed her suicide. Philo used the word in a literal sense: "But human affairs swing as on a scale with unequal *weights.*" τὰ δ' ἀνθρώπεια ὡς ἐπὶ ζυγοῦ ταλαντεύεται βάρεσιν ἀνίσοις (*On Joseph* 140).

In the Septuagint the Children of Israel expressed their fear of the Babylonian army by saying, "Neither the high mountains, nor the valleys, nor the hills, shall be able to bear their *weight.*" ὑποστήσονται τὸ βάρος αὐτῶν (Judith 7:4). The son of Sirach exhorted, "Take not up a *burden* above thy strength." βάρος ὑπὲρ σὲ μὴ ἄρῃς (Ecclesiasticus 13:2). In II Maccabees Antiochus was afflicted with a disease which "no one was able to bear because of the intolerable *burden* of the stench." διὰ τὸ τῆς ὀσμῆς ἀφόρητον βάρος (9:10).

One papyrus exhibits a tactful use of this word, ". . . but if this is carrying a *burden* [burdensome] to thee . . . ." εἰ δὲ τοῦτό σοι βάρος φέρει (*P. Oxy., VII,* 1062.14). In the *Epistle to Diognetus* (second century A.D.) the reflection of New Testament phraseology is evident. "But whoever takes up the *burden* of his neighbor . . . ." τὸ τοῦ πλησίον ἀναδέχεται βάρος (10.6). Most of these references connote a "burden" or "weight" which is too great to bear. This connotation is not necessary to the meaning of the word, but it is often found.

In the New Testament the earlier meanings may also be found. The laborers reproached the householder for paying all his workers the same wage, regardless of the time they had worked, saying, ". . . having made them equal to us, who have borne the *burden* of the day and the heat" (Matt. 20:12). βαστάσασι τὸ βάρος τῆς ἡμέρας. They implied that the "burden" of laboring all day was almost too much to bear, and hence they deserved a bonus. When the Jerusalem Council drew up its decisions in a letter, the letter read, "It seemed good . . . to lay upon you no greater *burden* than these necessary things" (Acts 15:28). μηδὲν πλέον ἐπιτίθεσθαι ὑμῖν βάρος. Doubtless they were thinking of the "yoke" which neither they nor their fathers had been able to bear (Acts 15:10).

When Paul wrote to the Thessalonians, he reminded them that he had not sought glory from men "when we were able to be in a *burden* [burdensome] as apostles of Christ" (I Thess. 2:6–7). δυνάμενοι ἐν βάρει εἶναι. Paul encouraged the Corinthians to endure their trials with hope, saying, "For our light affliction, which is temporary, is working for us a superabounding, eternal *weight* of glory" (II Cor. 4:17). καθ' ὑπερβολὴν εἰς ὑπερβολὴν αἰώνιον βάρος δόξης. The believer has such a staggering weight of glory laid up in the world to come that he could not bear it now. Finally, Paul exhorted the Galatians to be considerate of one another and urged them, "Bear ye one another's *burdens*" (Gal. 6:2). Ἀλλήλων τὰ βάρη βαστάζετε. The idea is to help a brother with a burden which is too great for him to bear. In the same context (Gal. 6:5) is another of these words, φορτίον, in a contrasting statement which is discussed in the next section.

φορτίον

The word φορτίον may also mean a "burden," but this term means a burden which is customary and suitable for a person or thing. Thus Xenophon used this word to refer to a soldier's pack: "And he was bearing a *pack.*" καὶ φορτίον ἔφερε (*Memorabilia* 3.13.6). Xenophon even used this word to refer to a woman's carrying a child in the womb. "But the woman, having received, bears this *burden.*" φέρει τὸ φορτίον τοῦτο (*Memorabilia* 2.25). In the plural it often has the meaning "wares" or "merchandise." Herodotus wrote of those who were "loading their vessels with the *wares* of Egypt and Assyria." ἀπαγινέοντας δὲ φορτία Αἰγύπτια (1.1).

In the Septuagint this word again means a burden which is fitting and expected to be borne. The son of Sirach mentioned the things which are naturally connected with an ass: "Fodder, a stick, and *burdens,* for an ass." Χορτάσματα καὶ ῥάβδος καὶ φορτία ὄνῳ (Ecclesiasticus 33:25; KJ 33:24). In Isaiah, idols which are carried by beasts of burden "are made a load, as a *burden* to the weary beast" (46:1). ὡς φορτίον κοπιῶντι. This is not, however, an invariable connotation, because the Psalmist referred to his iniquities by saying, "As a heavy *burden* they are too heavy for me" (Ps. 37:5; KJ Ps. 38:4). ὡσεὶ φορτίον βαρὺ ἐβαρύνθησαν ἐπ' ἐμέ. In this case the cognate words of the βάρος root have influenced the meaning.

BURDEN

After our Lord had upbraided certain cities for failing to repent, He gave His famous invitation, saying, "Take my yoke upon you . . . for my yoke is easy, and my *burden* is light" (Matt. 11:29–30). τὸ φορτίον μου ἐλαφρόν ἐστιν. The "burden" of Christ is a load which He expects men to bear. On another occasion Christ denounced the scribes and the Pharisees as those who "bind heavy *burdens* and lay them on men's shoulders" (Matt. 23:4). δεσμεύουσιν δὲ φορτία βαρέα. Here again the word from the βάρος root has made these ceremonial regulations a burden too great to be borne.

When Paul was being taken to Rome for trial, he warned those who were sailing with him of the coming dangers. "Men, I perceive that the voyage is about to be with injury and much loss, not only of the *cargo* and the ship, but also of our lives" (Acts 27:10). οὐ μόνον τοῦ φορτίου καὶ τοῦ πλοίου. This sense of "cargo" is also found in the papyri, one of which listed payment by Heraclas the boatman of 600 drachmae "for his *cargo*." ὑπὲρ τῶν φορτίων αὐτοῦ (*P. Oxy.*, VIII, 1153.9). The "cargo" means the load which the ship was designed to carry. Perhaps this sheds light on Paul's admonition to the Galatians: "For each one shall bear his own *load*"(Gal. 6:5). τὸ ἴδιον φορτίον βαστάσει. There are to be no shirkers among the Christian believers; every man should carry his own fitting load. In the same context Paul has exhorted, "Bear ye one another's *burdens*"(Gal. 6:2). Here the word βάρη refers to burdens which are too great to be borne. J. B. Lightfoot explains, "βάρη . . . suggests the idea of an adventitious and oppressive burden, which is not necessarily implied in the former φορτίον; so that βάρη points to a load of which a man may fairly rid himself when occasion serves, φορτίον to a load which he is expected to bear" (*St. Paul's Epistle to the Galatians,* p. 217). Such a distinction is clearly justified in the light of the literature which has been surveyed.

ὄγκος

This word occurs only once in the New Testament (Heb. 12:1) and not at all in the Septuagint. Sophocles' *Oedipus at Colonus* has the line "I'll waste no time or *trouble* whipping him." βραχεῖ σὺν ὄγκῳ καὶ χρόνῳ (line 1341). This metaphorical sense of "trouble" is rare; much more common is the literal meaning "bulk." Menander writes, "I never envied an expensive corpse; it comes to the same *bulk* [i.e. a handful of ashes] as a very cheap one." οὐπώποτ᾽ ἐζήλωσα πολυτελῆ νεκρόν· εἰς τὸν ἴσον ὄγκον τῷ σφόδρ᾽ ἔρχετ᾽ εὐτελεῖ (Fragments, p. 113, No. 394).

The writer to the Hebrews exhorted his readers, ". . . having laid aside every *encumbrance* and the easily besetting sin, let us be running with patience the race that is set before us" (Heb. 12:1). ὄγκος ἀποθέμενοι πάντα. Thus the ὄγκος is any "encumbrance" or "bulk" which would slow down a runner. B. F. Westcott explains, "The writer seems to have in mind the manifold encumbrances of society and business which would be likely to hinder a Christian convert. The duty of the convert would be to free himself from associations and engagements which, however innocent in themselves, hindered the freedom of his action" (*The Epistle to the Hebrews,* p. 393).

SUMMARY

The term βάρος refers to a heavy burden or weight, often with the implication that it is too heavy to be borne. On the other hand, φορτίον is a burden or load which is suitable for the person or thing and which may rightfully be expected to be borne. The ὄγκος is an encumbrance which may be no heavier than a garment, but which would slow down a runner.

2. Devil: διάβολος, δαίμων, δαιμόνιον

The noun διάβολος, *slanderer,* in classical Greek was an adjective, slanderous; in the New Testament, however, ὁ διάβολος is usually the devil or Satan. The term δαίμων, the old word for *deity,* came to mean *demon* or *evil spirit.* In the same way δαιμόνιον originally referred to a "divinity" but later came to mean *demon* or *evil spirit.*

διάβολος

From the same stem is διαβολή, the regular word for "slander." In Thucydides is the statement, "And in fact there was something of the kind afoot on the part of the ones who were having this accusation, and what he said was not altogether mere *slander."* ἦν δέ τι καὶ τοιοῦτον ἀπὸ τῶν τὴν κατηγορίαν ἐχόντων, καὶ οὐ πάνυ διαβολὴ μόνον τοῦ λόγου (8.91.3). Menander referred to a *"slanderous* old woman." διάβολος γραῦς (485, cited by Liddell and Scott, p. 343). In the papyri one writer made the statement, "If you learn that Aretius is going *to accuse* you about the copper, ..." ἐὰν οὖν μάθῃς ὅτι μέλλει διαβαλεῖν σε Ἀρητίων περὶ τῶν χαλκείνων (*P. Oxy.,* VI, 1158.22).

In the Septuagint, Queen Esther called the wicked Haman "the adversary." She described the plot against the Jews to King Ahasuerus, "For we are sold, both I and my people, unto destruction and plunder and slavery—we and our children to be bondmen and bondwomen I even overheard; for the *adversary* is not worthy of the court of the king" (Esth. 7:4). ἡμεῖς καὶ τὰ τέκνα ἡμῶν εἰς παῖδας καὶ παιδίσκας καὶ παράκουσα· οὐ γὰρ ἄξιος ὁ διάβολος τῆς αὐλῆς τοῦ βασιλέως. In some passages this word takes on the force of a proper name. The book of Job described one occasion in this manner: "And as it came to pass the same day, that behold! the angels of God came to present themselves before the Lord, the *devil* also came with them" (1:6). καὶ ἰδοὺ ἦλθον οἱ ἄγγελοι τοῦ θεοῦ παραστῆναι ἐνώπιον τοῦ κυρίου, καὶ ὁ διάβολος ἦλθεν μετ' αὐτῶν. Throughout chapters one and two of Job the Hebrew text reads "Satan," whereas the Septuagint has "the devil." The same substitution is found in the book of Chronicles as well: "And an *adversary* [Hebrew "Satan"] stood up in Israel and moved David to number Israel" (I Chron. 21:1). καὶ ἔστη διάβολος ἐν τῷ Ισραηλ καὶ ἐπέσεισεν τὸν Δαυιδ τὸν ἀριθμῆσαι τὸν

Ἰσραηλ. In Zechariah, Satan appears in the role of "the accuser" in a judicial scene. "And he showed me Joshua [Jesus] the high priest standing before the presence of the angel of the Lord, and the *devil* stood at his right hand to oppose him" (3:1). καὶ ὁ διάβολος εἱστήκει ἐκ δεξιῶν αὐτοῦ τοῦ ἀντικεῖσθαι αὐτῷ.

When the Synoptic Gospels relate the temptation of the Lord Jesus, they use the terms "Satan" and "the devil" interchangeably. As Matthew described it, "Then Jesus was led up into the desert by the Spirit to be tempted by the *devil*" (4:1). Τότε ὁ Ἰησοῦς ἀνήχθη εἰς τὴν ἔρημον ὑπὸ τοῦ πνεύματος πειρασθῆναι ὑπὸ τοῦ διαβόλου. Mark in this same context used "Satan" (1:13). On one occasion the Lord Jesus challenged the Jews by saying, "Ye are of your father, the *devil*, and the lusts of your father ye wish to be doing. He was a murderer from the beginning and did not stand in the truth, because there is no truth in him. Whenever he speaks the lie, he speaks of his own, because he is a liar and the father of it" (John 8:44). ὑμεῖς ἐκ τοῦ πατρὸς τοῦ διαβόλου ἐστὲ καὶ τὰς ἐπιθυμίας τοῦ πατρὸς ὑμῶν θέλετε ποιεῖν. James admonished his readers, "But resist the *devil*, and he will flee from you" (James 4:7). ἀντίστητε δὲ τῷ διαβόλῳ, καὶ φεύξεται ἀφ' ὑμῶν. In Revelation John described the casting down of the devil: "And the great dragon was cast down, the old serpent, the one who is called the *devil* and Satan, the one who deceives the whole world" (12:9). καὶ ἐβλήθη ὁ δράκων ὁ μέγας, ὁ ὄφις ὁ ἀρχαῖος, ὁ καλούμενος Διάβολος καὶ ὁ Σατανᾶς. The New Testament also uses this word in its basic sense of "slanderer." When Paul admonished Timothy concerning order in the church, he said, "Women likewise must be grave, not *slanderers*, temperate, faithful in all things" (I Tim. 3:11). γυναῖκας ὡσαύτως σεμνάς, μὴ διαβόλους. The same expression is found in Titus 2:3.

δαίμων

In classical Greek this word is sometimes used interchangeably with θεοί, "gods." Homer had Odysseus say, speaking of the storm deity, "But now the *deity* cast me down here upon this shore—with more evil yet to suffer, I must believe, before the *gods* relent." νῦν δ' ἐνθάδε κάββαλε δαίμων, ὄφρα τί που καὶ τῇδε πάθω κακόν· οὐ γὰρ ὀίω παύσεσθ', ἀλλ' ἔτι πολλὰ θεοὶ τελέουσι πάροιθεν (*Odyssey* 6.172–74). It is also used by Aeschylus to refer to the "evil genius" of the household of the Atreidae. Clytaemnestra said, "But I am willing, therefore, to make a sworn compact with the *Fiend* of the house of Pleisthenes that I will be content with what is done, hard to endure though it be." ἐγὼ δ' οὖν ἐθέλω δαίμονι τῷ Πλεισθενιδῶν ὅρκους (*Agamemnon* 1569). In the papyri the emperor Nero is described as "the good *genius* of the world." ἀγαθὸς δαίμων δὲ τῆς οἰκουμένης (*P. Oxy.*, VII, 1021.9).

DEVIL

This word occurs only once in the Septuagint. The prophet Isaiah warned the wicked with the words of the Lord, "But ye who have forsaken me and who forget my holy mountain, and who prepare a table for a *demon*, and who fill up mingled wine for Chance, I will give you unto the sword" (Isa. 65:11). ὑμεῖς δὲ οἱ ἐγκαταλιπόντες με καὶ ἐπιλανθανόμενοι τὸ ὄρος τὸ ἅγιόν μου καὶ ἑτοιμάζοντες τῷ δαίμονι τράπεζαν καὶ πληροῦντες τῇ τύχῃ κέρασμα.

The New Testament also uses this word only one time. When the Lord Jesus was casting out demons, Matthew's account states, "But the *demons* were beseeching him saying: If thou cast us out, send us into the herd of pigs" (8:31). οἱ δὲ δαίμονες παρεκάλουν αὐτὸν λέγοντες· εἰ ἐκβάλλεις ἡμᾶς, ἀπόστειλον ἡμᾶς εἰς τὴν ἀγέλην τῶν χοίρων. Thus the New Testament largely avoids this term, which has confusing pagan connotations, in favor of δαιμόνιον, our next word.

δαιμόνιον

Originally this word did have the sense of "divinity," as it does in Herodotus. On one occasion he wrote, "The Athenians too acknowledge that it was only one man of them who came safely back to Attica; but the Argives say that it was they, and the Athenians that it was the *divinity,* that destroyed the Attic army when this one man was saved alive." πλὴν Ἀργεῖοι μέν λέγουσι αὐτῶν τὸ Ἀττικὸν στρατόπεδον διαφθειράντων τὸν ἕνα τοῦτον περιγενέσθαι, Ἀθηναῖοι δὲ τοῦ δαιμονίου (5.87). However, this term early gained the sense of "demon," a lesser spirit which can communicate with men. When Xenophon mentioned the charge which was brought against Socrates, that he had rejected the gods acknowledged by the state, he said in defense that Socrates had offered sacrifices continually and had made use of divination, "For it had been commonly reported that as Socrates would say, his own *demon* guided him; it was out of this claim, it seems to me, that the charge of bringing in strange *divinities* arose." διετεθρύλητο γάρ, ὡς φαίη Σωκράτης τὸ δαιμόνιον ἑαυτῷ σημαίνειν· ὅθεν δὴ καὶ μάλιστά μοι δοκοῦσιν αὐτὸν αἰτιάσασθαι καινὰ δαιμόνια εἰσφέρειν (*Memorabilia* 1.1.2). The writer of one of the magical papyri warned, "Listen to me and turn away from this *demon*." εἰσάκουσόν μου καὶ ἀπόστρεψον τὸ δαιμόνιον τοῦτο (*P. Lond.,* 46.120). This meaning is not surprising, for the writer is acquainted with Judaism and perhaps Christianity.

In the Septuagint this word is not common, but it is clearly used concerning demons. In the Song of Moses, Moses related the sinfulness of the Israelites. One of his charges is, "They sacrificed to *demons* and not to God—to gods which they had not known" (Deut. 32:17). ἔθυσαν δαιμονίοις καὶ οὐ θεῷ, θεοῖς, οἷς οὐκ ᾔδεισαν. The psalmist gave assurance to

God's people that they need not fear "the thing which walks in darkness; nor of mischance and the *demon* of noonday" (Ps. 90:6; KJ Ps. 91:6). ἀπὸ πράγματος διαπορευομένου ἐν σκότει, ἀπὸ συμπτώματος καὶ δαιμονίου μεσημβρινοῦ. Isaiah prophesied of the destruction of Babylon, "And there the wild beasts shall make their abode, and their houses shall be filled with noise, and there the sirens shall make their abode, and there *demons* shall dance" (13:21). καὶ ἀναπαύσονται ἐκεῖ σειρῆνες, καὶ δαιμόνια ἐκεῖ ὀρχήσονται. There is an indication of a rite of exorcism in Tobit. When Tobit asked why he had to take along the heart, liver, and gall of the fish, the angel told him, "If a *demon* or evil spirit should trouble anyone, it is necessary to make a smoke with these things before the man or woman, and he will no longer be troubled at all." ἐάν τινα ὀχλῇ δαιμόνιον ἢ πνεῦμα πονηρόν, ταῦτα δεῖ καπνίσαι ἐνώπιον ἀνθρώπου ἢ γυναικός (6:7).

On numerous occasions the Lord Jesus is portrayed as casting out demons. "And he cast out many *demons,* and he was not permitting the *demons* to speak because they knew him" (Mark 1:34). καὶ δαιμόνια πολλὰ ἐξέβαλεν, καὶ οὐκ ἤφιεν λαλεῖν τὰ δαιμόνια, ὅτι ᾔδεισαν αὐτόν. When the Apostle Paul was testifying at Athens, the philosophers said, "He seems to be a preacher of strange *divinities*" (Acts 17:18). ξένων δαιμονίων δοκεῖ καταγγελεὺς εἶναι. Paul warned the Corinthians about the things which the Gentiles offered to idols: "But the things which they are sacrificing, they are sacrificing to *demons* and not to God" (I Cor. 10:20). ἀλλ᾽ ὅτι ἃ θύουσιν, δαιμονίοις καὶ οὐ θεῷ θύουσιν. Paul also gave warnings concerning the latter days: "But the Spirit says expressly that in latter times some shall depart from the faith, giving heed to deceiving spirits and teachings of *demons*" (I Tim. 4:1). προσέχοντες πνεύμασιν πλάνοις καὶ διδασκαλίαις δαιμονίων. In the book of Revelation the people who were not killed by the plagues still did not repent of their sins "that they should not worship *demons* and images" (9:20). ἵνα μὴ προσκυνήσουσιν τὰ δαιμόνια καὶ τὰ εἴδωλα.

SUMMARY

The word διάβολος refers to a "slanderer" or the "devil"; the word δαίμων means "deity" or "spirit" in the sense of "genius"; and the word δαιμόνιον has the meaning "divinity," "demon," or "evil spirit." The last two words could be used interchangeably in the New Testament for "demon," but they are never exchanged with διάβολος, which is the "devil," the ruler of the demons.

3. Glory: δόξα, ἔπαινος, τιμή

Originally *opinion*, δόξα later acquired the senses of *reputation, glory, brightness,* or *radiance;* ἔπαινος means *approval, recognition, praise.* τιμή, which may mean either *price* or *honor*, conveys a strong sense of *value*.

δόξα

Since this noun comes from the verb δοκέω which means "I think," it is only natural that it should mean "opinion." In one of his dialogues Plato related a question by Socrates: "But how, Protarchus, can there be true and false fears, or true and false expectations, or true and false *opinions?*" ἢ δόξαι ἀληθεῖς ἢ ψευδεῖς; (*Philebus* 36C). Archidamus exhorted his men, "It is but right, therefore, that we should show ourselves to be neither worse men than our fathers nor lacking in our own *reputation.*" μήτε τῶν πατέρων χείρους φαίνεσθαι μήτε ἡμῶν αὐτῶν τῆς δόξης ἐνδεεστέρους (Thucydides 2.11.2). In Aeschylus' *Eumenides* the chorus of furies express a similar thought: "And the *glories* [reputations] of men that vaunt themselves under the heavens waste away and are diminished into the ground at our black-robed assault." δόξαι τ᾽ ἀνδρῶν καὶ μάλ᾽ ὑπ᾽ αἰθέρι σεμναὶ τακόμεναι (line 368). In one of the papyri the writer hailed an official as the *"glory* of a city." δόξα πόλεως (*P. Oxy.,* I, 41.4).

In the Septuagint Jacob is portrayed as hearing the sons of Laban complain: "Jacob has taken all the things which were our father's, and out of the things which were our father's he has acquired all this *glory"* (Gen. 31:1). καὶ ἐκ τῶν τοῦ πατρὸς ἡμῶν πεποίηκεν πᾶσαν τὴν δόξαν ταύτην. The book of Proverbs has the statement, "He who binds a stone in a sling is like him who gives *glory* [reputation] to a fool" (26:8). ὃς ἀποδεσμεύει λίθον ἐν σφενδόνῃ, ὅμοιός ἐστιν τῷ διδόντι ἄφρονι δόξαν. But this word is also used regularly in ascribing glory to God. The psalmist sang triumphantly, "Lift up your gates, ye rulers, and be opened wide, ye everlasting gates, and the king of *glory* shall come in" (Ps. 23:7; KJ Ps. 24:7). καὶ ἐπάρθητε, πύλαι αἰώνιοι, καὶ εἰσελεύσεται ὁ βασιλεὺς τῆς δόξης. Isaiah prophesied boldly, "And the *glory* of the Lord will be seen, and all flesh will see the salvation of God" (Isa. 40:5). καὶ ὀφθήσεται ἡ δόξα κυρίου, καὶ ὄψεται πᾶσα σὰρξ τὸ σωτήριον τοῦ θεοῦ.

In the New Testament the meaning "opinion" is not found, but the sense of "honor" or "reputation" is found. Our Lord advised a guest to take the lowest place at a dinner so that when the host comes, he would say, "Friend, go up higher: then thou shalt have *honor* [reputation] before all the ones who are reclining with thee" (Luke 14:10). φίλε, προσανάβηθι ἀνώτερον· τότε ἔσται σοι δόξα ἐνώπιον πάντων τῶν συνανακειμένων σοι. The sense of worldly glory is frequent. At the temptation of the Lord Jesus, the devil "showed him all the kingdoms of the world and the *glory* of them" (Matt. 4:8). δείκνυσιν αὐτῷ πάσας τὰς βασιλείας τοῦ κόσμου καὶ τὴν δόξαν αὐτῶν. When the angel of the Lord announced the birth of the Lord Jesus to the shepherds, "the *glory* of the Lord shone round about them" (Luke 2:9). καὶ δόξα κυρίου περιέλαμψεν αὐτούς. This divine glory is certainly attributed to the Lord Jesus as well, for the writer to the Hebrews prayed for his readers, "The God of peace . . . make you perfect in every good thing to do his will, doing in us that which is well-pleasing in his sight through Jesus Christ, to whom be *glory* into the ages of the ages, Amen" (Heb. 13:20–21). ποιῶν ἐν ἡμῖν τὸ εὐάρεστον ἐνώπιον αὐτοῦ διὰ Ἰησοῦ Χριστοῦ, ᾧ ἡ δόξα εἰς τοὺς αἰῶνας τῶν αἰώνων. And by God's grace, the Apostle Paul teaches us, we will share in God's glory: "When Christ, who is our life, shall be manifested, then ye also shall be manifested with him in *glory*" (Col. 3:4). ὅταν ὁ Χριστὸς φανερωθῇ, ἡ ζωὴ ἡμῶν, τότε καὶ ὑμεῖς σὺν αὐτῷ φανερωθήσεσθε ἐν δόξῃ. At the present time this divine glory is far beyond what the believer can receive. Paul, in recounting his experience on the Damascus road, told the multitude, "But as I was not able to see from the *glory* [brightness] of that light, being led by the hand by those who were with me, I came into Damascus" (Acts 22:11). ὡς δὲ οὐκ ἐνέβλεπον ἀπὸ τῆς δόξης τοῦ φωτὸς ἐκείνου. True believers, however, shall be prepared for that glory, because God, writes Paul to the Thessalonians, "is calling you into his own kingdom and *glory*" (I Thess. 2:12). τοῦ καλοῦντος ὑμᾶς εἰς τὴν ἑαυτοῦ βασιλείαν καὶ δόξαν.

ἔπαινος

When Herodotus described how Deioces tried to become king of the Medes, he said that the Medes chose Deioces as judge because he was honest and just. "By doing these things he won no small *praise* from his fellow townsmen." ποιέων τε ταῦτα ἔπαινον εἶχε οὐκ ὀλίγον πρὸς τῶν πολιητέων (1.96). Xenophon recounted the instruction of Virtue to Heracles, saying, "The young rejoice to win the *praises* of the old; the elders rejoice greatly in the *honors* by the young." οἱ μὲν νέοι τοῖς τῶν πρεσβυτέρων ἐπαίνοις χαίρουσιν, οἱ δὲ γεραίτεροι ταῖς τῶν νέων τιμαῖς ἀγάλλονται (*Memorabilia* 2.1.33). Here praises are given to the young;

GLORY

honors to the old. When Antigone was led to her death, the chorus chanted, "Therefore with *praise* as your portion you go in fame to the vault of the dead." οὐκοῦν κλεινὴ καὶ ἔπαινον ἔχουσ' (Sophocles *Antigone* 817). In each of these examples the idea of "approval" or "public recognition" is very strong. A second century B.C. inscription recorded the phrase "to do the judgments worthily of *praise* and of *honors*." ἀξίως ἐπαίνου καὶ τιμῶν ποιεῖσθαι τὰς κρίσεις (*Priene,* 53.15).

In the Septuagint the judgment of the Lord on king Jehoram is proclaimed, and afterwards the simple statement is made that Jehoram "reigned in Jerusalem eight years and departed without *praise* and was buried" (II Chron. 21:20). καὶ ἐπορεύθη ἐν οὐκ ἐπαίνῳ καὶ ἐτάφη. This word is often applied to God as His due. When the ark was brought into the temple, David sang to God, *"Glory* and *praise* are before His face; strength and gladness are in His place" (I Chron. 16:27). δόξα καὶ ἔπαινος κατὰ πρόσωπον αὐτοῦ. The psalmist called God "the *Praise* of Israel" (Ps. 21:4; KJ Ps. 22:3). ὁ ἔπαινος Ισραηλ. On another occasion the psalmist said, "My tongue shall speak of thy righteousness—of thy *praise* the whole day" (Ps. 34:28; KJ Ps. 35:28). ἡ γλῶσσά μου μελετήσει τὴν δικαιοσύνην σου, ὅλην τὴν ἡμέραν τὸν ἔπαινόν σου.

The classical sense of "public recognition" or "approval" is not common in the New Testament, but it does occur, for Paul wrote to the Philippians, "As many things as are true, as many things as are reverend, as many things as are just, as many things as are pure, as many things as are lovely, as many things as are of good report, if there is any virtue, and if there is any *praise* [approval], keep on thinking about these things" (Phil. 4:8). εἴ τις ἀρετὴ καὶ εἴ τις ἔπαινος, ταῦτα λογίζεσθε. But in the same epistle Paul mentioned that the Philippians were filled with the fruit of righteousness "unto the *glory* and *praise* of God" (Phil. 1:11). εἰς δόξαν καὶ ἔπαινον θεοῦ. When Paul described the true Jew, he said that his "circumcision is of the heart in the spirit, not in the letter; whose *praise* is not of men, but of God" (Rom. 2:29). οὗ ὁ ἔπαινος οὐκ ἐξ ἀνθρώπων ἀλλ' ἐκ τοῦ θεοῦ. But praise may also come from human governments: "For the rulers are not a fear to the good work, but to the evil. Art thou wishing not to fear the authority? Do the thing which is good, and thou shalt have *praise* of the same" (Rom. 13:3). τὸ ἀγαθὸν ποίει, καὶ ἕξεις ἔπαινον ἐξ αὐτῆς. This word was also applied by the early church to one of their own number, for when Paul wrote to the Corinthians, he said, "And we have sent with him the brother whose *praise* in the Gospel is through all the churches" (II Cor. 8:18). τὸν ἀδελφὸν οὗ ὁ ἔπαινος ἐν τῷ εὐαγγελίῳ διὰ πασῶν τῶν ἐκκλησιῶν.

τιμή

This word occurs both with the sense of "honor" and with the sense of "price" throughout its history. When the aged Phoinix rebuked Achilles, he said, "But, Achilles, beat down your great wrath; it is not fitting for thee to have a pitiless heart. But even the very gods can bend, and their virtue and *honor* and strength are greater than ours." στρεπτοὶ δέ τε καὶ θεοὶ αὐτοί, τῶν περ καὶ μείζων ἀρετὴ τιμή τε βίη τε (Homer *Iliad* 9.498). Sometimes this word is used for the "honor" given by the gods to men, as when Menelaus addressed the Danaans as "Ye upon whom attend *honor* and glory from Zeus." ἐκ δὲ Διὸς τιμὴ καὶ κῦδος ὀπηδεῖ (Homer *Iliad* 17.251). When the herald in Aeschylus' *Agamemnon* came with bad news of the shipwreck of the fleet, he said, "It is not fitting to mar a day of happy omen by a tale of ill—the *honor* due to the gods keeps them apart." εὔφημον ἦμαρ οὐ πρέπει κακαγγέλῳ γλώσσῃ μιαίνειν· χωρὶς ἡ τιμὴ θεῶν (line 637). Herodotus used this word with the meaning of "price" when he said, "They were feeding the finest cattle in *price* which they could find." ἐσίτευον ἐξευρίσκοντες τιμῆς τὰ κάλλιστα (7.119). One of the papyri also used this word in the sense of "price" when the writer complained of "having come to the last extremity because of the [high] *price* of grain." εἰς πᾶν τι ἐληλυθυῖα διὰ τὴν τοῦ σίτου τιμήν (*P. Lond.*, 42.17). An inscription showed the other sense of the word by recording, "That there may be an opportunity of paying *honor* to the Augustus [emperor]." ἵνα ἀφορμὴ γένοιτο τῆς εἰς τὸν Σεβαστὸν τιμῆς (*Priene*, 105.16).

The Septuagint also used this word in both senses. Joseph commanded his steward: "Put my silver cup in the bag of the youngest and the *price* of his grain" (Gen. 44:2). καὶ τὴν τιμὴν τοῦ σίτου αὐτοῦ. In the other sense Abimelech said to Sarah, "I have given thy brother a thousand didrachme; these things shall be to thee for *honor* [adornment] to thy countenance and to the women with thee" (Gen. 20:16). ταῦτα ἔσται σοι εἰς τιμὴν τοῦ προσώπου σου. When the Lord challenged Job's self-righteousness, He said to him, "Assume then majesty and power, and array thyself with *glory* and *honor*" (Job 40:10). δόξαν δὲ καὶ τιμὴν ἀμφίεσαι. The psalmist, amazed over God's kindness to man, wrote, "Thou didst make him a little lower than the angels; with *glory* and *honor* thou didst crown him" (Ps. 8:6; KJ Ps. 8:5). δόξῃ καὶ τιμῇ ἐστεφάνωσας αὐτόν.

Both of these meanings are found in the New Testament. Paul reminded the Corinthians, "For ye were bought with a *price*" (I Cor. 6:20). ἠγοράσθητε γὰρ τιμῆς. He also admonished Timothy, "Let as many as are slaves under the yoke count their own masters worthy of all *honor*" (I Tim. 6:1). Ὅσοι εἰσὶν ὑπὸ ζυγὸν δοῦλοι, τοὺς ἰδίους δεσπότας πάσης

GLORY

τιμῆς ἀξίους ἡγείσθωσαν. Peter applied this word to the Lord Jesus when he said, "For he received from God the Father *honor* and *glory*" (II Pet. 1:17). λαβὼν γὰρ παρὰ θεοῦ πατρὸς τιμὴν καὶ δόξαν. The writer to the Hebrews used this word almost in the sense of a public "office." He spoke of the priesthood of the Lord Jesus by saying, "No one takes this *honor* to himself, but being called by God even as Aaron also was" (Heb. 5:4). οὐχ ἑαυτῷ τις λαμβάνει τὴν τιμήν. When God's purpose is about to be consummated, all the universe cries out to God saying, "To the One who is sitting upon the throne and to the Lamb be blessing and *honor* and *glory* and power into the ages of the ages" (Rev. 5:13). ἡ εὐλογία καὶ ἡ τιμὴ καὶ ἡ δόξα καὶ τὸ κράτος εἰς τοὺς αἰῶνας τῶν αἰώνων.

All three of these words occur in an eschatological context when the Apostle Peter wrote that the trial of your faith "may be found unto *praise* and *glory* and *honor* at the revelation of Jesus Christ" (I Pet. 1:7). εὑρεθῇ εἰς ἔπαινον καὶ δόξαν καὶ τιμὴν ἐν ἀποκαλύψει Ἰησοῦ Χριστοῦ. Plainly there was a distinction between these words or they would not be used in the same sentence together.

SUMMARY

These three words which are often used in connection with one another do have definite distinctions. The basic meaning of the word δόξα is "opinion," but this meaning is not found in the New Testament; there it has the sense of "glory," "reputation," or "brightness." The early meaning of ἔπαινος is "public recognition," but it usually means "praise." The basic sense of τιμή is "value," but again the usual meaning is either "price" or "honor." All of these words may be applied to the same subject because each one is high commendation from a different perspective.

4. Good: ἀγαθός, καλός

Both these words may refer to what is morally *good*, but with this distinction: ἀγαθός usually designates that which is good because its results are beneficial, whereas καλός denotes goodness which is evident to others. When these terms are used in the sense of *the good*, τὸ ἀγαθόν refers to that which is beneficial; τὸ καλόν to that which is good in an absolute sense (Lightfoot, *Notes on Epistles of St. Paul*, p. 81).

ἀγαθός

Helen described Agamemnon as "both a *noble* king and a valiant spearman." ἀμφότερον βασιλεύς τ' ἀγαθὸς κρατερός τ' αἰχμητής (Homer *Iliad* 3.179). Later in the *Iliad* Homer mentions "a certain Euchenor, son of Polyidus the seer, a man both rich and *good*." τις Εὐχήνωρ, Πολυΐδου μάντιος υἱός, ἀφνειός τ' ἀγαθός τε (13.664). Sophocles has Deianira speak ironically of "Heracles, being called the faithful and *good* one to us." Ἡρακλῆς, ὁ πιστὸς ἡμῖν κἀγαθὸς καλούμενος (*Trachinian Women* 541). Each of these examples portrays a beneficent man. In Plato's *Republic* Adeimantus said, "But thou indeed, O Socrates, tell me whether 'the *Good*' is knowledge or pleasure, or something different from these things?" ἀλλὰ σὺ δή, ὦ Σώκρατες, πότερον ἐπιστήμην τὸ ἀγαθὸν φῇς εἶναι, ἢ ἡδονήν, ἢ ἄλλο τι παρὰ ταῦτα; (506B). Some passages draw a clear contrast between these two words. In Xenophon, Socrates says to Pericles concerning his suggestions, "For any part of them which you carry out will be *good* to thee and *good* to the city." ὅ, τι μὲν γὰρ ἂν τούτων καταπράξῃς, καὶ σοὶ καλὸν ἔσται καὶ τῇ πόλει ἀγαθόν (*Memorabilia* 3.5.28). He means that it will appear good to Pericles and beneficial to the city.

When Abraham's servant prepared to go for a bride for Isaac, he took "ten camels from the camels of his master and from all the *good things* of his master which were his charge" (Gen. 24:10). δέκα καμήλους ἀπὸ τῶν καμήλων τοῦ κυρίου αὐτοῦ καὶ ἀπὸ πάντων τῶν ἀγαθῶν τοῦ κυρίου αὐτοῦ μεθ' ἑαυτοῦ. In the giving of the law, the Lord commanded, "Honor thy father and mother, in order that it may be well with thee and that thou mayest live long upon the *good* land which the Lord thy God gives thee" (Exod. 20:12). καὶ ἵνα μακροχρόνιος γένῃ ἐπὶ τῆς γῆς τῆς ἀγαθῆς, ἧς κύριος ὁ θεός σου δίδωσίν σοι. Eli, having heard of all the sins his sons were committing, gave them a mild reproof: "Stop doing thus, because the reports which I hear are not *good,* that the people will not serve God" (I Sam. 2:24). μὴ ποιεῖτε οὕτως, ὅτι οὐκ ἀγαθαὶ αἱ ἀκοαί, ἃς ἐγὼ ἀκούω, τοῦ μὴ δουλεύειν λαὸν θεῷ. The psalmist exhorted, "Depart from evil, and do *good,* and dwell forever" (Ps. 36:27; KJ Ps. 37:27). ἔκκλινον ἀπὸ κακοῦ καὶ ποίησον ἀγαθὸν καὶ κατασκήνου εἰς αἰῶνα αἰῶνος.

In the Sermon on the Mount the Lord Jesus said, "Therefore if ye, being evil, know how to give *good* gifts to your children, how much more will your Father who is in the heavens give *good things* to those who ask him?" (Matt. 7:11). εἰ οὖν ὑμεῖς πονηροὶ ὄντες οἴδατε δόματα ἀγαθὰ διδόναι τοῖς τέκνοις ὑμῶν, πόσῳ μᾶλλον ὁ πατὴρ ὑμῶν ὁ ἐν τοῖς οὐρανοῖς δώσει ἀγαθὰ τοῖς αἰτοῦσιν αὐτόν. The good gifts and good things are those that will benefit the recipients. When the Lord Jesus related the parable of the laborers in the vineyard, He told how the householder had paid all the laborers the same day's wage. Some laborers who had worked longer complained, but the householder replied, "Is it not lawful for me to do what I wish with what is mine? Or is thine eye evil because I am *good?*" (Matt. 20:15). ἢ ὁ ὀφθαλμός σου πονηρός ἐστιν ὅτι ἐγὼ ἀγαθός εἰμι; Here the man is clearly "generous" or "beneficent." In the parable of the talents the faithful servant brought his ten talents to present them to his lord, and his lord, recognizing how profitable he had been, said to him, "Well, *good* and faithful servant; thou wast faithful over a few things; I will appoint thee over many things" (Matt. 25:21). εὖ, δοῦλε ἀγαθὲ καὶ πιστέ.

In the epistles Paul taught that Christ died for the ungodly and added, "For hardly in behalf of a righteous man will anyone die; for perhaps in behalf of the *good* man some would even dare to die" (Rom. 5:7). ὑπὲρ γὰρ τοῦ ἀγαθοῦ τάχα τις καὶ τολμᾷ ἀποθανεῖν. Men are not concerned for a man who is merely righteous, but for a benefactor some would even die. When Paul dealt with human government, he said, "For rulers are not a fear to the *good* work, but to the evil. But art thou wishing not to fear the authority? Do thou the *good thing,* and thou shalt have praise from the same" (Rom. 13:3). οἱ γὰρ ἄρχοντες οὐκ εἰσὶν φόβος τῷ ἀγαθῷ ἔργῳ ἀλλὰ τῷ κακῷ. θέλεις δὲ μὴ φοβεῖσθαι τὴν ἐξουσίαν; τὸ ἀγαθὸν ποίει, καὶ ἕξεις ἔπαινον ἐξ αὐτῆς. Government does not usually bother what is beneficial to the community. "Let no corrupt word proceed out of your mouth," the apostle exhorted the believers, "but what is *good* unto edification of the need" (Eph. 4:29). πᾶς λόγος σαπρὸς ἐκ τοῦ στόματος ὑμῶν μὴ ἐκπορευέσθω, ἀλλὰ εἴ τις ἀγαθὸς πρὸς οἰκοδομὴν τῆς χρείας. The believer is to say only what is beneficial. The antonym with which ἀγαθός is most often contrasted is πονηρός, which is "evil" that results in evil, although ἀγαθός is used most freely in various combinations with its antonyms and synonyms. See Table I for a comparison of these combinations.

καλός

Since this word refers to goodness which is obvious to all, it often denotes what is "fair" or "beautiful," as when Athena changed herself into the form of a "woman, *beautiful* and tall." γυναικὶ καλῇ τε μεγάλῃ (Homer *Odyssey* 13.289). But the word also has a clear moral sense, for Ctesippus said, "For it is not *good* or just to rob of their due the guests of Telemachus." οὐ γὰρ καλὸν ἀτέμβειν οὐδὲ δίκαιον ξένους Τηλεμάχου (Homer *Odyssey* 20.294). Xenophon said of Socrates, "The problems he discussed were: What is devout, what is ungodly; what is *good*, what is shameful." τί εὐσεβές, τί ἀσεβές, τί καλόν, τί αἰσχρόν (*Memorabilia* 1.1.16). Herodotus uses both words in the same sentence in remarking, "For as I learn, the Massagetae have no experience of the *good things* of the Persians, nor are they well off in regard to great *good things*." ὡς γὰρ ἐγὼ πυνθάνομαι, Μασσαγέται εἰσὶ ἀγαθῶν τε Περσικῶν ἄπειροι καὶ καλῶν μεγάλων ἀπαθέες (1.207). The meaning is that the Massagetae, a primitive people, have no contact with the beneficial things of Persian civilization, nor of the things which are considered good in themselves. One papyrus mentioned "a box of very *good* grapes and a basket of *good* dates." κίστην σταφυλῆς λείαν καλῆς καὶ σφυρίδα φοίνικος καλοῦ (*P. Oxy.*, I, 116.19f). Again, the quality of the fruit was obvious.

Of the creation the Septuagint recorded at each stage, "And God saw that it was *good*" (Gen. 1:8, 10, 12, 18, and repeatedly). καὶ εἶδεν ὁ θεὸς ὅτι καλόν. It was evident that each thing created was the handiwork of God. In Eden, Scripture says, "God caused to spring up out of the ground every tree beautiful to the sight and *good* for food, and the tree of life in the midst of the garden, and the tree to know what was to be known of *good* and evil" (Gen. 2:9). ἐξανέτειλεν ὁ θεὸς ἔτι ἐκ τῆς γῆς πᾶν ξύλον ὡραῖον εἰς ὅρασιν καὶ καλὸν εἰς βρῶσιν καὶ τὸ ξύλον τῆς ζωῆς ἐν μέσῳ τῷ παραδείσῳ καὶ τὸ ξύλον τοῦ εἰδέναι γνωστὸν καλοῦ καὶ πονηροῦ. Here are both senses: food which is obviously "good," and a sharp contrast between what is morally "good" and what is "evil." The meaning "beautiful" is used when the inspired writer records that "the sons of God, having seen the daughters of men that they were *beautiful,* took to themselves wives of all which they chose" (Gen. 6:2). ἰδόντες δὲ οἱ υἱοὶ τοῦ θεοῦ τὰς θυγατέρας τῶν ἀνθρώπων ὅτι καλαί εἰσιν, ἔλαβον ἑαυτοῖς γυναῖκας ἀπὸ πασῶν, ὧν ἐξελέξαντο. The prophet Isaiah pleaded with

TABLE I
Occurrences of combinations of ἀγαθός and καλός with their antonyms in the New Testament

ἀγαθός and πονηρός	ἀγαθός and κακός	ἀγαθός and φαῦλος	ἀγαθός and καλός	καλός and κακός	καλός and πονηρός
Matt. 5:45. Matt. 7:11. Matt. 7:18. Matt. 12:34. Matt. 12:35. Matt. 20:15. Matt. 22:10. Matt. 25:21, 23, 26. Luke 6:45. Luke 11:13. Luke 19:17, 22. Rom. 12:9.	Mark 3:4. Luke 16:25. Rom. 2:7, 9, 10. Rom. 3:8. Rom. 7:19. Rom. 12:21. Rom. 13:3, 4. Rom. 16:19. I Thess. 5:15. I Pet. 3:10, 11. III John 11.	John 5:29. Rom. 9:11. II Cor. 5:10.	Matt. 7:17. Luke 8:15. Rom. 7:18. I Tim. 1:18, 19. I Tim. 5:10. I Tim. 6:18.	Rom. 7:21. Rom. 12:17. II Cor. 13:7. Heb. 5:11. I Pet. 2:12.	Matt. 7:17–18.

A TREASURY OF NEW TESTAMENT SYNONYMS

Israel, "Learn to do *well,* seek judgment" (Isa. 1:17). μάθετε καλὸν ποιεῖν, ἐκζητήσατε κρίσιν. This is clearly a moral context.

In the New Testament these same connotations may be found. While Jesus was teaching in the temple, "some were speaking concerning the temple, how it had been adorned with *beautiful* stones and offerings" (Luke 21:5). τινων λεγόντων περὶ τοῦ ἱεροῦ, ὅτι λίθοις καλοῖς καὶ ἀναθήμασιν κεκόσμηται. In the same sense the Lord Jesus spoke of the man who "was seeking *beautiful* pearls" (Matt. 13:45). ζητοῦντι καλοὺς μαργαρίτας. The Lord Jesus used the word with a strong moral sense when He said, "Let your light thus shine before men that they may see your *good* works and may glorify your father who is in heaven" (Matt. 5:16). οὕτως λαμψάτω τὸ φῶς ὑμῶν ἔμπροσθεν τῶν ἀνθρώπων, ὅπως ἴδωσιν ὑμῶν τὰ καλὰ ἔργα καὶ δοξάσωσιν τὸν πατέρα ὑμῶν. It should be obvious to all that these works are "good."

When Paul discussed the problems of sin and the law, he said, "I find then the law that, for me who wishes to do the *good,* for me the evil is present" (Rom. 7:21). εὑρίσκω ἄρα τὸν νόμον τῷ θέλοντι ἐμοὶ ποιεῖν τὸ καλόν, ὅτι ἐμοὶ τὸ κακὸν παράκειται. Paul really wished to do what is good in itself, but he could not without the power of the indwelling Spirit. To the Thessalonians he wrote, "But test all things; hold fast the *good"* (I Thess. 5:21). πάντα δὲ δοκιμάζετε, τὸ καλὸν κατέχετε. The believer ought to keep on holding that which is good in itself and is evident to others. The Christian standard of behavior before unsympathetic unbelievers is set down by the Apostle Peter: "Having your behavior among the Gentiles *good* [seemly], that in which thing they speak against you as evil-doers, they may, out of your *good* works which they behold, glorify God" (I Pet. 2:12). τὴν ἀναστροφὴν ὑμῶν ἐν τοῖς ἔθνεσιν ἔχοντες καλήν, ἵνα ἐν ᾡ καταλαλοῦσιν ὑμῶν ὡς κακοποιῶν, ἐκ τῶν καλῶν ἔργων ἐποπτεύοντες δοξάσωσιν τὸν θεόν. In Luke's account of the parable of the sower Christ used both adjectives to describe the same object: "But that in the *good* ground, these are the ones who, in a *noble* and *good* heart, having heard the word, keep holding it and keep bearing fruit with patience" (8:15). τὸ δὲ ἐν τῇ καλῇ γῇ, οὗτοί εἰσιν οἵτινες ἐν καρδίᾳ καλῇ καὶ ἀγαθῇ ἀκούσαντες τὸν λόγον κατέχουσιν καὶ καρποφοροῦσιν ἐν ὑπομονῇ. This heart is "good" in a sense which is evident to all and is beneficial to all.

SUMMARY

The word ἀγαθός means "good" in the sense of that which is beneficial in its results or actions. On the other hand καλός means "good" in the sense of that which is obvious to others as "good." If the article is used with these words, τὸ ἀγαθόν means "the good" in the sense of "the beneficial," whereas τὸ καλόν means "the good" in an absolute sense. Both Lightfoot and Hort strongly urge these distinctions in their writings; Westcott, however, seems to be unaware of any such distinctions.[1] There is certainly a realm in which these words overlap. The word ἀγαθός is usually contrasted with πονηρός, that which is "evil" in its results. Sometimes it is opposed to φαῦλος, that which is "worthless." It is nevertheless often contrasted with κακός, that which is "evil" in itself.[2] In the same way the usual antonym of καλός is κακός, but in one passage καλός is opposed to πονηρός.

[1] Lightfoot, *Notes on Epistles of St. Paul*, pp. 81, 86; Hort, *The First Epistle of St. Peter I. 1-II. 17*, pp. 134–35; Westcott, *Hebrews*, p. 325.
[2] For these combinations see Table I, p. 36.

5. Guardian: ἐπίτροπος, οἰκονόμος

The term ἐπίτροπος means *guardian, manager,* or *administrator*. The close synonym οἰκονόμος refers to a *steward, tutor, administrator,* or *treasurer*.

ἐπίτροπος

In relating the birth of Cyrus, Herodotus told how King Astyages "summoned Harpagus, a man of his household and most faithful of the Medes and who was *administrator* of all his possessions." καλέσας "Άρπαγον ἄνδρα οἰκήιον καὶ πιστότατόν τε Μήδων καὶ πάντων ἐπίτροπον τῶν ἑωυτοῦ (1.108). In another context Herodotus used this word in another sense. "The leader's place belonged by right to Pleistarchus the son of Leonidas; but he was yet a boy, and Pausanias his *guardian* and cousin." ἀλλ' ὁ μὲν ἦν ἔτι παῖς, ὁ δὲ τούτου ἐπίτροπός τε καὶ ἀνεψιός (9.10). Thucydides mentioned Sabylinthus, "the *guardian* of king Tharyps, who was still a boy." ἐπίτροπος ὢν Θάρυπος τοῦ βασιλέως ἔτι παιδὸς ὄντος (2.80).

The Septuagint described the great invasion of Judaea by Antiochus Eupator "and with him Lysias, his *guardian* and chancellor, each of them having a Greek force." καὶ σὺν αὐτῷ Λυσίαν τὸν ἐπίτροπον καὶ ἐπὶ τῶν πραγμάτων (II Maccabees 13:2). One of the papyri has this declaration: "I, Aurelius Hermodoras, *guardian* of the minors, have taken the oath on their behalf." Αὐρήλιος Ἑρμόδωρος . . . ἐπίτροπος τῶν ἀφηλίκων . . . ὤμοσα ὑπὲρ αὐτῶν (*P. Ryl.*, II, 109.18).

These same meanings may be found in the New Testament. When our Lord declared the parable of the workers in the vineyard, He said, "But when evening came, the Lord of the vineyard says to his *manager:* Call the workers and give them their wages" (Matt. 20:8). λέγει ὁ κύριος τοῦ ἀμπελῶνος τῷ ἐπιτρόπῳ αὐτοῦ. Here the context gives this term the idea of "foreman." Luke mentioned "Joanna the wife of Chuza, Herod's *administrator*" (8:3). Ἰωάννα γυνὴ Χουζᾶ ἐπιτρόπου Ἡρῴδου. It probably has the connotation of a political office in this passage.

The Apostle Paul discussed the freedom of the believer under God's grace and concluded that he is also the seed of Abraham and an heir according to the promise. Building upon this thought, Paul said, "But I say that as long a time as the heir is a child, he differs nothing from a slave although he is lord of all, but he is under *guardians* and *stewards* until the day appointed by the father" (Gal. 4:1-2). οὐδὲν διαφέρει δούλου κύριος πάντων ὤν, ἀλλὰ ὑπὸ ἐπιτρόπους ἐστὶν καὶ οἰκονόμους ἄχρι τῆς προθεσμίας τοῦ πατρός. There are two principal interpretations of the meaning of these two synonyms. Sir William Ramsay maintained that they applied to two different men: the ἐπίτροπος was a guardian of orphans up to the age of fourteen (this was equivalent to the Roman *tutor*), whereas the οἰκονόμος then administered the property until the children were twenty-five (this was equivalent to the Roman *curator*).[1] Under Syrian law the father could appoint both of these administrators for his children. The problem behind this interpretation is that no law in the ancient world allowed the father to specify the time that the children were to be considered mature. Consequently, some scholars hold that both of these terms refer to the same person and are not meant to be technical legal terms at all.[2] If this is the case, these two words would then refer to different aspects of the administration: the ἐπίτροπος would be the "guardian" supervising the whole life of the child; the οἰκονόμος would be the "steward" performing the financial responsibilities of the guardian.[3] Historical investigation has not yet found sufficient evidence to determine which of these two interpretations is correct.

οἰκονόμος

There is an interesting use of this word in Aeschylus' *Agamemnon:* "For there remains a fearful rushing back, a deceitful *house steward,* an unforgetting, child-avenging wrath." μίμνει γὰρ φοβερὰ παλίνορτος οἰκονόμος δολία μνάμων μῆνις τεκνόποινος (line 155). Xenophon describing the generous character of Cyrus, said, "But if he should see an able man who was justly a *steward* and who was furnishing [things needful] with which he might rule lands and who was making income, no such man would he deprive of anything, but he was always adding more [to him]." εἰ δέ τινα ὁρῴη δεινὸν ὄντα οἰκονόμον ἐκ τοῦ δικαίου καὶ κατασκευάζοντά τε ἧς ἄρχοι χώρας καὶ προσόδους ποιοῦντα (*Anabasis* 1.9.19).

In the Septuagint there are a number of examples of the use of this word, although most just name the office without mentioning the duties. When the officers of king Solomon's government were named, "Achiel was *steward"* (I Kings 4:6). Αχιηλ οἰκονόμος. Elah was the dissolute son of Baasha, who, while his servants conspired against him, "was drinking

---
[1] *A Historical Commentary on St. Paul's Epistle to the Galatians,* pp. 391-93.
[2] Ernest De Witt Burton, *The Epistle to the Galatians,* pp. 212-15.
[3] Herman N. Ridderbos, *The Epistle of Paul to the Churches of Galatia,* p. 152, notes 2 and 3.

himself drunk in the house of Osa, his *steward,* at Thersa" (I Kings 16:9). πίνων μεθύων ἐν τῷ οἴκῳ Ωσα τοῦ οἰκονόμου ἐν Θερσα. When Sennacherib, king of Assyria, invaded Palestine, Rabshakeh came to demand the surrender of Jerusalem. "And there went forth to him Eliakim the son of Chelkiah, the *steward,* and Somnas the scribe" (Isa. 36:3). καὶ ἐξῆλθεν πρὸς αὐτὸν Ελιακιμ ὁ τοῦ Χελκιου ὁ οἰκονόμος. The word is also found in II Kings 18:18 with the same meaning. King David had gathered a great treasure to use in adorning God's temple, but many of the nobles of Israel also made willing gifts for the temple, among whom were "the *overseers* of the king" (I Chron. 29:6). οἱ οἰκονόμοι τοῦ βασιλέως. In the book of Esther, King Ahasuerus made a feast for his subjects and provided wine for them to drink in the royal palace, "and thus the king wished and commanded the *stewards* to do his will" (1:8). οὕτως δὲ ἠθέλησεν ὁ βασιλεὺς καὶ ἐπέταξεν τοῖς οἰκονόμοις ποιῆσαι τὸ θέλημα αὐτοῦ. One of the papyri recorded the statement, "I have sent to you the *steward* Heraclides as you requested, to make arrangements about the vintage." ἀπέστειλα ὁ οἰκονόμος Ἡρακλείδην πρὸς σὲ καθὰ ἠξίωσας ἵνα τὴν διαταγὴν τῆς τρύγης ποιήσηται (P. Fay., 133.2).

When the Lord Jesus charged His disciples to watch and to be ready for the coming of the Son of Man, Peter wanted to know whether the Lord meant all believers or just the twelve. The Lord answered him, "Who then is the faithful and wise *steward,* whom the lord shall set over his household, to give them their measure of food in due season?" (Luke 12:42) τίς ἄρα ἐστὶν ὁ πιστὸς οἰκονόμος ὁ φρόνιμος, ὃν καταστήσει ὁ κύριος ἐπὶ τῆς θεραπείας; On another occasion the Lord Jesus spoke of an irresponsible steward: "There was a certain rich man, who had a *steward,* and this man was accused to him as wasting his goods" (Luke 16:1). ἄνθρωπός τις ἦν πλούσιος ὃς εἶχεν οἰκονόμον, καὶ οὗτος διεβλήθη αὐτῷ ὡς διασκορπίζων τὰ ὑπάρχοντα αὐτοῦ.

The Apostle Paul challenged his detractors by solemnly declaring, "Let a man so account us as ministers of Christ and *stewards* of the mysteries of God" (I Cor. 4:1). Οὕτως ἡμᾶς λογιζέσθω ἄνθρωπος ὡς ὑπηρέτας Χριστοῦ καὶ οἰκονόμους μυστηρίων θεοῦ. When Paul listed the qualifications for bishops, he began by saying, "For it is necessary for the bishop to be blameless as a *steward* of God" (Titus 1:7). δεῖ γὰρ τὸν ἐπίσκοπον ἀνέγκλητον εἶναι ὡς θεοῦ οἰκονόμον. The Apostle Peter exhorted every believer to serve God well, "even as each one received a gift, ministering it among yourselves as good *stewards* of the manifold grace of God" (I Pet. 4:10). ἕκαστος καθὼς ἔλαβεν χάρισμα, εἰς ἑαυτοὺς αὐτὸ διακονοῦντες ὡς καλοὶ οἰκονόμοι ποικίλης χάριτος θεοῦ.

Paul's use of this word in the sense "guardians and *stewards*" has

GUARDIAN

already been discussed under the former word, ἐπίτροπος. With a different connotation Paul wrote to the Romans, "Erastus, the *treasurer* of the city, sends greetings" (Rom. 16:23). ἀσπάζεται ὑμᾶς Ἔραστος ὁ οἰκονόμος τῆς πόλεως. Thus there is a strong sense of financial stewardship in these last two passages.

SUMMARY

The word ἐπίτροπος refers to an "administrator," which may further imply the "guardian" of a minor or the "manager" of an estate; the word οἰκονόμος refers to a "steward," which may imply the financial responsibility of an estate, a minor, or a city.

6. Possessions: κτήματα, ὑπάρξεις

Both of these words in the plural denote *possessions*. In the ordinary usage κτήματα designates "real estate," ὑπάρξεις, *personal property;* but this distinction was not immutable, and they are sometimes used interchangeably.

κτήματα

Homer described the treasures of Thebes in Egypt "where *possessions* in greatest store are laid up in men's houses." ὅθι πλεῖστα δόμοις ἐν κτήματα κεῖται (*Iliad* 9.382). When Odysseus finally arrived home, his swineherd warned him of the men who were wasting his possessions: "but at their ease they are wasting our *possessions* in an insolent manner, and there is no sparing." ἀλλὰ ἔκηλοι κτήματα δαρδάπτουσιν ὑπέρβιον, οὐδ᾽ ἔπι φειδώ (*Odyssey* 14.92). Herodotus portrayed Darius as saying, "For I knew that the most precious of all *possessions* is an understanding and loyal friend." ἐγνωκὼς ὅτι κτημάτων πάντων ἐστὶ τιμιώτατον ἀνὴρ φίλος συνετός τε καὶ εὔνοος (5. 24). In Sophocles' *Antigone* the chorus chants, "Love, unconquered in battle, Love, which falls on our *possessions.*" Ἔρως ἀνίκατε μάχαν, ἔΕρως, ὃς ἐν κτήμασι πίπτεις (line 782). One of the papyri has the statement "He will be master of many good things and *possessions.*" δεσπότης ἔσται πολλῶν ἀγαθῶν καὶ κτημάτων (*P. Ryl.*, I, 28.182).

In the Septuagint, Hosea prophesied, "And from thence I will give her for her *possessions* even the valley of Achor to open her understanding" (Hos. 2:17; KJ Hos. 2:15). καὶ δώσω αὐτῇ τὰ κτήματα αὐτῆς ἐκεῖθεν. The sense of "fields" or "agricultural land" is clear. When Joel cried out against the sins of his people, he said, "Mourn, ye *fields* [farms], for the wheat and barley, because the harvester is perished from the field" (Joel 1:11). θρηνεῖτε, κτήματα, ὑπέρ πυροῦ καὶ κριθῆς. The book of Wisdom says of the idolater, "When he makes his prayer concerning his *possessions* and his marriage and children, he is not ashamed to speak to that which is not alive." περὶ δὲ κτημάτων καὶ γάμων αὐτοῦ καὶ τέκνων προσευχόμενος (13:17). Even in the singular this word may still refer to "land," for Proverbs warns, "Do not encroach upon the *property* of orphans" (23:10). εἰς δὲ κτῆμα ὀρφανῶν μὴ εἰσέλθῃς.

POSSESSIONS

When the Lord Jesus told the rich young man to sell what he had and give to the poor, Scripture says, "But when the young man had heard this word, he went away sorrowing, for he was having many *possessions"* (Matt. 19:22). ἀπῆλθεν λυπούμενος· ἦν γὰρ ἔχων κτήματα πολλά. In the early church the voluntary sharing of goods was a mark of the great grace that was upon the believers. "And they were selling their *possessions* and *belongings,* and they were distributing them to all, even as anyone was having need" (Acts 2:45). καὶ τὰ κτήματα καὶ τὰς ὑπάρξεις ἐπίπρασκον καὶ διεμέριζον αὐτὰ πᾶσιν.

R. J. Knowling has confirmed this distinction in his explanation of the same passage: "τὰ κτήματα . . . τὰς ὑπάρξεις: according to their derivation, the former word would mean that which is acquired, and the latter that which belongs to a man for the time being. But in ordinary usage κτήματα was always used of real property, fields, lands, *cf.* 5:1, whilst ὑπάρξεις was used of personal property." However, Knowling admits that "the above distinction was not strictly observed" (Acts, in the *Expositor's Greek Testament,* II, 96). In the singular this word is also used for "property" in the sense of "land." "But a certain man, by name Ananias, with his wife Sapphira, sold *property"* (Acts 5:1). Ἀνὴρ δέ τις Ἀνανίας ὀνόματι σὺν Σαπφίρῃ τῇ γυναικὶ αὐτοῦ ἐπώλησεν κτῆμα. This is identified in the same context as "land" (verse 3).

ὑπάρξεις

An unusual use of both of these words in the singular appears in the writings of Dionysius of Halicarnassus, as he describes the actions of the tyrant Aristodemus, who was "seizing their [his subjects'] houses and lands and the rest of their *property,* reserving for himself the gold and silver and every *possession* that was worthy of a tyrant." οἰκίας δ᾽ αὐτῶν καὶ κλήρους καὶ τὴν λοιπὴν ὕπαρξιν ἀναλαβών, ἐξελόμενος χρυσὸν καὶ ἄργυρον καὶ εἴ τι ἄλλο τυραννίδος ἦν ἄξιον κτῆμα (*Roman Antiquities* 7.8.4). Thus Dionysius used these words loosely, practically reversing their usual meaning. Although ὑπάρξεις is scarce in the plural, it does occur in the singular in some of the papyri. One writes of "all his *property* valued at two hundred thousand sesterces." τὴν ὕπαρξιν αὐτοῦ πᾶσαν οὖσαν τιμήματος δουκηναρίας (*P. Oxy.*, X, 1274.14). Another is a legal document which begins, "My client Plutarchus leased from Demetria a *property* in the Oxyrhynchite nome." ὁ συνηγορούμενος Πλούταρχος ἐμισθώσατο παρὰ Δημητρίας τινὰ περὶ τὸν Ὀξυργχείτην ὕπαρξιν (*P. Oxy.,* IV, 707, 15).

In the Septuagint there is not a single occurrence of this word in the plural, but it does occur a few times in the singular. When King Josiah celebrated the passover, he dedicated thirty thousand sheep. "He dedicated also three thousand cattle; these were from the king's own *possession*" (II Chron. 35:7). ταῦτα ἀπὸ τῆς ὑπάρξεως τοῦ βασιλέως. The psalmist spoke concerning the Egyptian plagues that God "delivered up their cattle to hail and their *property* to the fire" (Ps. 77:48; KJ Ps. 78:48). παρέδωκεν εἰς χάλαζαν τὰ κτήνη αὐτῶν καὶ τὴν ὕπαρξιν αὐτῶν τῷ πυρί. The book of Proverbs also states, "Fathers bequeath house and *property* to children" (19:14). οἶκον καὶ ὕπαρξιν μερίζουσιν πατέρες παισίν.

Besides its occurrence in Acts 2:45, which has already been discussed, this word occurs only in Hebrews 10:34. The writer to the Hebrews, commending his readers, said, "For ye both sympathized with those who were in bonds, and took with joy the spoiling of your *possessions,* knowing that ye have for yourselves a better and an abiding *possession.*" καὶ τὴν ἁρπγὴν τῶν ὑπαρχόντων ὑμῶν μετὰ χαρᾶς προσεδέξασθε, γινώσκοντες ἔχειν ἑαυτοὺς κρείσσονα ὕπαρξιν καὶ μένουσαν. The writer is obviously using the participial form of the cognate verb as an exact parallel to the singular of ὑπάρξεις.

SUMMARY

In the plural both words mean "possessions." Commonly κτήματα signifies "real property" as distinguished from ὑπάρξεις, "personal property." Often, however, they are used interchangeably.

7. Power: βία, δύναμις, κράτος, ἰσχύς, ἐξουσία, ἐνέργεια

Each of these words denotes some form of *power*. The word βία means *force*. δύναμις, κράτος, and ἰσχύς all signify *power* or *strength*. The word ἐξουσία means *authority*. ἐνέργεια means *energy, working,* or *operation*. These words are all translated *power* by various English versions, with no attempt to distinguish them.

βία

Homer mentions Tlepolemus, "famed for his spear, who was born to *mighty* Heracles by Astyocheia." ὃν τέκεν Ἀστυόχεια βίῃ Ἡρακληείῃ (*Iliad* 2.658). In describing the suitors of Penelope Eumaeus speaks of them as men "whose insolence and *violence* reach an iron heaven." τῶν ὕβρις τε βίη τε σιδήρεον οὐρανὸν ἵκει (*Odyssey* 15.329). The chorus of maidens threaten suicide "before being plunged by *force* into a marriage that will pierce the heart." πρὶν δαΐκτορος βίᾳ καρδίας γάμου κυρῆσαι (Aeschylus *The Suppliant Maidens* 798). Herodotus states, "For when Histiaeus tried at night to enter Miletus by *force,* he was wounded." νυκτὸς γὰρ ἐούσης βίῃ ἐπειρᾶτο κατιὼν ὁ Ἱστιαῖος ἐς τὴν Μίλητον, τιτρώσκεται (6.5). One of the papyri has the idiom, "He is detained by *force.*" πρὸς βίαν ἔχεται (*P. Petr.,* III, 53n. 9).

The Septuagint relates that after Joseph died, "the Egyptians ruled over the children of Israel with *force*" (Exod. 1:13). κατεδυνάστευον οἱ Αἰγύπτιοι τοὺς υἱοὺς Ἰσραηλ βίᾳ. Isaiah, proclaiming the word of the Lord, said, "Into Egypt my people went down at the first to sojourn there, and to the Assyrians they were carried by *force*" (Isa. 52:4). καὶ εἰς Ἀσσυρίους βίᾳ ἤχθησαν. The book of Wisdom says of the ungodly, "By the *violence* of winds they shall be rooted out." ὑπὸ βίας ἀνέμων ἐκριζωθήσεται (4:4). Elsewhere Wisdom says, "And not even the *force* of fire prevailed to give light." καὶ πυρὸς μὲν οὐδεμία βία κατίσχυεν φωτίζειν (17:5).

In the New Testament βία occurs only in the book of Acts. When the officers arrested the apostles, "they were bringing them, not with *violence,* for they were fearing the people, lest they should be stoned" (Acts

5:26). ἦγεν αὐτούς, οὐ μετὰ βίας, ἐφοβοῦντο γὰρ τὸν λαόν. Having seized Paul in the temple, the Jewish mob beat him so severely that "when he came to the stairs, it came to pass that he was being borne by the soldiers because of the *violence* of the mob" (Acts 21:35). συνέβη βαστάζεσθαι αὐτὸν ὑπὸ τῶν στρατιωτῶν διὰ τὴν βίαν τοῦ ὄχλου. On the voyage to Rome Paul's ship ran aground at Malta, "but the stern was being destroyed by the *violence* [of the waves]" (Acts 27:41). ἡ δέ πρύμνα ἐλύετο ὑπὸ τῆς βίας.

δύναμις

Telemachus, addressing his mother's suitors, said, "I would indeed defend myself, if only I had the *power.*" ἦ τ᾽ ἂν ἀμυναίμην, εἴ μοι δύναμίς γε παρείη (Homer *Odyssey* 2.62). When Alexander urged Hector to lead on to the battle, he promised him, "We will not be lacking in valour, as much as we have *strength;* but beyond his *strength* no one is able to fight, no matter how eager he may be." ὅση δύναμίς γε πάρεστι. πὰρ δύναμιν δ᾽ οὐν ἔστι καὶ ἐσσύμενον πολεμίζειν (Homer *Iliad* 13.787). Herodotus used this word in the sense of "military power" when he mentioned that the Ionians took all of Sardis "except only the citadel, which was defended by Artaphrenes himself with great *power.*" τὴν δὲ ἀκρόπολιν ἐρρύετο αὐτὸς Ἀρταφρένης ἔχων ἀνδρῶν δύναμιν οὐκ ὀλίγην (5.100). A very different meaning is found in Thucydides when he speaks of the table-furniture of the Egestaeans, "which being of silver, although of small *value* in money, made a much greater display." ἃ ὄντα ἀργυρᾶ πολλῷ πλείω τὴν ὄψιν ἀπ᾽ ὀλίγης δυνάμεως χρημάτων παρείχετο (6.46). In his petition Apollonarion stated, "As long as I had the *power* I cultivated these things." ἐς ὅσον μὲν οὖν δύναμίς μοι ὑπῆρχεν (*P. Oxy.*, VI, 899.8).

In the Septuagint this word was used in the Song of Moses: "The chariots of Pharaoh and his *host* He cast into the sea" (Exod. 15:4). ἅρματα Φαραω καὶ τὴν δύναμιν αὐτοῦ ἔρριψεν εἰς θάλασσαν. Moses prayed to Jehovah, "Lord, Lord, thou didst begin to show to thy servant thy *strength* and thy *power* and thy *mighty* hand" (Deut. 3:24). Κύριε, κύριε, σὺ ἤρξω δεῖξαι τῷ σῷ θεράποντι τὴν ἰσχύν σου καὶ τὴν δυναμίν σου καὶ τὴν χεῖρα τὴν κραταιάν. The psalmist used another common phrase when he said, "Who is this King of glory? The Lord of *hosts,* He is the King of glory" (Ps. 23:10; KJ Ps. 24:10). τίς ἐστιν οὗτος ὁ βασιλεὺς τῆς δόξης; κύριος τῶν δυνάμεων, αὐτός ἐστιν ὁ βασιλεὺς τῆς δόξης. The last psalm commands, "Praise ye God in His holy places; praise ye Him in the firmament of His *power*"(Ps. 150:1). αἰνεῖτε αὐτὸν ἐν στερεώματι δυνάμεως αὐτοῦ.

The angel Gabriel, announcing to Mary the birth of Jesus, said, "The Holy Spirit shall come upon thee, and the *power* of the Highest shall overshadow thee" (Luke 1:35). πνεῦμα ἅγιον ἐπελεύσεται ἐπὶ σέ, καὶ δύναμις ὑψίστου ἐπισκιάσει σοι. In the public ministry of the Lord Jesus, His miracles caused astonishment. On one occasion the multitude said, "What is this word, that with *authority* and *power* he commands the unclean spirits, and they come out?" (Luke 4:36). τίς ὁ λόγος οὗτος, ὅτι ἐν ἐξουσίᾳ καὶ δυνάμει ἐπιτάσσει τοῖς ἀκαθάρτοις πνεύμασιν. The Lord had both the authority and the power to perform His miracles; in fact, they are often called "mighty works." "Then he began to upbraid the cities in which the most of his *mighty works* had been done" (Matt. 11:20). τότε ἤρξατο ὀνειδίζειν τὰς πόλεις ἐν αἷς ἐγένοντο αἱ πλεῖσται δυνάμεις αὐτοῦ. Before He ascended, the Lord promised the disciples, "But ye shall receive *power* after the Holy Spirit has come upon you" (Acts 1:8). ἀλλὰ λήμψεσθε δύναμιν ἐπελθόντος τοῦ ἁγίου πνεύματος ἐφ᾽ ὑμᾶς. Paul, writing to the Romans, declared, "For I am not ashamed of the Gospel; for it is the *power* of God unto salvation to every one who believes" (Rom. 1:16). οὐ γὰρ ἐπαισχύνομαι τὸ εὐαγγέλιον· δύναμις γὰρ θεοῦ ἐστιν εἰς σωτηρίαν.

κράτος

Homer used this word in the sense of sheer physical strength as opposed to guile when he recounted how Areïthous died: "Him Lycurgus slew by guile, and not by *might.*" τὸν Λυκόεργος ἔπεφνε δόλῳ, οὔ τι κράτεΐ γε (*Iliad* 7.142). In the *Odyssey* Homer described a smith tempering an ax by plunging it into cold water, "for from this is the *strength* of the iron." τὸ γὰρ αὖτε σιδήρου γε κράτος ἐστίν (9.393). Herodotus related that Megabyzus, when he argued for a ruling oligarchy, said, "I agree to all that Otanes says against tyranny, but when he bids you give *power* to the multitude, his judgment falls short of the best." τὰ δ᾽ ἐς τὸ πλῆθος ἄνωγε φέρειν τὸ κράτος, γνώμης τῆς ἀρίστης ἡμάρτηκε (3.81). Euripides represented Zeus as the god "who has *power* over all the other gods." ὃς τῶν μὲν ἄλλων δαιμόνων ἔχει κράτος (*The Daughters of Troy* 949). Thus this word connotes both physical strength and political sovereignty. A papyrus recorded this popular exclamation: "The *power* of the Romans forever!" εἰς ἐῶνα τὸ κράτος τῶν Ῥωμαίων (*P. Oxy.*, I, 41.i.2).

Before they entered Palestine, Moses warned the Israelites, "Say not in thy heart, My own *strength* and the *might* of my hand gained me this great *power*" (Deut. 8:17). μὴ εἴπῃς ἐν τῇ καρδίᾳ σου Ἡ ἰσχύς μου καὶ τὸ κράτος τῆς χειρός μου ἐποίησέν μοι τὴν δύναμιν τὴν μεγάλην ταύτην. The psalmist prayed, "My *strength* I guard with thee, because thou, O God, art my helper" (Ps. 58:10; KJ Ps. 59:9). τὸ κράτος μου, πρὸς σὲ φυλάξω. In another psalm it is written, "Once God spoke; these two things I heard, that *strength* belongs to God, and to thee, Lord, belongs mercy" (Ps. 61:12–13; KJ Ps. 62:11–12). ἅπαξ ἐλάλησεν ὁ θεός, δύο ταῦτα ἤκουσα, ὅτι τὸ κράτος τοῦ θεοῦ, καὶ σοί, κύριε, τὸ ἔλεος. Isaiah said of God, "The one who brings out his host by number shall call them all by name; from the great glory and in the *might* of his *strength* nothing escapes thee" (Isa. 40:26). ἀπὸ πολλῆς δόξης καὶ ἐν κράτει ἰσχύος οὐδέν σε ἔλαθεν.

In the Magnificat Mary said, "He showed *strength* with his arm" (Luke 1:51). ἐποίησεν κράτος ἐν βραχίονι αὐτοῦ. Paul prayed that the Colossians might increase in the knowledge of God, "being made powerful in all *power* according to the *might* of his glory unto all patience and longsuffering with joy" (Col. 1:11). ἐν πάσῃ δυνάμει δυναμούμενοι κατὰ τὸ κράτος τῆς δόξης αὐτοῦ. The writer to the Hebrews declared that Christ partook of flesh and blood "that through death he might bring to nothing the one who has the *power* of death, that is the devil" (Heb. 2:14). ἵνα διὰ τοῦ θανάτου καταργήσῃ τὸν τὸ κράτος ἔχοντα τοῦ θανάτου. In the book of Revelation John gave praise to the Lord Jesus: "To him be the glory and the *power* forever and ever" (1:6). αὐτῷ ἡ δόξα καὶ τὸ κράτος εἰς τοὺς αἰῶνας τῶν αἰώνων.

ἰσχύς

Aeschylus contrasted "brute strength" with "guile" in the words of Prometheus "How that it was not by *brute strength* nor by violence, but by guile that those who should gain the upper hand were destined to prevail." ὡς οὐ κατ᾽ ἰσχὺν οὐδὲ πρὸς τὸ καρτερὸν χρείη, δόλῳ δὲ τοὺς ὑπερσχόντας κρατεῖν (*Prometheus Bound* 214). Elsewhere Aeschylus wrote, "But yet the *might* of god is above all." θεοῦ δ᾽ ἔτ᾽ ἰσχὺς καθυπερτέρα (*Seven Against Thebes* 226). Plato related a speech of Aristophanes on the "hermaphrodite" in which he said, "Therefore they were of surprising *strength* and vigour, and so lofty in their ideas that they even conspired against the gods." ἦν οὖν τὴν ἰσχὺν δεινὰ καὶ τὴν ῥώμην (*Symposium* 190B). Jason says to Medea, "First, then, in Hellas thou didst dwell, instead of a barbaric land; thou knowest justice, and thou knowest to live by law without respect of *force*." καὶ δίκην ἐπίστασαι νόμοις τε χρῆσθαι μὴ πρὸς ἰσχύος χάριν (Euripides *Medea* 538). The writer of one of the papyri mentioned "his own *strength* and *power*." τὴν ἰδίαν ἰσχὺν καὶ δύναμιν (*P. Lond.* 1319.5).

Part of the judgment which the Lord pronounced upon Cain was "When thou tillest the ground, it will not henceforth yield to thee its *strength*" (Gen. 4:12). ὅτι ἐργᾷ τὴν γῆν, καὶ οὐ προσθήσει τὴν ἰσχὺν αὐτῆς δοῦναί σοι. In the song of Moses the Israelites sang, "Thy right

POWER

hand, O Lord, is glorious in *strength*" (Exod. 15:6). ἡ δεξιά σου, κύριε, δεδόξασται ἐν ἰσχύι. When Joshua prepared to attack Ai, Scripture says, "And Joshua chose out thirty thousand men, *mighty* in *strength* and sent them away by night" (Josh. 8:3). ἐπέλεξεν δὲ Ἰησοῦς τριάκοντα χιλιάδας ἀνδρῶν δυνατοὺς ἐν ἰσχύι. The psalmist prayed, "I will love thee, O Lord, my *strength*" (Ps. 17:2; KJ Ps. 18:1). ἀγαπήσω σε, κύριε ἡ ἰσχύς μου.

When the Lord Jesus was asked about the greatest commandment, He replied, "Thou shalt love the Lord thy God from thy whole heart and from thy whole soul and from thy whole mind and from thy whole *strength*" (Mark 12:30). ἀγαπήσεις κύριον τὸν θεόν σου ἐξ ὅλης τῆς καρδίας σου καὶ ἐξ ὅλης τῆς ψυχῆς σου καὶ ἐξ ὅλης τῆς διανοίας σου καὶ ἐξ ὅλης τῆς ἰσχύος σου. Paul spoke of the vengeance which is coming on those who obey not the Gospel, "who shall suffer punishment, eternal destruction from the face of the Lord and from the glory of his *strength*" (II Thess. 1:9). οἵτινες δίκην τίσουσιν ὄλεθρον αἰώνιον ἀπὸ προσώπου τοῦ κυρίου καὶ ἀπὸ τῆς δόξης τῆς ἰσχύος αὐτοῦ. When Peter said concerning the false teachers which should come, "Whereas angels, although they are greater in *strength* and *power,* do not bring a railing judgment against them before the Lord" (II Pet. 2:11), he used two of these words as close synonyms. ὅπου ἄγγελοι ἰσχύϊ καὶ δυνάμει μείζονες ὄντες οὐ φέρουσιν κατ᾽ αὐτῶν. The Apostle John saw the angels around the throne praising God and saying, "Worthy is the Lamb that has been slain to receive *power* and riches and wisdom and *strength* and honor and glory and blessing" (Rev. 5:12). ἄξιός ἐστιν τὸ ἀρνίον τὸ ἐσφαγμένον λαβεῖν τὴν δύναμιν καὶ πλοῦτον καὶ σοφίαν καὶ ἰσχὺν καὶ τιμήν.

ἐξουσία

Thucydides recounted the speech of the Corinthians in which they said, "But in the arrogance and *authority* of wealth they have wronged us in many other ways." ὕβρει δὲ καὶ ἐξουσίᾳ πλούτου πολλὰ ἐς ἡμᾶς ἄλλα τε ἡμαρτήκασι (1.38.6). Aristotle mentioned those "who are in more *authority.*" οἱ ἐν ἐξουσίᾳ μᾶλλον ὄντες (*Rhetoric* 2.6.9). In the *Symposium* Plato wrote, "The law has given *authority.*" ἐξουσίαν ὁ νόμος δέδωκε (182E). The petition of Dionysia also declared, "I esteem the law which gives me *authority.*" ἀξιῶ τοῦ νόμου διδόντος μοι ἐξουσίαν (*P. Oxy.* II, 237.6.17). In another petition a widow cried out against a man who had illegally taken her female slave: "He dared to carry off my slave, Theodora, although he had no *authority* over her." ἐτόλμησεν ἀποσπάσαι δούλην μου Θεοδώραν, μὴ ἔχων κατ᾽ αὐτῆς ἐξουσίαν (*P. Oxy.,* VIII, 1120.17 f).

When the ambassadors from Babylon came to Hezekiah, he showed them all of his treasures. "There was not a thing which Hezekiah did not show them in his house and in all his *authority"* (II Kings 20:13). ἐν τῷ αὐτοῦ καὶ ἐν πάσῃ τῇ ἐξουσίᾳ αὐτοῦ. Proverbs says, "A rule of righteousness gives *authority* to words" (17:14). ἐξουσίαν δίδωσιν λόγοις ἀρχὴ δικαιοσύνης. The book of Wisdom declares concerning God, "For thou hast *authority* over life and death." σὺ γὰρ ζωῆς καὶ θανάτου ἐξουσίαν ἔχεις (16:13). When the son of Sirach mentioned God's creation of man and the earth, he said, "And He gave them *authority* over the things which are upon it." καὶ ἔδωκεν αὐτοῖς ἐξουσίαν τῶν ἐπ' αὐτῆς (Ecclesiasticus 17:2).

The Lord Jesus warned the multitude to fear God: "Fear ye the one who, after he has killed, has *authority* to cast into Gehenna" (Luke 12:5). φοβήθητε τὸν μετὰ τὸ ἀποκτεῖναι ἔχοντα ἐξουσίαν ἐμβαλεῖν εἰς τὴν γέενναν. On one occasion the chief priests and elders challenged the Lord by saying, "With what *authority* art thou doing these things?" (Mark 11:28). ἐν ποίᾳ ἐξουσίᾳ ταῦτα ποιεῖς; When the Lord sent Ananias to restore sight to Saul, Ananias protested, "Here he has *authority* from the chief priests to bind all who call upon thy name" (Acts 9:14). ὧδε ἔχει ἐξουσίαν παρὰ τῶν ἀρχιερέων δῆσαι πάντας τοὺς ἐπικαλουμένους τὸ ὄνομά σου. Paul exhorted the Romans, "Let every soul be subject to the higher *authorities"*(Rom. 13:1). πᾶσα ψυχὴ ἐξουσίαις ὑπερεχούσαις ὑποτασσέσθω. There are some unusual uses of this word, as in John's description of the demonic horses: "For the *ability* of the horses is in their mouth and in their tails" (Rev. 9:19). ἡ γὰρ ἐξουσία τῶν ἵππων ἐν τῷ στόματι αὐτῶν ἐστιν. In the final words of the Lord to John, He promised, "Blessed are the ones who wash their robes, that they may have *authority* [right to] over the tree of life" (Rev. 22:14). ἵνα ἔσται ἡ ἐξουσία αὐτῶν ἐπὶ τὸ ξύλον τῆς ζωῆς.

ἐνέργεια

Although this word is not common before Aristotle, he used it with considerable freedom. In one passage he began, "If indeed the function of man is *activity* of soul according to rational principle." εἰ δή ἐστιν ἔργον ἀνθρώπου ψυχῆς ἐνέργεια κατὰ λόγον (*Nicomachean Ethics* 1.7.13). With a different sense Aristotle, citing a line from Euripides, said, "The word 'having sprung' expresses both *actuality* and metaphor." τὸ ἄξαντες ἐνέργεια καὶ μεταφορά (*Rhetoric* 3.11.2). The *Letter of Aristeas* declares, "But persuasion is being guided rightly by the *working* of God." θεοῦ δὲ ἐνεργείᾳ κατευθύνεται πειθώ (line 266).

The writer of the book of Wisdom claimed that God had given him gifts of knowledge "to know the constitution of the world and the *operation* of the elements." εἰδέναι σύστασιν κόσμου καὶ ἐνέργειαν στοιχείων

(7:17). Later he spoke of the wisdom "of the *working* of God." τῆς τοῦ θεοῦ ἐνεργείας (7:26). In another passage he said, "But he overcame the anger, not by *strength* of body, not by *operation* [efficiency] of weapons." οὐκ ἰσχύι τοῦ σώματος, οὐχ ὅπλων ἐνεργείᾳ (18:22). God struck Heliodorus with judgment, so that "he, through the divine *working*, was speechless and bereft of all hope and deliverance." ὁ μὲν διὰ τὴν θείαν ἐνέργειαν ἄφωνος (II Maccabees 3:29).

When Paul prayed for the believers, he seemed to pile together the words for power, praying that they might know "what is the superabounding greatness of his *power* unto us who believe, according to the *operation* of the *might* of his *strength*" (Eph. 1:19). τί τὸ ὑπερβάλλον μέγεθος τῆς δυνάμεως αὐτοῦ εἰς ἡμᾶς τοὺς πιστεύοντας κατὰ τὴν ἐνέργειαν τοῦ κράτους τῆς ἰσχύος αὐτοῦ. To the Philippians he wrote that the Lord Jesus Christ "shall transform the body of our humiliation, that it may be conformed to the body of his glory, according to the *working* by which he is able even to subdue all things to himself" (Phil. 3:21). κατὰ τὴν ἐνέργειαν τοῦ δύνασθαι αὐτὸν καὶ ὑποτάξαι αὐτῷ τὰ πάντα. Again to the Colossians he wrote concerning the resurrection of Christ, "Ye were raised with him through faith in the *working* of God, who raised him from the dead" (Col. 2:12). συνηγέρθητε διὰ τῆς πίστεως τῆς ἐνεργείας τοῦ θεοῦ τοῦ ἐγείραντος αὐτὸν ἐκ νεκρῶν. When Paul mentioned the advent of the antichrist and his followers, he said, "Because of this God sends them a *working* of error that they might believe the lie" (II Thess. 2:11). διὰ τοῦτο πέμπει αὐτοῖς ὁ θεὸς ἐνέργειαν πλάνης.

SUMMARY

The word βία means "force" or "violence," coming as it does from "life force." The word δύναμις signifies "power" or "strength," with a root meaning of "being able." κράτος designates "power" or "strength," with the connotation of "possession" or "mastery." ἰσχύς also expresses "power" or "strength," but from a root which means sheer "physical strength." The word ἐξουσία means "authority," "the power to decide." The last word, ἐνέργεια, means "energy," "working," "activity," or "operation."

8. Rain: ὑετός, βροχή, ὄμβρος

The regular word for *rain* in classical Greek was ὑετός. In Hellenistic times βροχή began to be used for *rain*, often with the sense of *heavy rain*, and in modern Greek βροχή has supplanted its predecessor as the word for *rain*. The strongest term of all was ὄμβρος, *thunderstorm*.

ὑετός

This was the word for "a common rain" (Liddell and Scott, p. 1046). Homer spoke of two oak trees that "through day upon day stand up to the wind and the *rain.*" αἵτ᾽ ἄνεμον μίμνουσι καὶ ὑετὸν ἤματα πάντα (*Iliad* 12.133). Interestingly, Herodotus turned the word into a superlative adjective: "Those are the *rainiest* of all winds." ἀνέμων πολλὸν τῶν πάντων ὑετιώτατοι (2.25). In the Septuagint this word is also the regular term for "rain." The Lord God spoke in warning to Noah, "For yet seven days and I will bring *rain* upon the earth" (Gen. 7:4). ἐγὼ ἐπάγω ὑετὸν ἐπὶ τὴν γῆν. The book of Job speaks of God as One "who gives *rain* upon the earth" (5:10). τὸν διδόντα ὑετὸν ἐπὶ τὴν γῆν. In the papyri the cognate verb is used in an Athenian prayer: "*Rain, rain,* O dear Zeus, upon the grainfields of the Athenians and their meadows." ὗσον, ὗσον, ω φίλε Ζεῦ, κατὰ τῆς ἀρούρας τῆς Ἀθηναίων (*M. Anton.* 5.7., cited in Moulton and Milligan, p. 648).

The Apostle Paul reminded the men of Lystra that God was "giving you from heaven *rains* and fruitful seasons . . ." (Acts 14:17). ὑμῖν ὑετοὺς διδούς. When Paul and his company were shipwrecked on the island of Malta, the natives of the island helped them greatly, "For they kindled a fire and received us all because of the standing *rain* and because of the cold" (Acts 28:2). διὰ τὸν ὑετὸν τὸν ἐφεστῶτα. The writer to the Hebrews stated, "For land which has drunk the *rain* which oftentimes comes upon it and brings forth herbs . . . receives blessing from God" (Heb. 6:7). τὸν ἐπ᾽ αὐτῆς ἐρχόμενον πολλάκις ὑετόν. When James spoke of the power of prayer, he used Elijah as an example. Elijah prayed, and it did not rain for three years and six months. "And again he prayed, and the heaven gave *rain,* and the earth brought forth her fruit" (James 5:18). ὁ οὐρανὸς ὑετὸν ἔδωκεν. The two witnesses in the book of Revelation are described as having the power "to shut the heaven in order that it may not rain a *rain* during the days of their prophecy" (11:6). ἵνα μὴ ὑετὸς βρέχῃ.

RAIN

βροχή

Because this word does not occur in classical Greek, Thayer classified it as a "Biblical" word (p. 694). More recent discoveries in the papyri, however, have shown him to have been wrong. The cognate verb βρέχω is common enough in classical literature with the meaning "to wet," "to irrigate," and in an impersonal sense "it rains." In one of the papyri which is dated A.D. 88–89 a lease of land was arranged "for four years [and] four *rains*." εἰς ἔτη τέσσαρα βροχὰς τέσσαρες (*P. Oxy.*, 280.5). Apparently if there was no rain, the year was not to count as one of the four lease years. There is also a sense of "adequate rain," because a brief shower would not be enough to make crops grow. In the Septuagint the meaning of "substantial rain" is also clear. The psalmist prayed, "Thou, O God, canst assign to thine inheritance a plentiful *rain* voluntarily" (Ps. 67:10; KJ Ps. 68:9). βροχὴν ἑκούσιον ἀφοριεῖς, ὁ θεός.

The New Testament uses this word in only one passage. Our Lord described in the Sermon on the Mount the wise man and the foolish building their respective houses, "and the *rain* came down, and the rivers [floods] came, and the winds blew . . ." (Matt. 7:25, 27). κατέβη ἡ βροχὴ καὶ ἦλθον οἱ ποταμοί. Here the word portrays a "torrential rain" which will produce flash flooding.

ὄμβρος

This is the classic term for a "thunderstorm." Homer described a winter torrent "rising suddenly as Zeus' *thunderstorm* makes heavy the water." ὅτ᾽ ἐπιβρίσῃ Διὸς ὄμβρος (*Iliad* 5.91). Again he mentioned a winter-swollen river "following a *thunderstorm* from Zeus." ὀπαζόμενος Διὸς ὄμβρῳ (*Iliad* 11.493). This was a common expression because thunderbolts were Zeus' characteristic weapons. Herodotus recorded a "furious *thunderstorm*" following a sea battle. ὄμβρος λάβρος (8.12). In the same book he described the Persians' communication system, which seems to have been similar to the "pony express"—their riders were "stayed neither by snow nor *thunderstorm* nor heat nor darkness from accomplishing their appointed course with all speed." οὔτε νιφετός, οὐκ ὄμβρος, οὐ καῦμα (8.98).

In the Septuagint the Song of Moses describes the prophet's words coming down "as a *thundershower* upon the grass" (Deut. 32:2). ὡσεὶ ὄμβρος ἐπ᾽ ἄγρωστιν. The son of Sirach commented in a different context, "For he [God] remembered the enemies in a *thunderstorm*." ἐμνήσθη τῶν ἐχθρῶν ἐν ὄμβρῳ (Ecclesiasticus 49:9). In the book of Wisdom the ungodly are said to be pursued "with strange rains and hails and inexorable *thunderstorms*." ξένοις ὑετοῖς καὶ χαλάζαις καὶ ὄμβροις (16:16).

A TREASURY OF NEW TESTAMENT SYNONYMS

This word also occurs only once in the New Testament. When the Lord Jesus reproached the multitude for failing to see the signs of the times, He said, "Whenever ye see a cloud rising in the west, immediately ye say, 'A *thunderstorm* comes,' and it happens thus" (Luke 12:54). εὐθέως λέγετε ὅτι ὄμβρος ἔρχεται.

SUMMARY

The word ὑετός is the usual word for "rain"; βροχή means a "heavy rain," and ὄμβρος a "thunderstorm."

9. Remembrance: ἀνάμνησις, ὑπόμνησις

The word ἀνάμνησις, *remembrance* or *recollection,* is used especially for something which comes spontaneously into memory. In contrast, ὑπόμνησις, designating a *reminder* given by another person, emphasizes the agent who is doing the reminding.

ἀνάμνησις

When Plato in *Phaedo* recounted Socrates' teaching on the immortality of the soul, he cited the statement of Cebes, "Your favorite teaching, O Socrates, that knowledge is simply *remembrance,* if it is true, also necessarily implies a previous time in which we have learned that which we now remember." εἰ ἀληθής ἐστιν, ὃν σὺ εἴωθας θαμὰ λέγειν, ὅτι ἡμῖν ἡ μάθησις οὐκ ἄλλο τι ἢ ἀνάμνησις τυγχάνει οὖσα (72E). Further on in the same dialogue is the statement "But the teaching concerning the *remembrance* and knowledge has been proven to me on trustworthy grounds." ὁ δὲ περὶ τῆς ἀναμνήσεως καὶ μαθήσεως λόγος δι᾽ ὑποθέσεως ἀξίας ἀποδέξασθαι εἴρηται (92D). This statement implies a spontaneous recollection.

In the instruction concerning the bread of the sanctuary the Lord said to Moses, "They shall be set before the Lord for loaves of *remembrance*" (Lev. 24:7). ἔσονται εἰς ἄρτους εἰς ἀνάμνησιν προκείμενα τῷ κυρίῳ. When the Israelites celebrated a festal occasion, the Lord commanded them, "Ye shall blow the trumpets over your burnt-offerings, and over the sacrifices of your peace-offerings; and it shall be to you for a *remembrance* before your God" (Num. 10:10). καὶ ἔσται ὑμῖν ἀνάμνησις ἔναντι τοῦ θεοῦ ὑμῶν. This word is found in the title of two of the Psalms. One is entitled, "A Psalm by David; for *remembrance* concerning a Sabbath" (Ps. 37:1; KJ Ps. 38). Ψαλμος τῷ Δαυιδ· εἰς ἀνάμνησιν περὶ σαββάτου. The other bears the title, "Unto the end; by David for a *remembrance,* that the Lord may save me" (Ps. 69:1–2; KJ Ps. 70). Εἰς τὸ τέλος· τῷ Δαυιδ εἰς ἀνάμνησιν, εἰς τὸ σῶσαί με κύριον. One of the papyri mentioned "*recollections* of [vows to pay] sacrifices." ἀναμνήσεις θυσιῶν (*Lysias* 194.22).

When the Lord Jesus instituted the sacrament of the Lord's Supper, He said, "This is my body which is given in your behalf; this do ye in *remembrance* of me" (Luke 22:19). τοῦτο ποιεῖτε εἰς τὴν ἐμὴν ἀνάμνησιν.

A TREASURY OF NEW TESTAMENT SYNONYMS

In relating the institution of the sacrament the Apostle Paul quoted these very words and added concerning the cup, "This do ye, as often as ye drink it, in *remembrance* of me" (I Cor. 11:24–25). τοῦτο ποιεῖτε, ὁσάκις ἐὰν πίνητε, εἰς τὴν ἐμὴν ἀνάμνησιν. Clearly the Lord Jesus expected His people to remember spontaneously His sacrifice for them.

The writer to the Hebrews mentioned the sacrifices which the Jews made year after year and which could not take away sin because "In them there is a *remembrance* of sins year by year" (Heb. 10:3). ἐν αὐταῖς ἀνάμνησις ἁμαρτιῶν κατ' ἐνιαυτόν. These sacrifices were a continual "calling to mind of sins" (Westcott, *Hebrews*, p. 306). Since the sacrifice on Calvary, however, the believer should spontaneously remember the Lord's great deliverance (I Cor. 11:24–25).

ὑπόμνησις

Thucydides described how the envoys of the Lacedaemonians addressed the Athenians, saying, "And do not receive what we say in a hostile way, nor feel that you are being instructed as though you were without understanding, but regard our words as merely a *reminder* to men who know how to come to a good decision." μηδ' ὡς ἀξύνετοι διδασκόμενοι, ὑπόμνησιν δὲ τοῦ καλῶς βουλεύσασθαι πρὸς εἰδότας ἡγησάμενοι (4.17.3). On another occasion one of the Athenian commanders exhorted his men because "he was wishing to make a *reminder* of their old-time confidence." ἐβούλετο ὑπόμνησιν ποιήσασθαι τοῦ θαρσεῖν (2.88.3).

In the Septuagint the psalmist prayed, "Thou art my Protector from my mother's belly," and the Codex Sinaiticus added, "My *reminder* is always in Thee" (Ps. 70:6; KJ Ps. 71:6). ἐν σοὶ ἡ ὑπόμνησίς μου διὰ παντός. The regular Septuagint reading (and the more accurate one) is "praise," ὕμνησις. The book of Wisdom described God's treatment of His enemies: "For they were being pricked unto a *reminder* of thy oracles and were being saved quickly." εἰς γὰρ ὑπόμνησιν τῶν λογίων σου ἐνεκεντρίζοντο (16:11). In II Maccabees is the statement, "Let these things which we have spoken suffice unto a *reminder* to you." ἕως ὑπομνήσεως ταῦθ' ἡμῖν εἰρήσθω (6:17). A late papyrus has the example, "You did not show a *reminder* to me concerning what you know." περὶ ὅ[ι] οἶδες οὐδεμίαν ὑπόμνησίν μοι ἐδηλώσας (*P. Oxy.*, XII, 1593.6).

When Paul wrote to his faithful helper Timothy, he mentioned that he was praying for him day and night, "Having received a *reminder* of the unfeigned faith which is in thee; which dwelt first in thy grandmother Lois, and thy mother Eunice" (II Tim. 1:5). ὑπόμνησιν λαβὼν τῆς ἐν σοὶ ἀνυποκρίτου πίστεως. Apparently some "reminder" of Timothy's genuine faith had just reached Paul's prison cell.

REMEMBRANCE

As long as the Apostle Peter was still alive, it was his dedicated purpose "to stir you up by a *reminder*" (II Pet. 1:13). διεγείρειν ὑμᾶς ἐν ὑπομνήσει. He wished his readers to have an abundant entrance into the Kingdom of God (II Pet. 1:11). In both of his epistles this was his concern: "This is now, beloved, the second epistle which I am writing to you, in both of which I am stirring up your sincere mind by a *reminder*" (II Pet. 3:1). ἐν αἷς διεγείρω ὑμῶν ἐν ὑπομνήσει τὴν εἰλικρινῆ διάνοιαν.

SUMMARY

The best meaning for ἀνάμνησις is a "remembrance" which comes spontaneously to mind; for ὑπόμνησις, a "reminder" which is given to a person by someone else.

10. Rest: ἀνάπαυσις, κατάπαυσις

The word ἀνάπαυσις, meaning *rest, respite,* a *ceasing,* or a *resting place,* connotes temporary rest as a preparation for further work. In contrast to this κατάπαυσις—*rest,* a *causing to stop,* or a *resting place*—implies a permanent rest.

ἀνάπαυσις

Thucydides recounted the speech of the Lacedaemonians in which they said, "Let us for ourselves choose peace instead of war and give a *respite* from evils to the other Hellenes." αὐτοί τε ἀντὶ πολέμου εἰρήνην ἑλώμεθα καὶ τοῖς ἄλλοις Ἕλλησιν ἀνάπαυσιν κακῶν ποιήσωμεν (4.20). In one of the papyri a seventy-year-old man begged for a *"respite"* from public duties. ἀναπαύσεως (*P. Flor.*, I, 57.56).

This is a common word in the Septuagint. When Noah sent the dove out of the ark, the Scripture said that "the dove, finding no *resting place* for its feet, returned to him into the ark" (Gen. 8:9). οὐχ εὑροῦσα ἡ περιστερὰ ἀνάπαυσιν τοῖς ποσὶν αὐτῆς ὑπέστρεψεν. The Israelites gathered twice as much manna on Friday, and Moses said to the elders, "Tomorrow is a sabbath, a holy *rest* to the Lord" (Exod. 16:23). σάββατα ἀνάπαυσις ἁγία τῷ κυρίῳ αὔριον. It is obvious in these two examples that the perch for the dove and the rest for the Israelites on their march to the promised land are only temporary. When the Lord instituted the feast of trumpets, He said, "In the seventh month, on the first day of the month, there shall be to you a *rest,* a memorial of trumpets" (Lev. 23:24). ἔσται ὑμῖν ἀνάπαυσις, μνημόσυνον σαλπίγγων. In the Shepherd Psalm, David said, "In a green place, there He caused me to dwell; by water of *rest* he brought me up" (Ps. 22:2; KJ Ps. 23:2). ἐπὶ ὕδατος ἀναπαύσεως ἐξέθρεψέν με. There are even passages in the prophets referring to the Millennium that use this word. Isaiah spoke of the great "Root of Jesse" with the words, "Unto him shall the nations hope; and his *resting place* shall be glorious" (Isa. 11:10). ἐπ᾽ αὐτῷ ἔθνη ἐλπιοῦσιν, καὶ ἔσται ἡ ἀνάπαυσις αὐτοῦ τιμή. This does not refer to the eternal state, but to the Millennium, as does another well-known passage: "And the works of righteousness shall be peace, and righteousness shall support *rest,* and they shall be confident forever" (Isa. 32:17). καὶ κρατήσει ἡ δικαιοσύνη ἀνάπαυσιν, καὶ πεποιθότες ἕως τοῦ αἰῶνος.

REST

"Take my yoke upon you and learn of me, for I am meek and lowly in heart, and ye shall find *rest* for your souls" (Matt. 11:29). καὶ εὑρήσετε ἀνάπαυσιν ταῖς ψυχαῖς ὑμῶν. The believer will not find absolute rest in this life, but he surely will find a rest which will prepare him for continued labor and service for the Lord. When the Lord spoke of the inability of mere human reformation to keep Satan's minions away, He said, "But the unclean spirit, whenever he goes forth from the man, passes through dry places seeking *rest* and does not find it" (Matt. 12:43). διέρχεται δι' ἀνύδρων τόπων ζητοῦν ἀνάπαυσιν, καὶ οὐχ εὑρίσκει. There is not even a temporary rest for this evil spirit. The four living creatures described by the Apostle John "have no *ceasing* day and night, saying, Holy, holy, holy, is the Lord God, the Almighty" (Rev. 4:8). ἀνάπαυσιν οὐκ ἔχουσιν ἡμέρας καὶ νυκτὸς λέγοντες· ἅγιος ἅγιος ἅγιος κύριος. Not even a temporary cessation interrupts their ascription of glory to the Lord God.

κατάπαυσις

After Herodotus had recounted the removal of tyrants in various cities, he said, "Thus indeed an *end* was made of despots in the cities." τυράννων μέν νυν κατάπαυσις ἐγίνετο ἀνὰ τὰς πόλιας (5.38). Later, Herodotus stated, "This then was how Demaratus came to an *end* of his kingship." κατὰ μὲν δὴ Δημαρήτου τὴν κατάπαυσιν τῆς βασιληίης οὕτω ἐγένετο (6.67). Both of these examples imply a "causing to stop" permanently.

The distinction between these two synonyms is not sharply maintained by the Septuagint. When Moses reminded the Israelites of the law of the sabbath, he said, "Six days thou shalt do works, but on the seventh day there shall be a *rest,* a holy one, a sabbath, a *rest* to the Lord" (Ex. 35:2). τῇ δὲ ἡμέρᾳ τῇ ἑβδόμῃ κατάπαυσις, ἅγιον, σάββατα, ἀνάπαυσις κυρίῳ. Since they are both used here in the same context, the translator probably meant to use them interchangeably. Moses described the moving and halting of the ark in the wilderness wanderings, saying, "And in the *resting* he said, Return, O Lord, unto the thousands of ten thousands in Israel" (Num. 10:35). καὶ ἐν τῇ καταπαύσει εἶπεν Ἐπίστρεφε, κύριε, χιλιάδας μυριάδας ἐν τῷ Ισραηλ. The meaning here is probably just "rest" with no thought of permanence. In many passages in the Septuagint, however, the context in which κατάπαυσις is used makes it clear that a "permanent rest" is meant. On one occasion Moses addressed the children of Israel and said, "For ye are not come for the present unto the *rest* and unto the inheritance, which the Lord your God gives you" (Deut. 12:9). οὐ γὰρ ἥκατε ἕως τοῦ νῦν εἰς τὴν κατάπαυσιν καὶ τὴν κληρονομίαν. The thought is surely a permanent rest. The psalmist mentioned God's rest twice; both times the permanence is the dominant idea. God is portrayed as saying, "As I swore in my wrath, They shall not enter into my *rest*"(Ps. 94:11; KJ Ps. 95:11). ὡς ὤμοσα ἐν τῇ ὀργῇ μου Εἰ εἰσελεύσονται εἰς τὴν κατάπαυσίν μου. The psalmist also spoke of the Lord permanently choosing Mount Zion and saying, "This is my *resting place* forever" (Ps. 131:14; KJ Ps. 132:14). Αὔτη ἡ κατάπαυσίς μου εἰς αἰῶνα αἰῶνος.

This word appears in only two New Testament books—Acts and the epistle to the Hebrews. Luke records Stephen's quoting of Isaiah 66:1, which says, "Heaven is my throne, and the earth is the footstool of my feet; what kind of house will ye build me, says the Lord; or what is the place of my *rest?*"(Acts 7:49). ἢ τίς τόπος τῆς καταπαύσεώς μου; This must mean God's eternal rest. The writer to the Hebrews also quotes from the Old Testament (Ps. 95:11), speaking of God's permanent rest: "As I swore in my wrath, They shall not enter into my *rest*" (Heb. 3:11). εἰς τὴν κατάπαυσίν μου. After he had quoted this passage twice more (4:3, 5), he said, "For the one who has entered into His *rest* has himself rested from his works even as God did from His own" (4:10). ὁ γὰρ εἰσελθὼν εἰς τὴν κατάπαυσιν αὐτοῦ καὶ αὐτὸς κατέπαυσεν ἀπὸ τῶν ἔργων αὐτοῦ. This usage certainly refers to what Richard Baxter aptly called "the saints' everlasting rest."

SUMMARY

The word ἀνάπαυσις means a temporary "rest," "respite," or "resting place" as a preparation for renewed labor, whereas the word κατάπαυσις refers to a permanent "rest," "resting place," or "ceasing," with the exception of a few passages in the Septuagint (such as Exod. 35:2) in which it is apparently used interchangeably with ἀνάπαυσις.

11. Righteousness: δικαίωμα, δικαίωσις, δικαιοσύνη

The endings on these three synonyms govern their distinct meanings. The ending -μα denotes the result of an action, giving δικαίωμα the sense of a *righteous deed, righteous claim,* or *ordinance.* Nouns which end in -σις denote an abstract action; hence, δικαίωσις refers to the action of accomplishing what is righteous—an action that in some contexts may mean *condemnation,* in others *a declaring righteous* or *justification.* Nouns ending in -συνη denote an abstract quality; δικαιοσύνη thus means *righteousness, justice,* or *righteous conduct.*

δικαίωμα

Aristotle regularly contrasts δικαίωμα with its antonym, ἀδίκημα, which means "injustice" or "wrong" (*Rhetoric* 1.13.1). Elsewhere he defines δικαίωμα more closely by saying, "But more correctly the general term is δικαιοπράγημα, δικαίωμα denoting the rectification of an act of injustice." καλεῖται δὲ μᾶλλον δικαιοπράγμα τὸ κοινόν, δικαίωμα δὲ τὸ ἐπανόρθωμα τοῦ ἀδικήματος (*Nicomachean Ethics* 5.7.7). Thucydides used this word in the sense of a "legal claim." "These, therefore, are the *legal claims* which we urge upon you—and they are adequate according to the laws of the Hellenes." Δικαιώματα μὲν οὖν τάδε πρὸς ὑμᾶς ἔχομεν, ἱκανὰ κατὰ τοὺς Ἑλλήνων νόμους (1.41). One of the papyri referred to a man who was sent to Alexandria "having with him the *justifying documents* for his case." ἔχοντα καὶ τὰ πρὸς τὴν κατάστασιν δικαιώματα (*P. Petr.,* II, 38c. 52).

In the Septuagint the word is used in the sense of "righteous ordinance" or "rule of rectitude," which has a wider meaning than just one of the ten commandments. When God appeared to Isaac, He reminded him that "Abraham thy father obeyed my voice and kept my charges and my commandments and my *righteous ordinances* and my rites" (Gen. 26:5). ἐφύλαξεν τὰ προτάγματά μου καὶ τὰς ἐντολάς μου καὶ τὰ δικαιώματά μου καὶ τὰ νόμιμά μου. After the Israelites had been delivered in the Exodus, the Lord dealt with them at the waters of Marah. "There he made for them *ordinances* and judgments, and there he proved them" (Exod.

15:25). ἐκεῖ ἔθετο αὐτῷ δικαιώματα καὶ κρίσεις. In the book of Job Elihu spoke of God's sending judgment on the wicked "because they turned aside from the law of God, and they did not acknowledge his *ordinances*"(34:27). ὅτι ἐξέκλιναν ἐκ νόμου θεοῦ, δικαιώματα δὲ αὐτοῦ οὐκ ἐπέγνωσαν. Baruch used the word in a different sense when he stated that the Israelites were not presenting their supplications before God "for the *righteous deeds* of our fathers and of our kings." ἐπὶ τὰ δικαιώματα τῶν πατέρων ἡμῶν καὶ τῶν βασιλέων ἡμῶν (2:19). The church fathers almost always reflect the usage of the Septuagint with the sense of "ordinance." Clement wrote to the Corinthians, "The commandments and *ordinances* of the Lord were written on the tables of your heart." τὰ προστάγματα καὶ τὰ δικαιώματα τοῦ κυρίου ἐπὶ τὰ πλάτη τῆς καρδίας ὑμῶν ἐγέγραπτο (I Clement 2:8).

This same meaning is found in the New Testament. Zacharias and Elisabeth were said to be both "righteous before God, walking in all the commandments and *ordinances* of the Lord blameless" (Luke 1:6). πορευόμενοι ἐν πάσαις ταῖς ἐντολαῖς καὶ δικαιώμασιν τοῦ κυρίου ἄμεμπτοι. The writer to the Hebrews referred to the old covenant as having "*ordinances* of divine service" (Heb. 9:1). δικαιώματα λατρείας. The closest that Paul came to this usage was his statement "Therefore if the uncircumcision should keep the *ordinances* of the law, shall not his uncircumcision be counted for circumcision?" (Rom. 2:26). ἐὰν οὖν ἡ ἀκροβυστία τὰ δικαιώματα τοῦ νόμου φυλάσσῃ. Paul, however, portrayed the unity of God's law by using this word in the singular. When Paul referred to those "haters of God" who have rejected the knowledge of God, he concluded his description of them by saying, "who, knowing the *ordinance* of God, that those who practice such things are worthy of death, not only do the same, but also take pleasure in those who do them" (Rom. 1:32). οἵτινες τὸ δικαίωμα τοῦ θεοῦ ἐπιγνόντες.

There has been a long dispute over the two uses of this word in Romans 5. In each use (5:16 and 5:18) the meaning is colored by the antonym with which it is contrasted. In verse 18 Paul states, "Therefore then as through one trespass [judgment came] unto all men unto condemnation; thus also through one *righteous deed* [the free gift came] unto all men unto justification of life." ὡς δι᾽ ἑνὸς παραπτώματος εἰς πάντας ἀνθρώπους εἰς κατάκριμα, οὕτως καὶ δι᾽ ἑνὸς δικαιώματος εἰς πάντας ἀνθρώπους εἰς δικαίωσιν ζωῆς. Here the contrast seems to be between a "wrong act" and a "righteous act." In verse 16, however, the meaning seems to be equivalent to δικαίωσις (Arndt and Gingrich, p. 197). Paul says, "And not as through one that sinned is the gift: for the judgment came out of one unto condemnation, but the free gift came out of many trespasses unto *justification*"(Rom. 5:16). τὸ μὲν γὰρ κρίμα ἐξ ἑνὸς εἰς κατάκριμα,

RIGHTEOUSNESS

τὸ δὲ χάρισμα ἐκ πολλῶν παραπτωμάτων εἰς δικαίωμα. Some scholars maintain that δικαίωμα means a "sentence of justification" in both verses (Kittel, II, p. 222). But even those who hold that this word has the same meaning in both verses admit it can hardly mean "a righteous act" in verse 16.[1] The idea of result implied by the -μα ending still fits both "condemnation" and "justification." But there also seems to be a sense of action in this last example.

A much easier example is found in the book of Revelation. John saw the consummation of God's purpose for the church in the triumphal marriage of the Lamb. His wife made herself ready: "And it was given to her that she should array herself with fine linen, bright and clean: for the fine linen is the *righteous deeds* of the saints" (19:8). τὸ γὰρ βύσσινον τὰ δικαιώματα τῶν ἁγίων ἐστίν. This is God's gracious purpose: not only does He declare man righteous by virtue of Christ's atonement, but He actually makes man righteous and grants that the church of Christ be arrayed in its own acts of righteousness.

δικαίωσις

This is a relatively rare word. In Thucydides' account of the "reign of terror" at Athens, he described some of the murders which took place and added, "No search was made for those who did the deed, nor if they were suspected was any *legal condemnation* made." εἰ ὑποπτεύοιντο δικαίωσις ἐγίγνετο (8.66.2). Pericles is reported to have said, "For it means enslavement just the same when either the greatest or the least *legal claim* is imposed by equals upon their neighbors, not by an appeal to justice but by dictation." τὴν γὰρ αὐτὴν δύναται δούλωσιν ἡ τε μεγίστη καὶ ἡ ἐλαχίστη δικαίωσις ἀπὸ τῶν ὁμοίων πρὸ δίκης τοῖς πέλας ἐπιτασσομένη (Thucydides 1.141.1). There is only one occurrence of this word in the Septuagint. The Lord commanded, "There shall be only one *statute* for both the proselyte and for the neighbor" (Lev. 24:22). δικαίωσις μία ἔσται τῷ προσηλύτῳ καὶ τῷ ἐγχωρίῳ. No examples of this word in the papyri have yet come to light.

In the New Testament the word occurs only twice, both times in the book of Romans. When Paul explained how Abraham was justified by faith, he mentioned the crucifixion and resurrection of the Lord Jesus Christ, saying, "Who was delivered for our trespasses, and was raised up for our *justification*" (Rom. 4:25). ὃς παρεδόθη διὰ τὰ παραπτώματα ἡμῶν καὶ ἠγέρθη διὰ τὴν δικαίωσιν ἡμῶν. Of all the different interpretations [2] perhaps the best is that He was delivered "because of our trespasses,"

---
[1] W. Sanday and A. Headlam, *The Epistle to the Romans*, p. 142.
[2] See Sanday and Headlam, *Romans*, p. 116, and Hodge, *Romans*, pp. 129–30.

looking backward to them, whereas He was raised up "in order to accomplish our justification," looking forward to His goal for those who believe in Him.

When Paul contrasted Adam and Christ, he said, "Therefore then as through one trespass [judgment came] unto all men unto condemnation; thus also through one righteous deed [the free gift came] unto all men unto *justification* of life" (Rom. 5:18). οὕτως καὶ δι' ἑνὸς δικαιώματος εἰς πάντας ἀνθρώπους εἰς δικαίωσιν ζωῆς. The context implies that the "action of God's justifying" produces life in the most abundant sense.

δικαιοσύνη

Although this word is not found in Homer or Hesiod, it is one of the most common legal and moral terms from the time of Herodotus on. Most often it has the legal sense of "justice." When Herodotus, describing how Deioces tried to become monarch, said that Deioces "began to profess and to practise *justice* more earnestly and zealously than ever." καὶ μᾶλλόν τι καὶ προθυμότερον δικαιοσύνην ἐπιθέμενος ἤσκεε (1.96). Herodotus reported a speech by Xerxes in which he commended the Ionians in his army by saying, "They gave proof of *justice* and faithfulness, and no evil intent." οἳ δὲ δικαιοσύνην καὶ πιστότητα ἐνέδωκαν, ἄχαρι δὲ οὐδέν (7.52). Aristotle, defining equity said, "We have next to speak of 'equity' and 'the equitable,' and of their relation to *'justice'* and to 'what is just' respectively." Περὶ δὲ ἐπιεικείας καὶ τοῦ ἐπιεικοῦς, πῶς ἔχει ἡ μὲν ἐπιείκεια πρὸς δικαιοσύνην τὸ δ' ἐπιεικὲς πρὸς τὸ δίκαιον, ἐχόμενόν ἐστιν εἰπεῖν (*Nicomachean Ethics* 5.10.1).

This word is not found often in the papyri, but when it is, it is usually with the sense of "justice." In a papyrus a man petitioned concerning a neighbor who had attacked his sheep "after the manner of a robber . . . contrary to *justice.*" ληστρικῷ τρόπῳ . . . παρὰ τὴν δικαιοσύνην.[3] In connection with judging, the *Epistle of Barnabas* asserted that *"righteousness* [justice] is the beginning and end of judgment." δικαιοσύνη, κρίσεως ἀρχὴ καὶ τέλος (*Epistle of Barnabus* 1.6).

By the time of the Septuagint some important developments had taken place. The first occurrence of the word in the Septuagint was in Abraham's response to God's promise. "And Abram believed in God, and it was counted to him for *righteousness"* (Gen. 15:6). καὶ ἐπίστευσεν Αβραμ τῷ θεῷ, καὶ ἐλογίσθη αὐτῷ εἰς δικαιοσύνην. This passage is, of course, often quoted in the New Testament. Sometimes this word has a definite connotation of "kindness." When Lot prayed to the Lord, he said, "Since thy servant found mercy in thy sight, and thou didst magnify thy *kindness*. . ."

[3] P. Jouguet, ed., *Papyrus de Theadelphie* 23. 9.

RIGHTEOUSNESS

(Gen. 19:19). ἐπειδὴ εὗρεν ὁ παῖς σου ἔλεος ἐναντίον σου καὶ ἐμεγάλυνας τὴν δικαιοσύνην σου. This meaning is so obvious in the Septuagint that the words for "righteousness" and "mercy" are sometimes used interchangeably.[4] The older connotation of "justice" is often found, however, as in the place where the Lord addressed Abraham saying that He knew that Abraham would command his household after him, "that they may keep the ways of the Lord to do *justice* and judgment" (Gen. 18:19). φυλάξουσιν τὰς ὁδοὺς κυρίου ποιεῖν δικαιοσύνην καὶ κρίσιν. Compared with the classical usage, the most distinctive use of this word in Biblical Greek is in the sense of "righteousness." A very familiar Psalm has the reading, "He led me in the paths of *righteousness* for His name's sake" (Ps. 22:3; KJ Ps. 23:3). ὡδήγησέν με ἐπὶ τρίβους δικαιοσύνης ἕνεκεν τοῦ ὀνόματος αὐτοῦ. This righteousness is pointedly linked with God's salvation: "The Lord made known His salvation; He manifested His *righteousness* before the nations" (Ps. 97:2; KJ Ps. 98). ἐγνώρισεν κύριος τὸ σωτήριον αὐτοῦ, ἐναντίον τῶν ἐθνῶν ἀπεκάλυψεν τὴν δικαιοσύνην αὐτοῦ.

In the New Testament the sense of "justice" is rare. When the Apostle John portrayed the return of Christ in glory, he said, "And I saw the heaven opened; and behold, a white horse, and the one who was sitting upon it is called Faithful and True, and with *justice* He judges and makes war" (Rev. 19:11). ὁ καθήμενος ἐπ' αὐτὸν πιστὸς καλούμενος καὶ ἀληθινός, καὶ ἐν δικαιοσύνῃ κρίνει. There is also a connotation of "kindness" in some contexts. In the Sermon on the Mount the Lord Jesus warned, "Beware that ye do not your *charity* before men in order to be seen by them" (Matt. 6:1). Προσέχετε δὲ τὴν δικαιοσύνην ὑμῶν μὴ ποιεῖν ἔμπροσθεν τῶν ἀνθρώπων. When the New Testament uses this word, it is usually with the meaning "righteousness." It is characteristic of John that he connects all righteousness with the Person of Christ. "Little children, let no one deceive you; the man who is doing *righteousness* is righteous, even as He is righteous" (I John 3:7). ὁ ποιῶν τὴν δικαιοσύνην δίκαιός ἐστιν, καθὼς ἐκεῖνος δίκαιός ἐστιν. When James quoted Genesis 15:6, he was arguing against a spurious profession of faith without the reality that produces a changed life. "We are simply given a straightforward and non-theological emphasising of the demand that faith should not be distorted by making it a substitute for works" (Kittel, II, 201). The works will surely follow a true faith.

The capstone of the New Testament teaching on "righteousness" was put in place by the Apostle Paul when he taught that righteousness can be given by God alone. The "righteousness of God" of which Paul speaks (Rom. 1:17) is the righteousness which God communicates, and hence is

[4] Edwin Hatch, *Essays in Biblical Greek*, pp. 49–51.

actually equivalent to "the salvation of God." [5] This was "an apart-from-law *righteousness* of God" (Rom. 3:21). χωρὶς νόμου δικαιοσύνη θεοῦ. It was "even a *righteousness* of God through faith in Jesus Christ" (Rom. 3:22). δικαιοσύνη δὲ θεοῦ διὰ πίστεως Ἰησοῦ Χριστοῦ. Paul also quoted Genesis 15:6 and went on to argue, "But to the one who does not work, but believes on the one who justifies the ungodly, his faith is reckoned for *righteousness*" (Rom. 4:3–5). λογίζεται ἡ πίστις αὐτοῦ εἰς δικαιοσύνην.

SUMMARY

The word δικαίωμα usually means a "righteous deed" or an "ordinance," because its ending denotes a result of what is righteous. The word δικαίωσις usually means "justification," with the stress on the action. The word δικαιοσύνη means "justice," "righteousness," or even "kindness," the ending referring to the abstract quality of the righteous.

[5] J. Jeremias, *The Central Message of the New Testament,* p. 55.

12. River: ποταμός, χείμαρρος

The word ποταμός is the general term for *river* or *stream*. χείμαρρος, a more specific term, designates a *winter torrent* or a *ravine* in which flood waters will flow in winter.

ποταμός

Homer taught that all rivers had their origin in the ocean, which he addressed as one of the gods. "Ocean, from whom all *rivers* are and the entire sea." ἐξ οὗπερ πάντες ποταμοὶ καὶ πᾶσα θάλασσα (*Iliad* 21.196). The term ποταμοί in this passage clearly designates all kinds of rivers. Aeschylus used this word to refer even to lava when he wrote of Mount Aetna pouring forth *"rivers* of fire." ποταμοὶ πυρός (*Prometheus Bound* 368). This same wide latitude of usage is found in the Septuagint. "A *river* issues out of Eden to water the garden" (Gen. 2:10). ποταμὸς δὲ ἐκπορεύεται ἐξ Εδεν ποτίζειν τὸν παράδεισον. When the Lord made His covenant with Abraham, He promised, "To thy seed I will give this land, from the *river* of Egypt unto the great *river,* the *river* Euphrates" (Gen. 15:18). δώσω τὴν γῆν ταύτην ἀπὸ τοῦ ποταμοῦ Αἰγύπτου ἕως τοῦ ποταμοῦ τοῦ μεγάλου, ποταμοῦ Εὐφράτου. A papyrus dated 258–53 B.C. refers to a time ". . . at the falling of the *river*" [the Nile]. περὶ τὴν ἀναχώρησιν τοῦ ποταμοῦ (*P. Petr.*, II, 13.19.10). Another papyrus speaks of the *"river* being somewhat backward in rising." τοῦ τε ποταμοῦ ποτε ἐνλιπέστερον ἀναβάντος (OGIS 56.13).

The Gospels describe the great multitudes that came to John the Baptist; "and they were being baptized by him in the Jordan *river,* confessing their sins" (Mark 1:5). ἐν τῷ Ἰορδάνῃ ποταμῷ. Speaking metaphorically, our Lord promised the true believer, "Even as the Scripture said: Out of his belly *rivers* of living water shall flow" (John 7:38). ποταμοὶ ἐκ τῆς κοιλίας αὐτοῦ ῥεύσουσιν. In the vision of the glories of the new heaven and the new earth the angel showed John "a *river* of water of life, shining as crystal" (Rev. 22:1). ποταμὸν ὕδατος ζωῆς λαμπρὸν ὡς κρύσταλλον. The general sense of "river" may have a more specific meaning in a given context. In the Sermon on the Mount the Lord described the wise man who built his house upon the rock: "and the rain came down, and the *rivers* [floods] came, and the winds blew, and beat upon that house, and it fell not: for it was founded upon a rock" (Matt. 7:25). καὶ ἦλθεν οἱ ποταμοί. The exposition of Broadus is particularly lucid here: "The rain descended, and (in consequence thereof) the rivers came (mountain torrents, rushing down the ravines, and swelling up to the site of the house), and these washed around the building, and would have washed the earth from under its foundations, had they rested mainly on the loose surface of the ground" (*Commentary on the Gospel of Matthew,* p. 170). Thus in this context οἱ ποταμοί is the equivalent of the term οἱ χείμαρροι, which is to be discussed next.

χείμαρρος

In classical Greek this term is commonly used as an adjective with the meaning "winter-swollen." Homer told how "Tydeus' son . . . went storming up the plain like a *winter-swollen* river." ποταμῷ πλήθοντι ἐοικὼς χειμάρρῳ (*Iliad* 5.88). Here χειμάρρῳ is a simple modifier which qualifies the meaning of "river." These two terms are often used with one another. Warning against mob rule, Herodotus wrote, "The people . . . ever rush headlong and drive blindly onward, like a *winter-swollen* river." χειμάρρῳ ποταμῷ εἴκελος (3.81).

It is only a small step to drop the noun "river" and to use the word χείμαρρος as a noun itself. This was certainly done. Sophocles' *Antigone* has a famous question, "Have you not seen the trees beside the *winter-torrent,* the ones that bend saving every leaf, while the ones that resist perish root and branch?" ὁρᾷς παρὰ ῥείθροισι χειμάρροις ὅσα δένδρων ὑπείκει (lines 712–14). In the Septuagint this term is applied to several streams which have strong seasonal fluctuations. On one occasion Jacob took his numerous family "and sent them over the *stream*" (Gen. 32:24; KJ 32:23). διέβη τὸν χειμάρρουν. This reference to the Jabbok can be paralleled with another to the Arnon: "From Aroer, which is on the edge of the *stream* of Arnon" (Deut. 2:36). ἐξ Αροηρ, ἥ ἐστιν παρὰ τὸ χεῖλος χειμάρρου Αρνων. In some seasons both of these streams would be ravines. The *Letter of Aristeas* also mentions that "other *winter-torrents,* as they are called, flow down." ἄλλοι δὲ χείμαρροι λεγόμενοι κατίασι (line 117).

There is only one occurrence of this word in the New Testament. "When Jesus had said these things [the upper-room discourse], he went forth with his disciples beyond the *ravine* [winter torrent] of the Kidron, where was a garden" (John 18:1). πέραν τοῦ χειμάρρου τοῦ Κεδρών. The amount of water in the Kidron depended strictly on the time of year.

RIVER

SUMMARY

The word ποταμός is the regular word for "river" and may be applied to every kind of river from the great Euphrates to a winter-torrent. The more limited term χείμαρρος is applied to a "stream" which may be a "winter-torrent" in one season and a dry "ravine" in another.

13. Son of God: υἱὸς θεοῦ, παῖς θεοῦ

The phrase υἱὸς θεοῦ designates a divine being, *a son of God;* in classical Greek it referred to a mythological *god,* but in later Greek it was a common title for the Roman emperors. On the other hand παῖς θεοῦ had a wider latitude of meaning; it could mean *son, child,* or *servant of God.*

υἱὸς θεοῦ

From earliest times υἱός was the regular word for *"son."* Homer wrote that Athena "made trial of the might and valour of Odysseus and his glorious *son.*" πειρήτιζεν ἡμὲν Ὀδυσσῆος ἠδ᾽ υἱοῦ κυδαλίμοιο (*Odyssey* 22.238). This word expresses a relationship not only between men but also between classical "gods." Zeus and Poseidon, for example, are "the two mighty *sons* of Cronos." δύω Κρόνου υἷε κραταιώ (Homer *Iliad* 13.345). The accent identifies the form as a dual. Later, this term was often applied to the deified Roman emperors. One papyrus recorded "the thirty-ninth year of the dominion of Caesar, *son of god.*" ἔτους ἐνάτου καὶ τριακοστοῦ τῆς καίσαρος κρατήσεως θεοῦ υἱοῦ (*P. Grenf.,* II, 40.4). Adolph Deissmann called attention to an inscription on a marble pedestal made while the emperor was still living which read, "Emperor, Caesar, *son of god,* the god Augustus." αὐτοκράτορα Καίσαρα θεοῦ υἱὸν θεὸν Σεβαστόν (*Light from the Ancient East,* p. 347).

In the Septuagint υἱός is one of the most common words, especially in the genealogical records. "And Adam knew Eve his wife, and she conceived and brought forth a *son"* (Gen. 4:25). ἔγνω δὲ Αδαμ Ευαν τὴν γυναῖκα αὐτοῦ, καὶ συλλαβοῦσα ἔτεκεν υἱόν. Although the phrase υἱὸς θεοῦ is scarce, it does occur in a few distinctive passages. "And the *sons of God,* having seen the daughters of men that were fair, took to themselves wives of all whom they chose" (Gen. 6:2). ἰδόντες δὲ οἱ υἱοὶ τοῦ θεοῦ τὰς θυγατέρας τῶν ἀνθρώπων ὅτι καλαί εἰσιν. Certainly this passage has been a battleground of conflicting interpretations; the interpretation that these "sons of God" were supernatural creatures is, however, a very ancient one (this is the view of the Book of Enoch, chapters 6–7). A great Messianic prophecy is often quoted in the New Testament: "I proclaim the decree of the Lord; the Lord said to me: Thou art my *Son;* today I have begotten thee" (Ps. 2:7). Κύριος εἶπεν πρός με Υἱός μου εἶ σύ. In view of the New

SON OF GOD

Testament interpretation, this statement must apply to Christ alone (Acts 13:33; Heb. 1:5, 5:5). In Theodotion's version of the book of Daniel, after the three Hebrews were cast into the burning furnace, King Nebuchadnezzar said, "Behold, I see four men having been loosed and walking about in the midst of the fire, and destruction is not on them, and the appearance of the fourth is like a *son of god"* (Dan. 3:92; KJ Dan. 3:25). καὶ διαφθορὰ οὐκ ἔστιν ἐν αὐτοῖς, καὶ ἡ ὅρασις τοῦ τετάρτου ὁμοία υἱῷ θεοῦ.

The Apostolic Fathers apply this phrase to the Lord Jesus, as in the *Martyrdom of Polycarp:* "For this One indeed we worship as the *Son of God,* but on the other hand the martyrs we love as disciples and imitators of the Lord." τοῦτον μὲν γὰρ υἱὸν ὄντα τοῦ θεοῦ προσκυνοῦμεν (17.3).

In the New Testament this phrase is one of the great titles of the Lord Jesus. When the angel announced the birth of Jesus to Mary, he prophesied that this would be His title. "The Holy Spirit shall come upon thee, and the power of the Highest shall overshadow thee; wherefore also that Holy Thing which is begotten shall be called the *Son of God"* (Luke 1:35). διὸ καὶ τὸ γεννώμενον ἅγιον κληθήσεται υἱὸς θεοῦ. After the Lord had stilled the storm, the disciples worshipped Him saying, "Truly thou art the *Son of God"* (Matt. 14:33). ἀληθῶς θεοῦ υἱὸς εἶ. Even the demons were crying out, "Thou art the *Son of God"* (Mark 3:11). σὺ εἶ ὁ υἱὸς τοῦ θεοῦ. At the crucifixion when the centurion saw the Lord release His spirit and saw the earthquake that followed, he confessed, "Truly this man was a *Son of God"* (Matt. 27:54). ἀληθῶς θεοῦ υἱὸς ἦν οὗτος. That Christ is the Son of God is one of the cardinal teachings of the Apostle John. Early in his Gospel he warned, "The one who is not believing has been condemned already, because he has not believed in the name of the unique *Son of God"* (John 3:18). ὅτι μὴ πεπίστευκεν εἰς τὸ ὄνομα τοῦ μονογενοῦς υἱοῦ τοῦ θεοῦ. And toward the end of his Gospel he affirmed that his purpose in writing his account of Christ's life was to bring his readers to a regenerating belief in this truth: "That ye may believe that Jesus is the Christ, the *Son of God,* and that believing ye may have life in his name" (John 20:31). ἵνα πιστεύητε ὅτι Ἰησοῦς ἐστιν ὁ χριστὸς ὁ υἱὸς τοῦ θεοῦ. That Christ is uniquely the Son of God was also one of the great doctrines of Paul. The Saviour he holds up to men is "Jesus Christ our Lord, who was declared to be the *Son of God* with power according to the spirit of holiness by the resurrection from the dead" (Rom. 1:4). τοῦ ὁρισθέντος υἱοῦ θεοῦ ἐν δυνάμει κατὰ πνεῦμα ἁγιωσύνης. Paul also taught that believers were made the sons of God by His grace. "For as many as are being led by the Spirit of God, these are *sons of God"* (Rom. 8:14). ὅσοι γὰρ πνεύματι θεοῦ ἄγονται, οὗτοι υἱοί εἰσιν θεοῦ. The words of Theodoret are particularly apt: "He on the one hand is a Son by nature, but we on the other hand by grace." ὁ μέν ἐστι φύσει υἱὸς ἡμεῖς δὲ χάριτι (Westcott, *Hebrews,* p. 50).

παῖς θεοῦ

In Homer παῖς is sometimes used for a "son," even of one of the "gods." He wrote, "Let there be one lord, one king, to whom the *son* [Zeus] of crooked-counselling Cronos has given the scepter and judgments." ᾧ ἔδωκε Κρόνου πάϊς ἀγκυλόμητις (*Iliad* 2.205). Once in a while it means "child." In another place Homer related the words of Odysseus: "For like little *children* or widow women they do wail each to the other longing to return home." ὥς τε γὰρ ἢ παῖδες νεαροὶ χῆραί τε γυναῖκες ἀλλήλοισιν ὀδύρονται οἶκόνδε νέεσθαι (*Iliad* 2.289). In later Greek the word means "servant." When Orestes finally comes home to avenge the death of Agamemnon, he cries, *"Porter! Porter!* Hear the knocking at the outer gate! Who's within? *Porter! Porter!"* παῖ παῖ, θύρας ἄκουσον ἑρκείας κτύπον. τίς ἔνδον, ω παῖ, παῖ (Aeschylus *The Libation Bearers* 652). Amid more comic circumstances Aristophanes has Strepsiades say, "But shall I not knock at the gate? *Porter!* Ho boy!" ἀλλ᾽ οὐχὶ κόπτω τὴν θύραν; παῖ, παιδίον (*The Clouds* 132). One of the papyri has the word παῖδες in the sense of "slaves" with a list of persons following (*Papyrus Grecs de Lille* I. 27).

The common word for "servant" in the Septuagint was παῖς. When the princes of Pharaoh admired the beauty of Sarah, Scripture says, "They treated Abram well on account of her, and he had sheep and oxen and asses, *men servants* and maid servants" (Gen. 12:16). καὶ ἐγένοντο αὐτῷ πρόβατα καὶ μόσχοι καὶ ὄνοι, παῖδες καὶ παιδίσκαι. Several of the great men in the Old Testament were called servants of God. The Lord said to Abraham, "Shall I hide from Abraham, my *servant,* the things which I am going to do?" (Gen. 18:17). Μὴ κρύψω ἐγὼ ἀπὸ Αβρααμ τοῦ παιδός μου ἃ ἐγὼ ποιῶ; When the Lord prepared Joshua to lead the children of Israel into Palestine, He said, "Therefore be strong and courageous, to watch and to do even as Moses, my *servant,* commanded thee" (Josh. 1:7). καθότι ἐνετείλατό σοι Μωυσῆς ὁ παῖς μου. The great passage which influenced the meaning of this phrase in the New Testament was the "servant of the Lord" section in Isaiah 40–66. One of the many uses of this phrase is, "Behold, my *Servant* shall be understanding and shall be exalted and highly glorified" (Isa. 52:13). Ἰδοὺ συνήσει ὁ παῖς μου καὶ ὑψωθήσεται καὶ δοξασθήσεται σφόδρα.

In the New Testament there is only one occurrence of this word with the meaning "son." After the Lord Jesus told the nobleman to go on his way, his child would live, Scripture says that while the nobleman was going home, "his servants met him saying that his *son* was living" (John 4:51). λέγοντες ὅτι ὁ παῖς αὐτοῦ ζῇ. A few more times the word occurs with the meaning "boy." When Eutychus fell out of the window during Paul's long sermon, he was taken up dead, but Paul prophesied that he would live: "And they led the *boy* alive, and they were greatly comforted" (Acts 20:12). ἤγαγον δὲ τὸν παῖδα ζῶντα. As in the Septuagint, a more common meaning is "servant." A certain centurion had a slave, δοῦλον, for whom he besought the Lord: "But say the word and let my *servant* be healed" (Luke 7:2, 7). ἀλλὰ εἰπὲ λόγῳ, καὶ ἰαθήτω ὁ παῖς μου. When the phrase παῖς θεοῦ is applied to the Lord Jesus, most probably it means "Servant of God" in the light of His identification with the "Servant of the Lord" in Isaiah. Matthew quoted Isaiah as referring to the Lord: "Behold my *servant* whom I have chosen; my beloved in whom my soul takes pleasure" (12:18). ἰδοὺ ὁ παῖς μου ὃν ᾑρέτισα. Peter, preaching to the multitude in Solomon's portico, declared, "The God of our fathers glorified His *Servant* Jesus" (Acts 3:13). ὁ θεὸς τῶν πατέρων ἡμῶν ἐδόξασεν τὸν παῖδα αὐτοῦ Ἰησοῦν. Again in the same sermon Peter stressed Christ the Servant: "To you first God, having raised up His *Servant,* sent Him to bless you" (Acts 3:26). ὑμῖν πρῶτον ἀναστήσας ὁ θεὸς τὸν παῖδα αὐτοῦ ἀπέστειλεν αὐτὸν εὐλογοῦντα ὑμᾶς. The Jews who heard Peter would certainly have seen the connection with the "Servant" passages in the Old Testament. In all probability this same meaning should be applied to the term παῖδα in the prayer of the early church after Peter was released from prison: "For of a truth in this city, against thy holy *Servant* Jesus, whom thou didst anoint, Herod and Pontius Pilate with Gentiles and the peoples of Israel were gathered together" (Acts 4:27). συνήχθησαν γὰρ ἐπ' ἀληθείας ἐν τῇ πόλει ταύτῃ ἐπὶ τὸν ἅγιον παῖδά σου Ἰησοῦν.

SUMMARY

The phrase υἱὸς θεοῦ manifests the deity of the Lord Jesus Christ. If "son of god" could be applied to deified Roman emperors, certainly it is fitting for Him who is "King of kings and Lord of lords." In contrast, the phrase παῖς θεοῦ links our Lord with the mighty "Servant of God" passages in Isaiah. The two phrases show the glory of Jesus Christ in two different aspects: that of the Mighty Servant and that of the Son of God.

14. Soul: καρδία, νοῦς, πνεῦμα, ψυχή

The word καρδία, *heart,* may refer to the physical organ or to the center of man's moral choice, intelligence, and emotion; νοῦς is the *mind,* that faculty which thinks and judges; πνεῦμα means either *breath* or *spirit,* the self-conscious part of man that wills, thinks, and feels; ψυχή may mean *life* or *soul:* it may refer to animal life or to the seat of the personal ego or *self.*

καρδία

This word often refers to the physical organ, as when Idomeneus speaks of the coward "whose *heart* beats loudly in his breast." οἱ κραδίη μεγάλα στέρνοισι πατάσσει (Homer *Iliad* 13.282. Note the Homeric spelling). Another common reference is to the seat of the emotions. Achilles says, "But my *heart* swells with wrath whenever I think of this." ἀλλά μοι οἰδάνεται κραδίη χόλῳ (Homer *Iliad* 9.646). Homer has Poseidon chide Apollo, saying, "Fool, thou hast a senseless *heart!*" νηπύτι', ὡς ἄνοον κραδίην ἔχες (*Iliad* 21.441). Homer said of Telemachus that he "nursed in his *heart* great grief for the smiting." δ' ἐν μὲν κραδίῃ μέγα πένθος ἄεξε (*Odyssey* 17.489). An interesting use from the extra-Biblical statements of the Lord Jesus is in Logion 3, which reads: "And my *soul* grieves over the sons of men, because they are blind in *heart.*" καὶ πονεῖ ἡ ψυχή μου ἐπὶ τοῖς υἱοῖς τῶν ἀνθρώπων ὅτι τυφλοί εἰσιν τῇ καρδίᾳ αὐτῶν (*P. Oxy.*, I, 1, p. 3). This certainly refers to the spiritual nature of man.

Before the flood, God saw that the wickedness of man was great, "and every man was considering in his *heart* diligently the evil things all day long" (Gen. 6:5). καὶ πᾶς τις διανοεῖται ἐν τῇ καρδίᾳ αὐτοῦ ἐπιμελῶς ἐπὶ τὰ πονηρά. When the Lord called Moses to build the tabernacle, He promised him, "To every man of an understanding *heart* I have given understanding, and they shall make all the things which I commanded thee" (Exod. 31:6). παντὶ συνετῷ καρδίᾳ δέδωκα σύνεσιν, καὶ ποιήσουσιν πάντα, ὅσα σοι συνέταξα. The raiding Danites invited Micah's priest to go with them, and Scripture says, "The *heart* of the priest rejoiced" (Judg. 18:20). ἠγαθύνθη ἡ καρδία τοῦ ἱερέως. In her hymn of praise Hannah said, "My heart was strengthened by the Lord" (I Sam. 2:1). ἐστερεώθη ἡ καρδία μου ἐν κυρίῳ. David prayed to God, saying, "A broken and a humble *heart,* O God, thou wilt not despise" (Ps. 50:19; KJ Ps. 51:17). καρδίαν συντετριμμένην καὶ τεταπεινωμένην ὁ θεὸς οὐκ ἐξουθενώσει. The prophet Jeremiah said, "The *heart* is deep beyond all things; so also is a man; who then shall know him?" (Jer. 17:9). βαθεῖα ἡ καρδία παρὰ πάντα, καὶ ἄνθρωπός ἐστιν· καὶ τίς γνώσεται αὐτόν;

In the Sermon on the Mount the Lord Jesus said, "Blessed are the pure in *heart,* because they shall see God" (Matt. 5:8). μακάριοι οἱ καθαροὶ τῇ καρδίᾳ, ὅτι αὐτοὶ τὸν θεὸν ὄψονται. John, quoting Isaiah 6:10 concerning the unbelieving Jews, said, "He hardened their *heart,* lest they should see with their eyes and understand with their *heart*"(John 12:40). ἐπώρωσεν αὐτῶν τὴν καρδίαν, ἵνα μὴ ἴδωσιν τοῖς ὀφθαλμοῖς καὶ νοήσωσιν τῇ καρδίᾳ. When Paul, speaking of the consequences of man's revolt against God, said, "Wherefore God gave them up in the lusts of their *hearts"* (Rom. 1:24). διὸ παρέδωκεν αὐτοὺς ὁ θεὸς ἐν ταῖς ἐπιθυμίαις τῶν καρδιῶν αὐτῶν. Paul assured the Corinthians, "For I have said before that ye are in our *hearts* to die together and to live together" (II Cor. 7:3). προείρηκα γὰρ ὅτι ἐν ταῖς καρδίαις ἡμῶν ἐστε εἰς τὸ συναποθανεῖν καὶ συζῆν.

νοῦς

When Circe changed the crew of Odysseus into swine, they had the shape of swine "but their *minds* were unchanged even as before." αὐτὰρ νοῦς ἦν ἔμπεδος, ὡς τὸ πάρος περ (Homer *Odyssey* 10.240). In his description of the Greek victory over the Persians at Salamis, Herodotus said that the Greeks fought orderly, "but the foreigners were by now disordered, nor were they doing anything with the *mind* [*i.e.* logically or wisely]." τῶν δὲ βαρβάρων οὔτε τεταγμένων ἔτι οὔτε σὺν νόῳ ποιεόντων οὐδέν (8.86). Herodotus used this word very differently when he said, "But this is the *meaning* [literally *mind*] of the thing which he was wishing to say." οὗτος δὲ ὁ νόος τοῦ ῥήματος τὸ ἐθέλει λέγειν (7.162). Both "mind" and "soul" were used by Plato in his recounting the words of Socrates concerning the orator, "When he applies to our *souls* the words which he speaks, and in all his actions, and if he gives any gift, he will give it, and if he takes anything away, he will take it, always having this thought before his *mind:* how justice may be engendered in the *souls* of his fellow-citizens." τοὺς λόγους προσοίσει ταῖς ψυχαῖς, οὓς ἂν λέγῃ, καὶ τὰς πράξεις ἁπάσας, καὶ δῶρον ἐάν τι διδῷ, δώσει, καὶ ἐάν τι ἀφαιρῆται, ἀφαιρήσεται, πρὸς τοῦτο ἀεὶ τὸν νοῦν ἔχων, ὅπως ἂν αὐτοῦ τοῖς πολίταις δικαιοσύνη μὲν ἐν ταῖς ψυχαῖς γίγνηται (*Gorgias* 504D).

In the Septuagint when the magicians had, like Moses, turned the river to blood, "Pharaoh returned and entered his house, and did not set his *mind* even to this" (Exod. 7:23). ἐπιστραφεὶς δὲ Φαραω εἰσῆλθεν εἰς τὸν οἶκον αὐτοῦ καὶ οὐκ ἐπέστησεν τὸν νοῦν αὐτοῦ οὐδὲ ἐπὶ τούτῳ. Job cried out in despair, "If I sinned, what am I able to do to thee, O Thou who knowest the *mind* of men?" (Job 7:20). εἰ ἐγὼ ἥμαρτον, τί δύναμαί σοι πρᾶξαι, ὁ ἐπιστάμενος τὸν νοῦν τῶν ἀνθρώπων; The book of Proverbs warns, "Give not thy wealth to women, nor thy *mind* and life unto that which destroys counsel" (24:71; KJ 31:3). μὴ δῷς γυναιξὶ σὸν πλοῦτον καὶ τὸν νοῦν καὶ βίον εἰς ὑστεροβουλίαν. Isaiah asked the rhetorical question, "Who knew the *mind* of the Lord, and who became his counsellor, who has taught him?" (Isa. 40:13). τίς ἔγνω νοῦν κυρίου, καὶ τίς αὐτοῦ σύμβουλος ἐγένετο, ὃς συμβιβᾷ αὐτόν; In a late papyrus a woman bringing a petition against her husband who has deserted her adds, "By him I have also had two children, and I have no *mind* for another man." ἐξ οὗ καὶ ἐπαιδοποιησάμην παιδία δύο, μὴ ἔχουσα κατὰ νοῦν ἄλλον (*P. Tebt.*, II, 334.8).

When the risen Lord appeared to the disciples, Scripture says, "Then he opened their *mind* in order that they might understand the Scriptures" (Luke 24:45). τότε διήνοιξεν αὐτῶν τὸν νοῦν τοῦ συνιέναι τὰς γραφάς. The Apostle Paul concluded his discussion of law and sin by saying, "Therefore then I myself serve with the *mind* the law of God, but with the flesh the law of sin" (Rom. 7:25). ἄρα οὖν αὐτὸς ἐγὼ τῷ μὲν νοῒ δουλεύω νόμῳ θεοῦ. Later on, Paul exhorted believers, "And be not conformed to this age, but be ye transformed by the renewing of your *mind*"(Rom. 12:2). καὶ μὴ συσχηματίζεσθε τῷ αἰῶνι τούτῳ, ἀλλὰ μεταμορφοῦσθε τῇ ἀνακαινώσει τοῦ νοός. When Paul discussed the problem of tongues, he said, "For if I should pray in a tongue, my *spirit* prays, but my *mind* is unfruitful" (I Cor. 14:14). ἐὰν γὰρ προσεύχωμαι γλώσσῃ, τὸ πνεῦμά μου προσεύχεται, ὁ δὲ νοῦς μου ἄκαρπός ἐστιν. In his letter to the Philippians Paul promised, "And the peace of God, which passes all *mind*, shall guard your *hearts* and thoughts in Christ Jesus" (4:7). καὶ ἡ εἰρήνη τοῦ θεοῦ ἡ ὑπερέχουσα πάντα νοῦν φρουρήσει τὰς καρδίας ὑμῶν καὶ τὰ νοήματα ὑμῶν ἐν Χριστῷ Ἰησοῦ.

πνεῦμα

This word can refer to "wind." In his description of a sea battle, Thucydides said, "But when the *wind* began to come up, and the ships, already being hemmed in on both sides, were being thrown into confusion by the violence of the wind." ὡς δὲ τό τε πνεῦμα κατῄει καὶ αἱ νῆες ἐν ὀλίγῳ ἤδη οὖσαι ὑπ' ἀμφοτέρων, τοῦ τε ἀνέμου τῶν τε πλοίων (2.84.3). Aeschylus used this word to mean "breath" when he described the desert march: "But one after another our men sank down, but fortunate indeed was the one whose *breath* of life was exhausted most quickly." πῖπτον δ᾽ ἐπ᾽ ἀλλήλοισιν· ηὐτύχει δέ τοι ὅστις τάχιστα πνεῦμ᾽ ἀπέρρηξεν βίου (*The Persians* 507). The meaning "spirit" occurs in Euripides: "But since her *spirit* departed in that death-stroke, no man had the same task." ἐπεὶ δ᾽ ἀφῆκε πνεῦμα θανασίμῳ σφαγῇ (*Hecuba* 571). In the papyri a certain much-abused Flavius complained, "so that at last the very *breath* of my life [salvation] is in danger." ὡς λοιπὸν εἰς αὐτὸ τὸ τῆς σωτηρίας πνεῦμα δυστυχῖν με (*P. Oxy.*, VI, 904.7).

The first occurrence of this word in the Septuagint is in the beginning of God's creation. "But the earth was invisible and unfurnished, and darkness was over the abyss, and the *Spirit* of God was brought upon above the water" (Gen. 1:2). καὶ πνεῦμα θεοῦ ἐπεφέρετο ἐπάνω τοῦ ὕδατος. When the Lord saw the wickedness of man on the earth, He said, "My *Spirit* shall not continue in these men forever, because they are flesh" (Gen. 6:3). οὐ μὴ καταμείνῃ τὸ πνεῦμά μου ἐν τοῖς ἀνθρώποις τούτοις εἰς τὸν αἰῶνα. After Joseph had interpreted Pharaoh's dreams, Pharaoh said, "Can we find such a man as this, who has the *spirit* of God in him?" (Gen. 41:38). μὴ εὑρήσομεν ἄνθρωπον τοιοῦτον, ὃς ἔχει πνεῦμα θεοῦ ἐν αὐτῷ; In preparation for the building of the tabernacle, the Lord called Bezaleel and said of him, "I filled him with a divine *spirit* of wisdom and understanding and knowledge in every workmanship" (Exod. 31:3). ἐνέπλησα αὐτὸν πνεῦμα θεῖον σοφίας καὶ συνέσεως καὶ ἐπιστήμης ἐν παντὶ ἔργῳ. When Ahab failed to persuade Naboth to sell him his vineyard, Scripture says, "And the *spirit* of Ahab became troubled, and he laid himself down on his bed and covered his face and would not eat" (I Kings 20:4; KJ I Kings 21:4). καὶ ἐγένετο τὸ πνεῦμα Αχααβ τεταραγμένον, καὶ ἐκοιμήθη ἐπὶ τῆς κλίνης αὐτοῦ.

There are a few passages in the New Testament in which this word means "wind." The Lord Jesus said to Nicodemus, "The *wind* blows where it wishes, and thou hearest the sound of it" (John 3:8). τὸ πνεῦμα ὅπου θέλει πνεῖ. But often it refers to the "spirit" of man. In the Sermon on the Mount the Lord said, "Blessed are the poor in the *spirit*, because theirs is the Kingdom of the heavens" (Matt. 5:3). μακάριοι οἱ πτωχοὶ τῷ πνεύματι. When Stephen was being stoned, he prayed, "Lord Jesus, receive my *spirit*" (Acts 7:59). κύριε Ἰησοῦ, δέξαι τὸ πνεῦμά μου. Paul in the same context used the word to refer both to the Spirit of God and to the human spirit. "The *Spirit* Himself bears witness with our *spirit* that we are the children of God" (Rom. 8:16). αὐτὸ τὸ πνεῦμα συμμαρτυρεῖ τῷ πνεύματι ἡμῶν ὅτι ἐσμὲν τέκνα θεοῦ. The writer to the Hebrews used two of this group of words when he said, "For the Word of God is living and active and sharper than any two-edged sword, piercing even to the dividing of *soul* and *spirit"* (Heb. 4:12). καὶ διϊκνούμενος ἄρχι μερισμοῦ ψυχῆς καὶ πνεύματος.

ψυχή

Homer said of the slaying of Pandarus by Diomedes, "But there his *life* and his strength were undone." τοῦ δ' αὖθι λύθη ψυχή τε μένος τε (*Iliad* 5.296). But Homer also used the word for a disembodied "spirit." As Achilles slept, "then the *spirit* of hapless Patroclus came to him there." ἦλθε δ' ἐπὶ ψυχὴ Πατροκλῆος δειλοῖο (*Iliad* 23.65). In his discussion of Egypt Herodotus stated, "But indeed the Egyptians were the first to teach that the *soul* of man is immortal." πρῶτοι δὲ καὶ τόνδε τὸν λόγον Αἰγύπτιοι εἰσὶ οἱ εἰπόντες, ὡς ἀνθρώπου ψυχὴ ἀθάνατος ἐστί (2.123). Xenophon said of Socrates, "But he trained both his *soul* and his body by following a system which would give him a life of confidence and security." Διαίτῃ δὲ τήν τε ψυχὴν ἐπαίδευσε καὶ τὸ σῶμα (*Memorabilia* 1.3.5).

In the Septuagint account of creation the Lord says, "And to all the beasts of the earth, and to all the birds of the air, and to every creeping thing that creeps upon the earth, which has in it *animal life* [soul of life], I have also thus given every green herb for food" (Gen. 1:30). καὶ παντὶ ἑρπετῷ τῷ ἕρποντι ἐπὶ τῆς γῆς, ὃ ἔχει ἐν ἑαυτῷ ψυχὴν ζωῆς, πάντα χόρτον χλωρὸν εἰς βρῶσιν. Later in the account of creation Scripture says, "And God formed the man, dust from the earth, and breathed into his face a breath of life, and the man became a living *soul"* (Gen. 2:7). καὶ ἐνεφύσησεν εἰς τὸ πρόσωπον αὐτοῦ πνοὴν ζωῆς, καὶ ἐγένετο ὁ ἄνθρωπος εἰς ψυχὴν ζῶσαν. Before they entered the land of Canaan, Moses warned the Israelites, "Take heed to thyself, and keep thy *soul* diligently" (Deut. 4:9). πρόσεχε σεαυτῷ καὶ φύλαξον τὴν ψυχήν σου σφόδρα. A sneering retort was Satan's answer to the Lord's claims about Job: "Skin for skin; all that a man has he will give for his *life"* (Job 2:4). Δέρμα ὑπὲρ δέρματος· ὅσα ὑπάρχει ἀνθρώπῳ, ὑπὲρ τῆς ψυχῆς αὐτοῦ ἐκτείσει. David prophesied concerning the resurrection of the Messiah "that thou wilt not leave my *soul* in Hades, nor suffer thy Holy One to see corruption" (Ps. 15:10; KJ Ps. 16:10). ὅτι οὐκ ἐγκαταλείψεις τὴν ψυχήν μου εἰς ᾅδην.

In the Magnificat Mary said, "My *soul* magnifies the Lord, and my *spirit* rejoiced in God my Saviour" (Luke 1:46). Μεγαλύνει ἡ ψυχή μου τὸν κύριον, καὶ ἠγαλλίασεν τὸ πνεῦμά μου ἐπὶ τῷ θεῷ τῷ σωτῆρί μου. The Lord Jesus taught His disciples "And stop fearing those who kill the body, but are not able to kill the *soul;* but rather fear the one who is able to destroy both *soul* and body in Gehenna" (Matt. 10:28). καὶ μὴ φοβεῖσθε ἀπὸ τῶν ἀποκτεννόντων τὸ σῶμα, τὴν δὲ ψυχὴν μὴ δυνα-

SOUL

μένων ἀποκτεῖναι· φοβεῖσθε δὲ μᾶλλον τὸν δυνάμενον καὶ ψυχὴν καὶ σῶμα ἀπολέσαι ἐν γεέννῃ. In the parable of the rich fool the rich man said to his soul, *"Soul,* thou hast many good things laid up for many years; rest, eat, drink, be merry" (Luke 12:19). ψυχή, ἔχεις πολλὰ ἀγαθὰ κείμενα εἰς ἔτη πολλά. When Paul was completing the first missionary journey, he returned through the cities he had visited, "confirming the *souls* of the disciples, exhorting them to continue in the faith" (Acts 14:22). ἐπιστηρίζοντες τὰς ψυχὰς τῶν μαθητῶν. Paul prayed for the Thessalonians, "May your *spirit* and *soul* and body be preserved whole blamelessly in the coming of our Lord Jesus Christ" (I Thess. 5:23). ὁλόκληρον ὑμῶν τὸ πνεῦμα καὶ ἡ ψυχὴ καὶ τὸ σῶμα ἀμέμπτως ἐν τῇ παρουσίᾳ τοῦ κυρίου ἡμῶν Ἰησοῦ Χριστοῦ τηρηθείη.

SUMMARY

Each of these words refers to the inner life of man as well as to other things. The word καρδία means "heart," either the physical organ or the center of man's personal life, the source of moral choice, intelligence, emotion, and feeling. νοῦς is the "mind," that faculty which thinks and makes moral judgments. πνεῦμα can mean "breath" or "spirit," that is, the self-conscious principle which wills, thinks, and feels. The word ψυχή means "life" or "soul." It can refer to animal life, but it can also refer to the seat of the personal ego, the "self" or "soul." Each of these terms can thus denote the whole spiritual nature of man, as opposed to the physical nature.

15. Stranger: ξένος, πάροικος, παρεπίδημος

Of these three words ξένος has the widest range of meaning. Its general sense is *a stranger*. But it may refer specifically to a stranger not working in a land he is just passing through; or it may also mean a *guest* or even a *host*. On the other hand, πάροικος, designating a *sojourner,* one who dwells in a foreign land, may have the technical sense of a *stranger licensed to work*. The word παρεπίδημος means a *sojourner* who is settled only for a time in a foreign land.

ξένος

This word may be applied to both parties when two strangers meet. Although strangers were suspicious of one another, when one obviously befriended another he could be termed a *beloved stranger*. Telemachus offers Athena a gift "which shall be to thee an heirloom gift, such as beloved *strangers* give to *strangers.*" ὅ τοι κειμήλιον ἔσται ἐξ ἐμεῦ, οἷα φίλοι ξεῖνοι ξείνοισι διδοῦσι (Homer *Odyssey* 1.313). Zeus is known as the "avenger of suppliants and *strangers.*" ἐπιτιμήτωρ ἱκετάων τε ξείνων τε (Homer *Odyssey* 9.270). Homer also uses the word to mean "guest." "For a *guest* of his, king of men, Euphetes, had given it to him to wear in battle." ξεῖνος γάρ οἱ ἔδωκεν ἄναξ ἀνδρῶν Εὐφήτης ἐς πόλεμον φορέειν (*Iliad* 15.532). Herodotus has the statement, "For they were calling the foreigners '*strangers.*'" ξείνους γὰρ ἐκάλεον τοὺς βαρβάρους (9.11). In one of the papyri the writer complained of someone's having despised him because he was a *stranger:* καταφρονήσας μου ὅτι ξένος εἰμί (*P. Magd.* 8.11).

When Boaz made provision for Ruth, she fell before him and said, "Why did I find favor in thine eyes that thou shouldest notice me, since I am a *stranger?*" (Ruth 2:10). τί ὅτι εὗρον χάριν ἐν ὀφθαλμοῖς σου τοῦ ἐπιγνῶναί με; καὶ ἐγώ εἰμι ξένη. In telling Saul how to find Samuel, the young girls said to Saul, "The people will not eat until he comes, because he will bless the sacrifice, and after these things the *guests* eat" (I Sam. 9:13). ὅτι οὗτος εὐλογεῖ τὴν θυσίαν, καὶ μετὰ ταῦτα ἐσθίουσιν οἱ ξένοι. When King David had to flee from Absalom, he said to Ittai the Gittite, "Why art thou also going with us? return and dwell with the king because thou art a *stranger* and because thou art an exile from thine own place" (II Sam. 15:19). ἐπίστρεφε καὶ οἴκει μετὰ τοῦ βασιλέως, ὅτι ξένος εἶ σὺ καὶ ὅτι μετῳκηκας σὺ ἐκ τοῦ τόπου σου. Job protested to his three friends, "But the *stranger* did not lodge outside, but my door was open to every comer" (Job 31:32). ἔξω δὲ οὐκ ηὐλίζετο ξένος, ἡ δὲ θύρα μου παντὶ ἐλθόντι ἀνέῳκτο.

In the Olivet Discourse the Lord Jesus prophesied, concerning the judgment of the nations, of His saying to the "sheep" on His right hand, "For I was hungry, and ye gave me to eat; I was thirsty, and ye gave me to drink; I was a *stranger,* and ye took me in" (Matt. 25:35). ἐδίψησα καὶ ἐποτίσατέ με, ξένος ἤμην καὶ συνηγάγετέ με. When Paul was witnessing in the market place, certain of the philosophers said of him, "He seems to be a preacher of *strange* divinities" (Acts 17:18). ξένων δαιμονίων δοκεῖ καταγγελεὺς εἶναι. Paul reminded believers that at one time they were "alienated from the commonwealth of Israel and *strangers* from the covenants of the promise" (Eph. 2:12). ἀπηλλοτριωμένοι τῆς πολιτείας τοῦ Ἰσραηλ καὶ ξένοι τῶν διαθηκῶν τῆς ἐπαγγελίας. Using the word in a different sense, Paul mentioned "Gaius, my *host,* and of the whole church" (Rom. 16:23). Γάϊος ὁ ξένος μου καὶ ὅλης τῆς ἐκκλησίας.

πάροικος

Thucydides relates that the Acarnanians and Amphilochians "were now afraid that the Athenians, if they had the town in their possession, would prove more troublesome *neighbors* [than the Ambraciots]." νῦν δ᾽ ἔδεισαν μὴ οἱ Ἀθηναῖοι ἔχοντες αὐτὴν χαλεπώτεροι σφίσι πάροικοι ὦσιν (3.113.6). When the messenger comes in with news of Haemon's death, he cries, "*Neighbors* of Cadmus and Amphion's house, there is no kind of state in human life which I dare to envy or to blame." Κάδμου πάροικοι καὶ δόμων Ἀμφίονος (Sophocles *Antigone* 1155). In one papyrus Zosimus promised to invite "both all the citizens and *sojourners* and inhabitants and Romans and *strangers* and slaves." τούς τε πόλιτας πάντας καὶ παροίκους καὶ κατοίκους καὶ Ῥωμαίους καὶ ξένους καὶ δούλους (*Priene,* 113.38f).

In the Septuagint the Lord said to Abraham, "Know assuredly that thy seed shall be *sojourners* in a land not their own" (Gen. 15:13). γινώσκων γνώσῃ ὅτι πάροικον ἔσται τὸ σπέρμα σου ἐν γῇ οὐκ ἰδίᾳ. When the Lord gave instructions concerning the passover, He said to Moses, "A *sojourner* or a hireling shall not eat of it" (Exod. 12:45). πάροικος ἢ μισθωτὸς οὐκ ἔδεται ἀπ᾽ αὐτοῦ. A man brought news of King Saul's death to David, expecting a reward, "and David said to the young man who had told him, Whence art thou? And he said, I am the son of a *sojourner*—an Amalekite" (II Sam. 1:13). καὶ εἶπεν Υἱὸς ἀνδρὸς παροίκου Αμαληκίτου ἐγώ εἰμι. The psalmist prayed to the Lord, "I am a *sojourner* in the earth;

do not hide thy commandments from me" (Ps. 118:19; KJ Ps. 119:19). πάροικος ἐγώ εἰμι ἐν τῇ γῇ· μὴ ἀποκρύψῃς ἀπ' ἐμοῦ τὰς ἐντολάς σου.

Stephen recounted the promise to Abraham, "that his seed should be a *sojourner* in a foreign land" (Acts 7:6). ὅτι ἔσται τὸ σπέρμα αὐτοῦ πάροικον ἐν γῇ ἀλλοτρίᾳ· To the believers Paul wrote, "Therefore then ye are no longer *strangers* and *sojourners,* but ye are fellow citizens with the saints and the household of God" (Eph. 2:19). ἄρα οὖν οὐκέτι ἐστέ ξένοι καὶ πάροικοι, ἀλλὰ ἐστέ συμπολῖται τῶν ἁγίων καὶ οἰκεῖοι τοῦ θεοῦ. The Apostle Peter exhorted, "Beloved, I beseech you as *sojourners* and *outsiders* to abstain from fleshly lusts, which war against the soul" (I Pet. 2:11). Ἀγαπητοί, παρακαλῶ ὡς παροίκους καὶ παρεπιδήμους ἀπέχεσθαι τῶν σαρκικῶν ἐπιθυμιῶν. Apparently the reference is to "sojourners who settle for work" and "sojourners who are in a place briefly" and who have no official connection with the state they are in.

παρεπίδημος

Although this is a relatively scarce word, there is an inscription which refers to "a multitude, people of the country and *sojourners.*" πλῆθος ἐπιχώριον καὶ παρεπίδημον (OGIS, 383.150). In the Septuagint, when Abraham went to the sons of Heth after Sarah had died to obtain a tomb, he said to them, "I am a *sojourner* and an *outsider* among you; give me therefore the possession of a burying place among you" (Gen. 23:4). πάροικος καὶ παρεπίδημος ἐγώ εἰμι μεθ' ὑμῶν. The psalmist prayed, "Hear my prayer, O Lord, and give ear to my petition; hold not thy peace at my tears, because I am a *sojourner* with thee and an *outsider* even as all my fathers were" (Ps. 38:13; KJ Ps. 39:12). ὅτι πάροικος ἐγώ εἰμι παρὰ σοὶ καὶ παρεπίδημος καθὼς πάντες οἱ πατέρες μου.

The writer to the Hebrews spoke of the heroes of faith and added, "These all died in faith, not having received the promises, but having seen them afar off and having greeted them, and having confessed that they were *strangers* and *sojourners* upon the earth" (Heb. 11:13). καὶ ὁμολογήσαντες ὅτι ξένοι καὶ παρεπίδημοί εἰσιν ἐπὶ τῆς γῆς. Peter began his first epistle, "Peter, an apostle of Jesus Christ, to the chosen *sojourners* [exiles (Arndt and Gingrich, p. 631).] of the dispersion" (I Pet. 1:1). Πέτρος ἀπόστολος Ἰησοῦ Χριστοῦ ἐκλεκτοῖς παρεπιδήμοις διασπορᾶς.

SUMMARY

The word ξένος means "stranger," but it has a variety of secondary meanings; it may mean a stranger who is just passing through a country and does not live in it, or it may refer to a "guest" or a "host." The word πάροικος denotes "one who dwells alongside," either as a "neighbor" or

STRANGER

as a "sojourner," often with the sense of a "sojourner who settles in order to work"; παρεπίδημος also means a "sojourner," but one who is an "outsider," one who is settled only for a time in a land but who does not work in it. Sometimes, however, these words are grouped together with no strong distinctions between them.

16. Strife: ἔρις, ἐριθεία

The King James Version translates both of these words on occasion as *strife* (Rom. 1:29; II Cor. 12:20), but there is some distinction between them: ἔρις means *strife, contention,* or *rivalry;* ἐριθεία, *selfishness, contentiousness,* or *personal ambition.*

ἔρις

This word is often used of the "strife" of battle. Homer has King Agamemnon answer Achilles, "Most hateful to me art thou of the kings, nurtured by Zeus, for always are *strife* and wars and battles dear to thee." ἔχθιστος δέ μοί ἐσσι διοτρεφέων βασιλήων· αἰεὶ γάρ τοι ἔρις τε φίλη πόλεμοί τε μάχαι τε (*Iliad* 1.177). Odysseus challenged Eurymachus, "For if we two might have a *contest* [rivalry] in working in the season of spring, when the long days come, at mowing the grass, ..." εἰ γὰρ νῶϊν ἔρις ἔργοιο γένοιτο (*Odyssey* 18.366). In one place Herodotus mentioned, "But at this very time the Spartans themselves had a *contest* [feud] on hand with the Argives concerning the country called Thyrea." κατ' αὐτὸν τοῦτον τὸν χρόνον συνεπεπτώκεε ἔρις ἐοῦσα πρὸς Ἀργείους περὶ χώρου καλεομένου Θυρέης (1.82). Once in a while this word is used with a good connotation as a *rivalry* that produces good results. Aeschylus portrayed the goddess Athena as saying to the chorus of the Furies, "Our *rivalry* in doing good forever is victorious." νικᾷ δ' ἀγαθῶν ἔρις ἡμετέρα διὰ παντός (*Eumenides* 975). The writer of one of the papyri warned with his challenge, "Know thou that I have passion unconquerable when *strife* takes hold of me." γίνωσκε ὅτι θυμὸν ἀνίκητον ἔχω ὅταν ἔρις λάβῃ με (*P. Grenf.,* 1.21).

Only three times in the Septuagint does this word occur, all three times in the book of Ecclesiasticus. In one place the son of Sirach says, "*Strife* hastily begun kindles a fire, and hasty fighting sheds blood." ἔρις κατασπευδομένη ἐκκαίει πῦρ, καὶ μάχη κατασπεύδουσα ἐκχέει αἷμα (Ecclesiasticus 28:11). In another context he states that both for the rich and the poor there is "wrath and jealousy and trouble and disquiet and fear of death and anger and *strife.*" καὶ φόβος θανάτου καὶ μηνίαμα καὶ ἔρις (Ecclesiasticus 40:5). To this list he adds the things that were created for the wicked: "Death and bloodshed and *strife* and sword." θάνατος καὶ αἷμα καὶ ἔρις καὶ ῥομφαία (Ecclesiasticus 40:9). There is a similar list in Clement when he exhorts the Corinthians to be casting away "all iniquity and evil, covetousness, *strifes,* both malice and deceit." πᾶσαν ἀδικίαν καὶ πονηρίαν, πλεονεξίαν, ἔρεις, κακοηθείας τε καὶ δόλους (I Clement 35. 5; note use of variant form of plural ending instead of ἔριδες)

In the New Testament this word is found in the terrible list of vices that characterize man apart from God. Paul charged that sinful mankind was "full of envy, murder, *strife,* deceit, malice" (Rom. 1:29). μεστοὺς φθόνου φόνου ἔριδος δόλου κακοηθείας. Part of the burden that Paul had to bear was that "some preach Christ even because of envy and *strife,* but others also because of good will" (Phil. 1:15). τινὲς μὲν καὶ διὰ φθόνον καὶ ἔριν, τινὲς δὲ καὶ δι᾽ εὐδοκίαν. Whenever Paul heard that there was strife in any church, he spoke strongly against it. He wrote to the Corinthians that the household of Chloe had made known to him that "there were *strifes* among you" (I Cor. 1:11). ὅτι ἔριδες ἐν ὑμῖν εἰσιν. Paul exhorted his faithful helper Titus "to avoid foolish questionings and genealogies and *strife* and fightings concerning the law" (Titus 3:9). μωρὰς δὲ ζητήσεις καὶ γενεαλογίας καὶ ἔριν καὶ μάχας νομικὰς περιΐστασο. The only other two times that it occurs, it is used along with ἐριθεία.

ἐριθεία

If the former word is common in extra-Biblical literature, this one is certainly scarce. In classical literature it is found in only one work by Aristotle, where it has the sense of "canvassing for public office" with a dishonest connotation (*Politics* 5. 2. 6, cited by Liddell and Scott, p. 578). The word itself comes from the verb ἐριθεύομαι, which means "I work for hire." This may have an entirely innocent sense, as its cognate does in one of the papyri which mentions "wool *workers*" in the sense of "weavers." ἐρίθοις ἐρίων (*P. Hibeh,* I, 121. 34). But one who works for wages may do so only for the money, and it is this connotation of "selfishness" that dominates the use of this word in the New Testament. "Its general meaning is plain enough. It describes a wrong attitude in the doing of work and in the holding of office" (William Barclay, *Flesh and Spirit,* p. 53).

Although this word does not occur at all in the Septuagint, it does occur in a number of places in the New Testament, always with a bad connotation. Paul wrote of God's impartial judgment: "But to the ones who, out of *selfishness,* are even disobeying the truth and are being persuaded by unrighteousness, wrath and anger [shall be]" (Rom. 2:8). τοῖς δὲ ἐξ ἐριθείας καὶ ἀπειθοῦσι τῇ ἀληθείᾳ πειθομένοις δὲ τῇ ἀδικίᾳ, ὀργὴ καὶ θυμός. Paul writing to the Philippians, exhorted them that they should be "doing nothing according to *selfishness* or according to vain glory, but in lowliness of mind each counting one another better than himself" (Phil. 2:3). μηδὲν κατ' ἐριθείαν μηδὲ κατὰ κενοδοξίαν. Any "contentiousness" here would be from "personal ambition." James also warned his readers, "But if ye have bitter jealousy and *selfishness,* stop glorying" (James 3:14). εἰ δὲ ζῆλον πικρὸν ἔχετε καὶ ἐριθείαν. In one place Paul expressed concern to the Corinthians lest he should find among them "*strife,* jealousy, wraths, *personal ambitions,* backbitings, whisperings" (II Cor. 12:20). ἔρις, ζῆλος, θυμοί, ἐριθεῖαι, καταλαλιαί, ψιθυρισμοί. Since both words are used in the same context in this passage, there is clearly a distinction between them: the distinction between "strife" and "selfish acts." When Paul lists the works of the flesh, he names these two words together again: "idolatry, sorcery, enmities, *strife,* jealousies, wraths, *selfish ambitions,* divisions, heresies" (Gal. 5:20). εἰδωλολατρία, φαρμακεία, ἔχθραι, ἔρις, ζῆλος, θυμοί, ἐριθεῖαι, διχοστασίαι, αἱρέσεις.

SUMMARY

The word ἔρις refers to "strife," "contention," or "rivalry," always with an evil connotation in the New Testament, but with the potentiality for a neutral sense. The word ἐριθεία means "selfishness," "selfish ambition," or "contentiousness." The basic contrast seems to be "love of fighting" on the one hand and "love of self" on the other.

17. Sword: μάχαιρα, ῥομφαία

The μάχαιρα was a *large knife* or a *short sword*, a common weapon among the Greeks. The ῥομφαία on the other hand was a large *broadsword*, little used among the Greeks though often used by other nations.

μάχαιρα

This was the usual military weapon and a common personal implement among the Greeks and the Romans. One of the scenes on the great shield of Achilles depicted a festive gathering in which "the young men carried golden *knives* that hung from silver belts." μαχαίρας εἶχον χρυσείας ἐξ ἀργυρέων τελαμώνων (Homer *Iliad* 18.597). Herodotus recorded that Cleomenes "asked a *dagger*" from his guard and slashed himself to death. αἰτέει μάχαιραν (6.75). In recounting the fighting between the Greeks and the Persians, Herodotus mentioned that the Greeks "defended themselves with their *swords*." ἀλεξομένους μαχαίρῃσι (7.225).

When God called Abraham to sacrifice Isaac, Abraham "took also the fire in his hand and the *knife*"(Gen. 22:6). ἔλαβεν δὲ καὶ τὸ πῦρ μετὰ χεῖρα καὶ τὴν μάχαιραν. The psalmist said of wicked men, "Their tongue is a sharp *sword*"(Ps. 56:5; KJ Ps. 57:4). ἡ γλῶσσα αὐτῶν μάχαιρα ὀξεῖα. In a papyrus dated 114 B.C. a man is described as "armed with a *sword.*" ἐν μαχαίρῃ (*P. Tebt,* I, 16. 14). In another some military police are called "*sword*-bearers." μαχαιροφόροι (*P. Oxy.,* II, 294. 20). This is a common usage.

The New Testament shows a similar usage. When Judas led the mob out to seize the Lord Jesus, there was "with him a great crowd with *swords* and staves" (Matt. 26:47). μετὰ μαχαιρῶν καὶ ξύλων. One of the deeds recorded against Herod Agrippa I was that "he slew James, the brother of John, with the *sword*" (Acts 12:2). ἀνεῖλεν Ἰάκωβον τὸν ἀδελφὸν Ἰωάννου μαχαίρῃ. The writer to the Hebrews stated that the Word of God is "sharper than any two-edged *sword*" (Heb. 4:12). τομώτερος ὑπὲρ πᾶσαν μάχαιραν δίστομον. In the same vein the Apostle Paul exhorted believers to put on the full armor of God and to take "the *sword* of the Spirit, which is the Word of God" (Eph. 6:17). τὴν μάχαιραν τοῦ πνεύματος. This usage is particularly fitting, because all the armor which he mentioned was the usual equipment of the Roman soldier, and the short sword was the regular weapon for Roman troops. Using this word figuratively, Paul urged believers to render all obedience to governmental authority, "but if thou shouldest do evil, be afraid; for he is not bearing the *sword* in vain" (Rom. 13:4). οὐ γὰρ εἰκῇ τὴν μάχαιραν φορεῖ. Human governments have the authority to execute criminals. In the book of Revelation John describes the rider on the red horse and adds, "To him was given a great *sword*"(6:4). ἐδόθη αὐτῷ μάχαιρα μεγάλη. This is in contrast to the sword which our Lord bears in that book (19:15).

ῥομφαία

This is the large broadsword which the Thracians in particular customarily carried. Plutarch described the Thracians as "having straight *swords* of heavy iron swaying from their right shoulders." ὀρθὰς ῥομφαίας βαρυσιδήρους ἀπο τῶν δεξιῶν ὤμων ἐπισείοντες (*Aemil.* 18, cited in Hastings, *Dictionary of the Bible,* IV, 634). In the *Epistle of Barnabas* is the petition, "Spare my soul from the *sword.*" φεῖσαί μου τῆς ψυχῆς ἀπὸ ῥομφαίας (5.13). It is typical that the Septuagint uses this term for the great sword of Goliath. David stood over the Philistine and "took his *sword* and slew him" (I Sam. 17:51). ἔλαβεν τὴν ῥομφαίαν αὐτοῦ καὶ θανάτωσεν αὐτόν. After the Lord had driven Adam and Eve out of the garden of Eden, He placed there the Cherubim "and the whirling, flaming *sword,* to keep the way of the tree of life" (Gen. 3:24). καὶ τὴν φλογίνην ῥομφαίαν τὴν στρεφομένην. When Gideon made his night attack against the Midianites, the Israelites broke their pitchers, brandished their torches, blew their trumpets, "and cried, A *sword* for the Lord and for Gideon" (Judg. 7:20). καὶ ἀνέκραξαν Ῥομφαία τῷ κυρίῳ καὶ τῷ Γεδεων. The psalmist cried out, "The *swords* of the enemy have utterly come to an end" (Ps. 9:7; KJ Ps. 9:6). τοῦ ἐχθροῦ ἐξέλιπον αἱ ῥομφαῖαι εἰς τέλος.

In a poignant passage in the New Testament the angel warned Mary of the death of her Son and said, "And a *sword* shall pierce through thine own soul" (Luke 2:35). καὶ σοῦ δὲ αὐτῆς τὴν ψυχὴν διελεύσεται ῥομφαία. The four horsemen in the book of Revelation were given "authority over the fourth part of the earth, to kill with the *sword* and with famine and with death" (Rev. 6:8). ἐξουσία ἐπὶ τὸ τέταρτον τῆς γῆς, ἀποκτεῖναι ἐν ῥομφαίᾳ καὶ ἐν λιμῷ. Our Lord is described as "the one who has the sharp two-edged *sword*" (Rev. 2:12). ὁ ἔχων τὴν ῥομφαίαν τὴν δίστομον τὴν ὀξεῖαν. At the end of the battle of Armageddon the Lord Jesus will return to earth to take over the reins of government, and the book of Revelation prophesies, "Out of His mouth comes a sharp *sword,* that with it He should smite the nations" (Rev. 19:15). ἐκπορεύεται ῥομφαία ὀξεῖα. This whole wicked age is portrayed as coming to a bloody end. "And the rest were slain

SWORD

with the *sword* of the one who is sitting upon the horse" (Rev. 19:21). οἱ λοιποὶ ἀπεκτάνθησαν ἐν τῇ ῥομφαίᾳ τοῦ καθημένου·

SUMMARY

The μάχαιρα was a short sword or a large knife, the usual weapon of the Greeks and the Romans; the ῥομφαία was a great broadsword commonly used by other nations.

18. Trickery: κυβεία, μεθοδεία, πανουργία

This group of words applies to very devious conduct. The word κυβεία signifies *dice playing* or *trickery;* μεθοδεία denotes *method, scheming,* or, in the plural, *wiles;* πανουργία refers to *craftiness, villainy,* or what the Elizabethans would have called *knavery*.

κυβεία

In the *Phaedrus* Plato has Socrates say that the Egyptian god Theuth had "invented numbers and arithmetic and geometry and astronomy, and also draughts and *dice playing* and, most important indeed, letters." ἀριθμόν τε καὶ λογισμὸν εὑρεῖν καὶ γεωμετρίαν καὶ ἀστρονομίαν, ἔτι δὲ πεττείας τε καὶ κυβείας, καὶ δὴ καὶ γράμματα (274D). Xenophon also said of Socrates, "But he considered that praying as those who pray for gold or silver or kingly power or some other of such things was nothing different than if he should pray how *dice playing* or a battle or some other of the manifestly uncertain things should turn out." τοὺς δ' εὐχομένους χρυσίον ἢ ἀργύριον ἢ τυραννίδα ἢ ἄλλο τι τῶν τοιούτων οὐδὲν διάφορον ἐνόμιζεν εὔχεσθαι ἢ εἰ κυβείαν ἢ μάχην ἢ ἄλλο τι εὔχοιντο τῶν φανερῶς ἀδήλων ὅπως ἀποβήσοιτο (*Memorabilia* 1.3.2). The writer of one of the papyri used the cognate verb form in his petition "Make me to win *playing dice.*" ποίησόν μοι κυβεύοντα νικῆσαι (*P. Lond.*, 121.424).

The word does not occur in the Septuagint and occurs only once in the New Testament. Paul urged the believers to unity and maturity "that we may no longer be children, tossed to and fro and carried about by every wind of teaching in the *trickery* of men, in *craftiness,* unto the *scheming* of deceit" (Eph. 4:14). ἵνα μηκέτι ὦμεν νήπιοι, χλυδωνιζόμενοι καὶ περιφερόμενοι παντὶ ἀνέμῳ τῆς διδασκαλίας ἐν τῇ κυβείᾳ τῶν ἀνθρώπων, ἐν πανουργίᾳ πρὸς τὴν μεθοδείαν τῆς πλάνης. Evidently κυβεία is "chance trickery," whereas μεθοδεία is planned, deliberate "scheming," and πανουργία is general "craftiness" which can express itself in either kind of deception.

μεθοδεία

This word is both scarce and late in Greek literature. In one of his homilies Chrysostom said, "For such is always the devil's way: he puts forward everything in a *scheming,* and not in a straightforward manner, that we may be on our guard." Τοιοῦτος γὰρ ἀεὶ ὁ διάβολος, μεθοδείᾳ πάντα, καὶ οὐκ ἐξ εὐθείας προβάλλει, ἵνα φυλαττώμεθα (*Homily* 2.5 on Col.). Obviously Chrysostom is indebted to the New Testament usage of this word. The papyri use this word in a strictly neutral sense; one official receipt for rents states that the writer is faithful in discharging the function of an agent "in *method* corresponding to the account given by you of receipt and expenditure." πρὸς τὴν μεθοδίαν ἀκολούθως τῷ δοθέντι ὑπὸ σοῦ λόγῳ τοῦ τε λήμματος καὶ τοῦ ἐξωδιασμοῦ (*P. Oxy.*, VIII, 1134. 9).

Although this word does not occur in the Septuagint, the cognate verb does occur one time. When Mephibosheth met king David, he said concerning his evil servant Ziba, "*He defrauded* [slandered] thy servant to my lord the king, but my lord the king is as an angel of God" (II Sam. 19:28; KJ II Sam. 19:27). μεθώδευσεν ἐν τῷ δούλῳ σου πρὸς τὸν κύριόν μου τὸν βασιλέα.

Other than the passage already discussed under the first word, there is only one occurrence of this word in the New Testament. Paul exhorted the believers, "Put ye on the whole armor of God in order that ye may be able to stand against the *schemes* [wiles] of the devil" (Eph. 6:11). ἐνδύσασθε τὴν πανοπλίαν τοῦ θεοῦ πρὸς τὸ δύνασθαι ὑμᾶς στῆναι πρὸς τὰς μεθοδείας τοῦ διαβόλου. The connotation of evil plotting or scheming is very strong in this example. The devil is a master strategist.

πανουργία

Aeschylus portrayed Eteocles as saying, "For a godly man, having embarked together with sailors hotly bent on a certain *villainy,* perishes together with the heaven-detested crew." ἢ γὰρ ξυνεισβὰς πλοῖον εὐσεβὴς ἀνὴρ ναύταισι θερμοῖς καὶ πανουργίᾳ τινὶ ὄλωλεν ἀνδρῶν σὺν θεοπτύστῳ γένει (*Seven Against Thebes* 603). Creon, speaking of bribery, says, "It shows men how to do *villainy* and to know unholiness in every deed." πανουργίας δ' ἔδειξεν ἀνθρώποις ἔχειν, καὶ παντὸς ἔργου δυσσέβειαν εἰδέναι (Sophocles *Antigone* 300). In discussing virtue and ability Aristotle said, "There is indeed a certain power [faculty] called Cleverness, which is the capacity for doing the things mentioned before that leads to the aim we intend and thus attains it. Therefore, if the aim is good [noble], it is praiseworthy, but if it is base, it is *villainy;* wherefore we say that both prudent men and *villains* are clever." ἂν μὲν οὖν ὁ σκοπὸς ᾖ καλός, ἐπαινετή ἐστιν, ἂν δὲ φαῦλος, πανουργία· διὸ καὶ τοὺς φρονίμους δεινοὺς καὶ τοὺς πανούργους φαμέν εἶναι (*Nicomachean Ethics* 6.12.9). In the papyri an edict states, "I proclaim that people shall abstain from such *craftiness.*" παραγγέλλω τῆς τοιαύτης πανουργίας ἀπέχεσθαι (*P. Oxy.*, II, 237.8.12).

In a rather confused paraphrase of Balaam's prophecy, the Septuagint reads, "Even if Beor has a nest of *craftiness,* the Assyrians will take thee captive" (Num. 24:22). καὶ ἐὰν γένηται τῷ Βεωρ νεοσσιὰ πανουργίας, Ἀσσύριοί σε αἰχμαλωτεύσουσιν. When Joshua started destroying the inhabitants of Canaan, the men of Gibeon formed a plan: "And they themselves worked even with *craftiness* and went and took supplies, prepared and took old sacks on their asses and old wineskins, rent and having been bound up" (Josh. 9:4). καὶ ἐποίησαν καί γε αὐτοὶ μετὰ πανουργίας. Proverbs was written "that he might give to the innocent *craftiness"* (1:4). ἵνα δῷ ἀκάκοις πανουργίαν.

When the scribes and the chief priests tried to ensnare the Lord Jesus with the question about giving tribute to Caesar, Scripture says of the Lord, "But having perceived their *craftiness,* he said to them, Show me a denarius" (Luke 20:23). κατανοήσας δὲ αὐτῶν τὴν πανουργίαν εἶπεν πρὸς αὐτούς. The Apostle Paul wrote, "For the wisdom of this world is foolishness with God. For it has been written, He takes the wise in their own *craftiness"* (I Cor. 3:19). γέγραπται γάρ· ὁ δρασσόμενος τοὺς σοφοὺς ἐν τῇ πανουργίᾳ αὐτῶν. Later, Paul, speaking of his ministry, said, "But we renounced the hidden things of shame, not walking in *craftiness,* nor using the Word of God deceitfully" (II Cor. 4:2). μὴ περιπατοῦντες ἐν πανουργίᾳ. The serpent is the epitome of "craftiness," and accordingly, Paul warned, "But I fear, lest by any means, as the serpent deceived Eve in his *craftiness,* your minds should be corrupted" (II Cor. 11:3). ὡς ὁ ὄφις ἐξηπάτησεν Εὔαν ἐν τῇ πανουργίᾳ αὐτοῦ.

SUMMARY

Since the word κυβεία comes from κύβος, a "cube" or "die," it is natural for it to mean "dice playing"; dicing in turn lends itself to deception, so that the usual meaning is "chance trickery." On the other hand, μεθοδεία means "method" or systematic "scheming" and deliberate "plotting." The word πανουργία means literally "being ready to do everything"; hence, the usual sense is "craftiness" or "villainy" which will use either "method" or "chance" to deceive.

19. Well: φρέαρ, πηγή

The word φρέαρ means *well, cistern,* or *pit,* whereas πηγή designates a *spring* or *fountain.*

φρέαρ

Homer distinguished φρέαρ from "spring" when saying of the ocean, "And all springs and all deep *wells* have their waters of him." καὶ πᾶσαι κρῆναι καὶ φρείατα μακρὰ νάουσιν (*Iliad* 21.197; note the Homeric spelling). This term also means "cistern." Thucydides spoke of the great plague of Athens, in which it was thought that its enemies had poisoned the cisterns, and mentioned the great thirst of the victims, some of whom actually "plunged into the *cisterns.*" εἰς φρέατα καταβαίνειν (2.48–49). This word does not necessarily indicate water.

In the Septuagint the psalmist prayed concerning the wicked, "But thou, O God, shalt bring them down into the *pit* of destruction" (Ps. 54:24; KJ Ps. 55:23). σὺ δέ, ὁ θεός, κατάξεις αὐτοὺς εἰς φρέαρ διαφθορᾶς. The Septuagint also says of the region of Sodom and Gomorrah, "But the salt valley had *many pits* of asphalt" (Gen. 14:10). ἡ δὲ κοιλὰς ἡ ἁλυκὴ φρέατα φρέατα ἀσφάλτου. However, with qualifying words this term can even refer to a "spring." When the Lord opened the eyes of Hagar, "she saw a *well* of living [spring] water" (Gen. 21:19). εἶδεν φρέαρ ὕδατος ζῶντος.

Some of the papyri indicate the man-made characteristics of a "well." In a papyrus dated 126 B.C. a testator willed a "vineyard and the *wells* of baked brick in it." ἔδαφος ἀμπελῶνος, καὶ τὰ ἐν τούτωι φρέατα ἐξόπτης πλίνθου (*P. Grenf.,* I, 21.8). Another papyrus dated A.D. 81–96 mentions "a stone *well.*" φρέατρος λιθίνου (*P. Oxy;* VIII, 1105. 10).

These same usages are found in the New Testament. When the woman at the well addressed Jesus, she said, "Sir, thou hast no bucket, and the *well* is deep" (John 4:11). τὸ φρέαρ ἐστιν βαθύ. During the catastrophic judgments of the Revelation, a certain star fell from heaven to earth, "and he opened the *pit* of the abyss" (Rev. 9:2). τὸ φρέαρ τῆς ἀβύσσου. In one passage the context does not determine whether the meaning is "well" or "pit." Our Lord said, "Of which of you shall a son or an ox fall into a *well* [or pit] . . ." (Luke 14:5). εἰς φρέαρ πεσεῖται.

A TREASURY OF NEW TESTAMENT SYNONYMS

πηγή

In contrast to the term above, πηγή refers to naturally flowing water. Homer spoke of the "nymphs who live in the lovely groves, and the *springs* of rivers." πηγὰς ποταμῶν (*Iliad* 20.9). Often the sense is metaphorical, such as when Sophocles in *Antigone* has the chorus say, "The *fountains* of my tears I can refrain no more." πηγὰς δύναμαι δακρύων (line 803). Sometimes this sense of "spring" shades into the meaning of "source." In Aeschylus' *The Persians* the ghost of Darius exclaimed, "The *spring* of evils is found." πηγὴ κακῶν (line 743).

The Septuagint translates one of the Psalms, "The *fountains* of waters were seen" (Ps. 17:16; KJ Ps. 18:15). ὤφθησαν αἱ πηγαὶ τῶν ὑδάτων. The first use of this word in the Septuagint is a strange translation of the Hebrew word for "mist": "But a *fountain* ascended out of the earth and watered the whole face of the earth" (Gen. 2:6). πηγὴ δὲ ἀνέβαινεν ἐκ τῆς γῆς. The account of the flood recorded, "On this day all the *fountains* of the abyss were burst open" (Gen. 7:11). τῇ ἡμέρᾳ ταύτῃ ἐρράγησαν πᾶσαι αἱ πηγαὶ τῆς ἀβύσσου. After the Exodus the Israelites came to Elim, "and there was there twelve *springs* of water and seventy palm trees" (Exod. 15:27). καὶ ἦσαν ἐκεῖ δώδεκα πηγαὶ ὑδάτων.

The author of *The Shepherd of Hermas* mentioned the creatures which "were given to drink from the *springs* of the mountain." ἐποτίζοντο ἐκ τῶν πηγῶν τοῦ ὄρους (Sim. 9.1.8.). There is an express contrast between these two terms in one of the papyri. The author said, "How, therefore, wilt thou possess a living *fountain* and not a [mere] *well?*" πῶς οὖν πηγὴν ἀέναον ἕξεις καὶ μὴ φρέαρ; (*M. Anton.* 8.51, cited in Moulton and Milligan, p. 648).

James, exhorting his readers concerning the evils of the tongue, wrote, "The *fountain* does not send forth from the same opening the sweet and the bitter, does it?" (James 3:11). ἡ πηγὴ . . . βρύει. With a figurative meaning the Lord Jesus promised, "The water that I shall give him shall become in him a *fountain* of water springing up unto eternal life" (John 4:14). πηγὴ ὕδατος ἁλλομένου. Here the King James Version confuses these terms by calling this a "well." It is really a much more striking image which Christ gives of a natural fountain pouring forth water from within the believer.

This word is used with a variety of connotations; in one passage it refers to a "flow" of blood. When Christ healed a woman, the Word recorded, "The *fountain* of her blood was dried up" (Mark 5:29). ἡ πηγὴ τοῦ αἵματος αὐτῆς. In describing the consummation of all things, our Lord promised John, "I will give to the one who thirsts of the *fountain* of the water of life freely" (Rev. 21:6). ἐκ τῆς πηγῆς τοῦ ὕδατος τῆς ζωῆς.

SUMMARY

The φρέαρ is an artificial well, whereas the πηγή is a natural or spontaneous flow of water, such as a spring or fountain. The φρέαρ is purposely dug and may be only a dry pit, but the πηγή exists in nature.

20. Word: λόγος, ρῆμα

Although there are a multitude of specific meanings for the word λόγος, they may all be grouped in two major categories: (1) *word* or *statement* and (2) *thought* or *reason*. The word ρῆμα means a *word* or *thing*.

λόγος

In the first category of "word" this term is used in Homer only in the plural with the sense of "talk." Athena accuses Calypso of hindering Odysseus from returning home by saying, "she keeps on coaxing him with her beguiling *talk*, to turn his mind from Ithaca." *αἰεὶ δὲ μαλακοῖσι καὶ αἱμυλίοισι λόγοισι* (Homer *Odyssey* 1.56). There are several interesting usages in Herodotus. In one passage he says, "Their religious observances are, as they say in a *word* [i.e. 'briefly'], innumerable." *μυρίας ὡς εἰπεῖν λόγῳ* (2.37). In another place he mentions a certain queen, Tomyris, to whom "Cyrus sent a message in *pretence* of wooing her." *πέμπων ὁ Κῦρος ἐμνᾶτο τῷ λόγῳ* (1.205). This seems to mean "in word" and not "in deed." Sometimes this term has the meaning of "narrative" and in the plural signifies "history": "Among the many rulers of this city of Babylon (of whom I shall make mention in my Assyrian *history*). . . ." *τῶν ἐν τοῖσι Ἀσσυρίοισι λόγοισι μνήμην ποιήσομαι* (1.184). Thucydides used this word in the sense of "statement": "Here is an excellent illustration of the truth of my *statement*." *παράδειγμα τόδε τοῦ λόγου οὐκ ἐλάχιστόν ἐστι* (1.2). In Sophocles it has the meaning of "assertion." Theseus says to Oedipus, "You'd get no more assurance than by my *word*." *οὔκουν πέρα γ᾽ ἂν οὐδὲν ἢ λόγῳ φέροις* (*Oedipus at Colonus* 651).

In the sense of "thought" or "reason" this word is also used by Herodotus. "But in true *reason* this dress is not originally Ionian, but Carian." *ἔστι δὲ ἀληθεῖ λόγῳ* (5.88). It has the meaning of "opinion" or "purpose" in some contexts. "But it was necessary in the *opinion* of those [i.e. the Persians] that not even a firebearer should be saved alive." *ἔδει δὲ μηδὲ πυρφόρον τῷ ἐκείνων λόγῳ ἐκφυγόντα περιγενέσθαι* (8.6).

There is much less variety of usage in the Septuagint; most of the examples have the meaning "statement" or "speech." When Lamech recited his verse to his wives, he said, "Adah and Zillah, hear my voice; Ye wives of Lamech, listen carefully to my *speech*" (Gen. 4:23). *γυναῖκες*

WORD

Λαμεχ, ἐνωτίσασθέ μου τοὺς λόγους. The sons of Jacob made a dishonest agreement with Hamor and Shechem, "and their *proposal* pleased Hamor and Shechem" (Gen. 34:18). καὶ ἤρεσαν οἱ λόγοι ἐναντίον Εμμωρ. When Moses was in Mount Sinai before the Lord for forty days and forty nights, "He wrote upon the tables these *words* of the covenant, the ten *commandments*"(Exod. 34:28). ἔγραψεν τὰ ῥήματα ταῦτα . . . τοὺς δέκα λόγους. This statement presents an interesting contrast between these two terms: ῥῆμα meaning "word" and λόγος meaning "statement." There is a similar distinction in the charge of Eliphaz against Job: "But had there been a true *word* in thy *statements*, none of these evils would have happened to thee" (Job 4:12). εἰ δέ τι ῥῆμα ἀληθινὸν ἐγεγόνει ἐν λόγοις σου, οὐδὲν ἄν σοι τούτων κακὸν ἀπήντησεν. These passages are good illustrations of the distinction between these two words. "λόγος never means a *word* in the grammatical sense, as the mere name of a thing or act, (these being expressed by ἔπος, ὄνομα, ῥῆμα, Lat. vocabulum), but rather a *word as the thing referred to, the material* not *the formal* part" (Liddell and Scott, p. 901). Another common use of this word in the prophets is illustrated by the statement of Isaiah, "Hear ye a *word* of the Lord, O rulers of Sodom" (Isa. 1:10). Ἀκούσατε λόγον κυρίου, ἄρχοντες Σοδομων. Here the connotation is that of a "message."

In one of the papyri is the statement, "But no sooner had the son of Psintaes departed from Memphis than he took no further account of the *matter.*" τοῦ δὲ τοῦ Ψινταέους υἱοῦ ἐκ τῆς Μέμφεως χωρισθέντες, οὐκέτι οὐδένα λόγον ἐποήσατο (*P. Par,* 26.31). The sense of a financial "account" for a business transaction is also common in the papyri. One writer mentioned a sum of money paid "unto an *account* of clothing." εἰς λόγον ἱματισμοῦ (*P. Oxy.,* XII, 1441.7).

In his attempted synthesis of Greek and Hebrew thought, Philo dealt with this term. He seemed to approach John's use of the word without actually having had God's revelation to guide him. During his discussion of the creation, he said, "But that invisible light perceptible only by mind has come into being as an image of the Divine *Word* who brought it within our understanding." τὸ δὲ ἀόρατον καὶ νοητὸν φῶς ἐκεῖνο θείου λόγου γέγονεν εἰκὼν τοῦ διερμηνεύσαντος τὴν γένεσιν αὐτοῦ (*On the Creation* 31). Philo even went so far as to call the Logos (Word) "a second God." δεύτερος θεός (*Questions and Solutions in Genesis* 2.62).

In the New Testament most of these meanings can be found. When the centurion came to the Lord, beseeching Him to heal his servant, he said, "But only say with a *word,* and my servant shall be healed" (Matt. 8:8). ἀλλὰ μόνον εἰπὲ λόγῳ. Sometimes "word" is contrasted with "deed." The Apostle John exhorted believers, "Let us not love in *word,* neither in tongue,

A TREASURY OF NEW TESTAMENT SYNONYMS

but in deed and truth" (I John 3:18). μὴ ἀγαπῶμεν λόγῳ μηδὲ τῇ γλώσσῃ, ἀλλὰ ἐν ἔργῳ καὶ ἀληθείᾳ. The scribes and the chief priests were always trying to ensnare our Lord. On one occasion they sent out spies, "who feigned themselves to be righteous men, in order that they might seize his *speech,* so that they might betray him to the rule and authority of the governor" (Luke 20:20). ἵνα ἐπιλάβωνται αὐτοῦ λόγου, ὥστε παραδοῦναι αὐτόν. The financial sense of a business "account" appears when Paul says to the Philippians, "Not that I seek the gift, but I seek the fruit which abounds to your *account"* (Phil. 4:17). ἀλλὰ ἐπιζητῶ τὸν καρπὸν τὸν πλεονάζοντα εἰς λόγον ὑμῶν.

When the Apostle Peter rebuked Simon the sorcerer for trying to buy the Holy Spirit, he said, "There is neither part nor lot to thee in this *matter,* for thy heart is not right before God" (Acts 8:21). οὐκ ἔστιν σοι μερὶς οὐδὲ κλῆρας ἐν τῷ λόγῳ τούτῳ. After describing how the Lord had led him, Peter said to Cornelius, "Wherefore also I came without contradicting when I was summoned. I ask, therefore, for what *reason* ye sent for me?" (Acts 10:29). πυνθάνομαι οὖν, τίνι λόγῳ μεταπέμψασθέ με; The prophets in the Old Testament had spoken of the "Word," meaning God's message for man; the New Testament continued this use of λόγος. In the great high-priestly prayer, the Lord Jesus said to the Father, "I have given to them Thy *Word"* (John 17:14). ἐγὼ δέδωκα αὐτοῖς τὸν λόγον σου. "Message" is a common meaning of λόγος.

The most striking use of this term is found at the beginning of the Gospel of John: "In the beginning was the *Word,* and the *Word* was with God, and the *Word* was God" (1:1). Ἐν ἀρχῇ ἦν ὁ λόγος, καὶ ὁ λόγος ἦν πρὸς τὸν θεόν, καὶ θεὸς ἦν ὁ λόγος. This metaphysical use of the word combined both ideas of "word" and of "thought." It is well known that both Greek and Hebrew thought had prepared the way for this doctrine, but the theological doctrine of the "Logos" has its foundation in Scripture alone. Although Paul had already taught the transcendence and preexistence of the Person of Christ, as well as the meaning of His incarnation, it was John who connected these truths with the word λόγος. John taught plainly that the Lord Jesus Christ was a great supernatural Person who was distinct from the Father but who was truly God; that this Person was in existence before the universe was created, and that this same Person became flesh for the sake of man. "It is admitted on all hands that his central affirmation, 'the Word became flesh,' which underlies all he wrote, is absolutely new and unique" (Westcott, *John,* p. XV). Neither Philo nor any other earlier writer had a concept even similar to this.[1]

The references in patristic literature to Christ as the Word are based

[1] Archibald Alexander, "Logos," *International Standard Bible Encyclopaedia,* III, 1911–17.

on this passage in John's Gospel and his other teaching on the Person of Christ. To Ignatius God is the One "who manifested Himself through Jesus Christ His Son, who is His *Word* proceeding from silence." ὅς ἐστιν αὐτοῦ λόγος ἀπὸ σιγῆς προελθών (*Ignatius to the Magnesians* 8.2). The *Epistle to Diognetus* speaks of the mysteries given to the disciples, "to whom the *Word* appeared and revealed them, speaking boldly." οἷς ἐφανέρωσεν ὁ λόγος φανείς, παρρησίᾳ λαλῶν (11.2).

Thus the word λόγος may have a great variety of meanings. Under the idea "word" it may mean "statement," "talk," "history," "proposal," "matter," or "account"; under the idea of "thought" it may mean "opinion" or "reason."

ῥῆμα

The first occurrence of this word in prose is in Herodotus, who, in explaining a previous statement, wrote, "Of which *saying* this is the meaning, that Gelon's army was the most notable part of the Greek army, even as the spring is of the year." οὗτος δέ ὁ νόος τοῦ ῥήματος τὸ ἐθέλει λέγειν (7.162). Sophocles has Oedipus confront Creon saying, "They see both me and thee; and they also see that when I am hurt I have only *words* to avenge it!" καὶ φρονοῦσ᾽ ὅτι ἔργοις πεπονθὼς ῥήμασίν σ᾽ ἀμύνομαι (*Oedipus at Colonus* 873). Oedipus has only "words" or "names" rather than material means with which to avenge himself. Thucydides also made a distinction between words or names and material reality: "For many men, though they can still clearly foresee the dangers into which they are drifting, are lured on by the power of a seductive *word*—the thing called disgrace—until, the victims of a phrase, they are plunged into calamities." πολλοῖς γὰρ προορωμένοις ἔτι ἐς οἷα φέρονται τὸ αἰσχρὸν καλούμενον ὀνόματος ἐπαγωγοῦ δυνάμει ἐπεσπάσατο, ἡσσηθεῖσι τοῦ ῥήματος (5.111). In the strictest grammatical sense ῥῆμα referred to a verb instead of a noun, which was denoted by ὄνομα (Aristotle *Poetics* 20.9). Plato used it in this technical sense several times. In one place he wrote, "And again from nouns and *verbs* we shall finally construct something great and fair and complete." καὶ πάλιν ἐκ τῶν ὀνομάτων καὶ ῥημάτων μέγα ἤδη τι καὶ καλὸν καὶ ὅλον συστήσομεν (*Cratylus* 425A).

Sometimes this term is used with different connotations in the same context. In the Septuagint, after Abraham had met Melchizedek, the passage reads, "After these *things* [events] a *word* of the Lord came to Abram in a vision" (Gen. 15:1). Μετὰ δὲ τὰ ῥήματα ταῦτα ἐγενήθη ῥῆμα κυρίου. The psalmist prayed, "Give ear to my *words,* O Lord" (Ps. 5:2; KJ Ps. 5:1). τὰ ῥήματά μου ἐνώτισαι, κύριε. Solomon in the book of Proverbs exhorted the reader, "Son, forget not my rules, but let thy heart keep my *words"* (3:1). τὰ δὲ ῥήματά μου τηρείτω σὴ καρδία. One of the papyri has the phrase "from the *words* of the former ordinance." ἐκ τῶν ῥημάτων τοῦ προτέρου διατάγματος.[2]

In the New Testament our Lord warned, "But I say to you that every idle *word* which men shall speak, they shall render an account concerning it in the day of judgment" (Matt. 12:36). ὅτι πᾶν ῥῆμα ἀργὸν ὃ λαλήσουσιν οἱ ἄνθρωποι. The angel assured Mary, *"Nothing* [literally: "not everything"] shall be impossible with God" (Luke 1:37). οὐκ ἀδυνατήσει παρὰ τοῦ θεοῦ πᾶν ῥῆμα. After the Lord Jesus had given some difficult teaching to His disciples, He explained to them, "The *words* which I have spoken to you are spirit and are life" (John 6:63). τὰ ῥήματα ἃ ἐγὼ λελάληκα ὑμῖν πνεῦμά ἐστιν. This statement implies that the words, not just the concepts, have God's power resting upon them. In the great high-priestly prayer, the Lord Jesus said to the Father, "The *words* which thou gavest me I have given to them, and they have received them" (John 17:8). τὰ ῥήματα ἃ ἔδωκάς μοι δέδωκα αὐτοῖς. This declaration teaches a verbal inerrancy in the revelation of God to man and contradicts the liberal idea that man could not receive the true "words" of God. In his first epistle Peter stated, "But the *Word* of the Lord abides forever. And this is the *Word* which was preached unto you" (I Pet. 1:25). τὸ δὲ ῥῆμα κυρίου μένει εἰς τὸν αἰῶνα. τοῦτο δέ ἐστιν τὸ ῥῆμα τὸ εὐαγγελισθὲν εἰς ὑμᾶς. Thus both λόγος and ῥῆμα may refer to the "message" of God to man.

SUMMARY

Although the word λόγος may range in specific meaning from "word," "statement," "talk," "history," "matter," "account," "thought," "opinion," and "reason," it does not mean a grammatical word. The word ῥῆμα does refer to a grammatical "word," as well as the idea of "thing." Both terms are used to refer to the revelation which God has granted to man. λόγος is the larger term, and ῥῆμα the more specific. Westcott makes the distinction that ὁ λόγος τοῦ θεοῦ is "the whole message of the Gospel," whereas θεοῦ ῥῆμα is "some special utterance . . . , such as that which marks the confession of faith, apprehended in its true character as an utterance of God: Rom. 10:8; Eph. 5:26" (*Hebrews*, p. 149). Thus in Hebrews 6:1 the "word" (λόγος) refers to the whole Gospel, but in Hebrews 6:5 the "word" (ῥῆμα) refers to a single promise which can bring salvation.

[2] Eger, Kornemann, and Meyer, *Griechische Papyri zu Giessen*, I, 40. 2. 7.

Verbs

1. I Anoint: ἀλείφω, χρίω

Both of these words started out with the same meaning——*I anoint, I smear,*——but by the time of the New Testament they were clearly distinguished. By then ἀλείφω referred to an anointing for adornment or for medicinal purposes, whereas χρίω indicated a religious anointing in a metaphorical sense, such as the anointing with the Holy Spirit.

ἀλείφω

In Homer this word is often used for the anointing that follows a bath. Homer said of Odysseus, "But when he had washed his whole body and *had anointed* himself with oil, he put on the clothes which the virgin had given him." αὐτὰρ ἐπεὶ δὴ πάντα λοέσσατο καὶ λίπ᾽ ἄλειψεν (*Odyssey*, 6.227). Thucydides described the practice of the Greek athletes in preparation for the contests: "And first they made themselves naked and, after openly unclothing, *anointed* themselves with oil when they exercised in contests." ἐγυμνώθησάν τε πρῶτοι καὶ ἐς τὸ φανερὸν ἀποδύντες λίπα μετὰ τοῦ γυμνάζεσθαι ἠλείψαντο (1.6.5). When Ischomachus tried to persuade his wife to give up cosmetics, he threatened to use some himself, "*by smearing* my cheeks with red lead and *painting* myself under the eyes with rouge." μίλτῳ ἀλειφόμενος καὶ τοὺς ὀφθαλμοὺς ὑπαλειφόμενος ἀνδρεικέλῳ (Xenophon *Oeconomicus* 10.5). One papyrus mentions a yoke-band "which *thou wilt* carefully *grease.*" ὃ καὶ ἀλείψεις ἐπιμελῶς (*P. Fay.*, 121.6).

When Naomi gave advice to Ruth in securing Boaz as the kinsman-redeemer, she said, "But thou shalt wash and *anoint* thyself and put thy raiment upon thyself, and thou shalt go up to the threshing-floor" (Ruth 3:3). σὺ δὲ λούσῃ καὶ ἀλείψῃ καὶ περιθήσεις τὸν ἱματισμόν σου. In another example Elisha asked the poor widow what he could do for her, and she replied, "Thy handmaid has nothing in the house, but only oil with which *I shall anoint myself*" (II Kings 4:2). οὐκ ἔστιν τῇ δούλῃ σου οὐθὲν ἐν τῷ οἴκῳ ὅτι ἀλλ᾽ ἢ ὃ ἀλείψομαι ἔλαιον. There are a few places in which this word has a strongly religious connotation. In the consecration of the tabernacle χρίω is used again and again, but ἀλείφω occurs in one verse. The Lord commanded Moses, "And thou shalt take the oil of the anointing, and *thou shalt anoint* the tabernacle. . . . And *thou shalt anoint* the altar. . . . And *thou shalt anoint* them in the same way in which *thou didst anoint* their father" (Exod. 40:9, 10, 15). καὶ λήμψῃ τὸ ἔλαιον τοῦ χρίσματος καὶ χρίσεις τὴν σκηνήν. . . . καὶ χρίσεις τὸ θυσιαστήριον. . . . καὶ ἀλείψεις αὐτούς, ὃν τρόπον ἤλειψας τὸν πατέρα αὐτῶν.

In the Sermon on the Mount the Lord Jesus spoke of those who try to appear to others to be fasting, and commanded, "But while thou art fasting, *anoint* thy head, and wash thy face" (Matt. 6:17). σὺ δὲ νηστεύων ἄλειψαί σου τὴν κεφαλήν. After the Lord had sent forth the twelve, Scripture recorded that "they were casting out many demons and *were anointing* with oil many who were sick and were healing them" (Mark 6:13). καὶ δαιμόνια πολλὰ ἐξέβαλλον, καὶ ἤλειφον ἐλαίῳ πολλοὺς ἀρρώστους καὶ ἐθεράπευον. This was a common practice both for medicinal and religious purposes. Also the bodies of the dead were anointed. After the sabbath of the crucifixion, the women bought spices "that they might come and *anoint* him" (Mark 16:1). ἵνα ἐλθοῦσαι ἀλείψωσιν αὐτόν. James, instructing the elders concerning the sick, said, "Let them pray over him, *anointing* him with oil in the name of the Lord" (James 5:14). προσευξάσθωσαν ἐπ᾽ αὐτὸν ἀλείψαντες ἐλαίῳ ἐν τῷ ὀνόματι τοῦ κυρίου. Here again the religious sense blends with the medicinal (Luke 10:34).

χρίω

This word like ἀλείφω refers to anointing after a bath. Helen said concerning Odysseus, "But when I was bathing him and *anointing* him with oil." ἀλλ᾽ ὅτε δή μιν ἐγὼ λόεον καὶ χρῖον ἐλαίῳ (Homer *Odyssey* 4.252). In another place Homer described how Odysseus went in search of a deadly poison "that he might have some with which *to smear* his bronze-tipped arrows." ὄφρα οἱ εἴη ἰοὺς χρίεσθαι χαλκήρεας (*Odyssey* 1.262). In a dream the daughter of Polycrates saw her father "washed by Zeus and *anointed* by the sun." χρίεσθαι δὲ ὑπὸ τοῦ ἡλίου (Herodotus 3.124). Herodotus described the barbaric Libyans who let half their hair grow long and shave the other half, "and *they paint* their bodies with red." τὸ δὲ σῶμα χρίονται μίλτῳ (4.191). As late as the third century of the Christian era the word is applied to the anointing of camels with oil: "The reclining camels *were anointed.*" ἐχρίσθησαν οἱ προκείμενοι κάμηλοι (*P. Flor.*, III, 364.24).

In Biblical Greek, however, this word is restricted to the religious meaning. A typical example is the anointing of the tabernacle. "And it came to pass on the day that Moses completed the setting-up of the tabernacle, he *anointed* it and sanctified it" (Num. 7:1). καὶ ἐγένετο ᾗ ἡμέρᾳ συνετέλεσεν Μωυσῆς ὥστε ἀναστῆσαι τὴν σκηνὴν καὶ ἔχρισεν αὐτήν. This is the regular word for the anointing of kings before God. "And Samuel

I ANOINT

anointed Saul king there before the Lord in Gilgal" (I Sam. 11:15). καὶ ἔχρισεν Σαμουηλ ἐκεῖ τὸν Σαουλ εἰς βασιλέα ἐνώπιον κυρίον ἐν Γαλγαλοις. But the psalmist applied this word to the Messiah: "Thou didst love righteousness and didst hate lawlessness, on account of this God, thy God, *anointed* thee with the oil of gladness" (Ps. 44:8; KJ Ps. 45:7). ἠγάπησας δικαιοσύνην καὶ ἐμίσησας ἀνομίαν· διὰ τοῦτο ἔχρισέν σε ὁ θεὸς ὁ θεός σου ἔλαιον ἀγαλλιάσεως. In Theodotion's version of Daniel the angel described the seventy weeks which were necessary, among other things, "to *anoint* a Holy of Holies" (Dan. 9:24). τοῦ χρῖσαι ἅγιον ἁγίων.

The New Testament uses this word especially for the anointing which rested on the Lord Jesus Christ. Since His name is Christ, the Anointed (Χριστός), this is most appropriate. The Lord Jesus Himself said, "The Spirit of the Lord is upon me, because he *anointed* me to preach the Gospel to the poor" (Luke 4:18). πνεῦμα κυρίου ἐπ' ἐμέ, οὗ εἵνεκεν ἔχρισέν με εὐαγγελίσασθαι πτωχοῖς. Peter explained to Cornelius about "Jesus of Nazareth, how God *anointed* him with the Holy Spirit and with power" (Acts 10:38). Ἰησοῦν τὸν ἀπὸ Ναζαρέθ, ὡς ἔχρισεν αὐτὸν ὁ θεὸς πνεύματι ἁγίῳ καὶ δυνάμει. The writer to the Hebrews quoted and applied to Christ Psalm 45:7, which has already been treated (Heb. 1:9). But this word is also applied to the anointing which rests upon believers. The Apostle Paul stated boldly, "But the one who is establishing us with you in Christ, and who *has anointed* us, is God" (II Cor. 1:21). ὁ δὲ βεβαιῶν ἡμᾶς σὺν ὑμῖν εἰς Χριστὸν καὶ χρίσας ἡμᾶς θεός.

SUMMARY

For the most part, Trench's distinction is true: "ἀλείφειν is the mundane and profane, χρίειν the sacred and religious, word" (*Synonyms*, pp. 136–37). But outside the New Testament this distinction does not always hold; the former word is used with a strong religious sense and the latter sometimes with no religious connotation. Still, it generally is true that ἀλείφω designates an anointing for adornment or medicinal uses, whereas χρίω implies a religious anointing.

2. I Answer: ἀποκρίνομαι, ὑπολαμβάνω

In the middle voice ἀποκρίνομαι means *I answer;* in some contexts ὑπολαμβάνω may mean *I answer*—but from there on these two words are radically different. The root meaning of ἀποκρίνομαι is *I set apart* or *I distinguish.* From this meaning it is a logical step to *I distinguish a difference of opinion*—that is, *I answer.* In contrast, ὑπολαμβάνω means basically *I take up,* but here again it is a short step to *I take up what is said*—that is, *I answer.*

ἀποκρίνομαι

In classical Greek the root meaning is the common one. Herodotus observed, "Since indeed from earliest times the Hellenic *was* always *distinguished* from the barbaric race by its greater cleverness and its freedom from silly foolishness." ἐπεί γε ἀπεκρίθη ἐκ παλαιτέρου τοῦ βαρβάρου ἔθνεος τὸ Ἑλληνικὸν ἐόν (1.60). The Athenians, wrote Thucydides, were incensed against the Lacedaemonians "so that they *answered* the envoys angrily and sent them away." ὥστε χαλεπῶς πρὸς τοὺς πρέσβεις ἀποκρινάμενοι ἀπέπενπψαν (5.42.2). In the *Gorgias,* Plato wrote, "But failing to notice that *I have* not yet *answered* that, he asks if I do not consider it a fine thing. But *I will* not *answer* whether I consider rhetoric a fine or a base thing, until I *have* first *answered* what it is." ἀλλ᾽ αὐτὸν λέληθα οὔπω ἀποκεκριμένος, ὁ δὲ ἐπανερωτᾷ, εἰ οὐ ἡγοῦμαι εἶναι. ἐγὼ δὲ αὐτῷ οὐκ ἀποκρινοῦμαι πρότερον, εἴτε καλὸν εἴτε αἰσχρὸν ἡγοῦμαι εἶναι τὴν ῥητορικήν, πρὶν ἂν πρῶτον ἀποκρίνωμαι ὅ τι ἐστίν (463C). In the papyri this word is often used for a legal "reply" by a lawyer: "Severus and Heliodorus, advocates, *replied* that the late governor [praefect] Titianus heard a similar plea." Σεουήρου καὶ Ἡλιοδώρου ῥητόρων ἀποκρειναμένων Τειτιανον τὸν ἡγεμονεύσαντα ὁμοίας ὑποθέσεως ἀκούσαντα (*P. Oxy.*, II, 237.7.33).

Scripture describes how Abraham began interceding for Sodom: "And Abraham *answered* and said, Now I began to speak to my Lord" (Gen. 18:27). καὶ ἀποκριθεὶς Αβρααμ εἶπεν Νῦν ἠρξάμην λαλῆσαι πρὸς τὸν κύριον. This is the customary meaning throughout the Septuagint: "And Moses *answered* and said" (Exod. 4:1). ἀπεκρίθη δὲ Μωυσῆς καὶ εἶπεν. In a less stereotyped expression the psalmist said, "And *I will answer* those who reproach me, that I have hoped upon thy word" (Ps. 118:42; KJ Ps. 119:42). καὶ ἀποκριθήσομαι τοῖς ὀνειδίζουσί με.

The New Testament usage is very close to these Septuagint expressions. Matthew wrote, "At that time Jesus *answered* and said, I thank thee, Father, Lord of heaven and earth" (Matt. 11:25). ἐν ἐκείνῳ τῷ καιρῷ ἀποκριθεὶς ὁ Ἰησοῦς εἶπεν· ἐξομολογοῦμαί σοι. Since the context indicates no dialogue between persons, the meaning must be "He continued saying"—a typically Hebrew idiom. But the word is also found in the strictest sense as an answer to a question. When the Jews wished to find out who John the Baptist was, they asked him, "Art thou the prophet? And *he answered:* No" (John 1:21). ὁ προφήτης εἶ σύ; καὶ ἀπεκρίθη· οὔ. Sometimes the questions are merely implied. When Peter and John had healed the lame man at the temple, the multitude marveled. "But when Peter saw it, *he answered* the people, Men, Israelites, why marvel ye at this?" (Acts 3:12). ἰδὼν δὲ ὁ Πέτρος ἀπεκρίνατο πρὸς τὸν λαόν.

ὑπολαμβάνω

The basic meaning "I take up" is often found in classical Greek. Herodotus relates the story of the singer Arion's being cast overboard by the crew: "but a dolphin (they say) *took up* Arion on his back and bore him to Taenarus." τὸν δὲ δελφῖνα λέγουσι ὑπολαβόντα ἐξενεῖκαι ἐπὶ Ταίναρον (1.24). Herodotus also uses a different expression: "But she said *in reply.* " ἡ δὲ ὑπολαβοῦσα ἔφη (1.11). In Thucydides the Athenians advise the Melians, "Take up each point, and do not make a single speech but judge ye *by replying* immediately to any of our statements that seems unsatisfactory." ἀλλὰ πρὸς τὸ μὴ δοκοῦν ἐπιτηδείως λέγεσθαι εὐθὺς ὑπολαμβάνοντες κρίνετε (5.85). Not only is it possible to take up a reply, it is also possible to take up a supposition, and this meaning is found especially in the papyri. One writer said, *"They supposed* that they would be killed." ὑπελαμβάνοσαν φονευθήσεσθαι (*P. Grenf.* II, 36.10).

This same meaning is found in the Septuagint when the man of God warned king Amaziah: "Because if *thou thinkest* to strengthen thyself with any of these [Ephraimites], the Lord will rout thee before thy enemies" (II Chron. 25:8). ὅτι ἐὰν ὑπολάβῃς κατισχῦσαι ἐν τούτοις. But in the Septuagint the usual meaning is "I answered." When the Lord challenged Satan with the righteousness of Job, "the devil *answered* and said to the Lord, Skin for skin" (Job 2:4). ὑπολαβὼν δὲ ὁ διάβολος εἶπεν τῷ κυρίῳ. Later on in the debate between Job and his three friends, this phrase begins each speech: "But Eliphaz the Thaimanite *answered* and said, Should replies be

87

made many times to thee in distress?" (Job 4:1). ὑπολαβὼν δὲ Ελιφας ὁ Θαιμανίτης λέγει. This is the stereotyped introductory phrase throughout the book of Job (6:1; 8:1; 9:1; 11:1, etc.).

This word is rare in the New Testament, but it does occur with each of these meanings. When the Lord Jesus ascended up into heaven, Scripture says, "The cloud *took* him *up* from their sight" (Acts 1:9). νεφέλη ὑπέλαβεν αὐτόν. The Lord Jesus taught Simon the Pharisee a lesson in forgiveness by telling him of the two men who were forgiven, one much and the other less. Jesus asked, "Which of them will love him more? Simon *answered* and said, *I suppose* the one to whom he forgave more" (Luke 7:43). ἀποκριθεὶς Σίμων εἶπεν· ὑπολαμβάνω ὅτι ᾧ τὸ πλεῖον ἐχαρίσατο. In another context the Lord Jesus was teaching love for one's neighbor, and a lawyer who wished to justify himself asked, "Who is my neighbor? Jesus *answered* and said, A certain man went down from Jerusalem to Jericho, and he fell among robbers" (Luke 10:30). ὑπολαβὼν ὁ Ἰησοῦς εἶπεν· ἄνθρωπός τις κατέβαινεν. The sense of "taking up" the question to give a reply is obvious in this passage.

SUMMARY

In some contexts both of these words may mean "I answer." The word ἀποκρίνομαι comes to this meaning from the meaning "I distinguish" or "I set apart." The word ὑπολαμβάνω arrives at this meaning from "I take up," which is actually a more common meaning in the New Testament.

3. I Complete: καταρτίζω, τελειόω

Both of these words may mean *I complete* or *I prepare,* but they arrive at these meanings from different directions. The basic meaning of καταρτίζω is *I fit together well,* from which derive such meanings as *I restore, I perfect, I reconcile.* The root meaning of τελειόω is *I bring to maturity* or *I bring to an end,* which leads to the meanings *I finish, I perfect, I accomplish,* or *I develop.*

καταρτίζω

Herodotus related that the people of Miletus were greatly troubled by factions for two generations "until the Parians *reconciled* them." μέχρι οὗ μιν Πάριοι κατήρτισαν (5.28). Histiaeus, in a speech, urged, "Now therefore send me away on my journey to Ionia quickly, that *I may restore* that country to its former peace." νῦν ὦν ὡς τάχος ἄπες με πορευθῆναι ἐς Ἰωνίην, ἵνα τοι κεῖνά τε πάντα καταρτίσω ἐς τὠυτό (5.106). Elsewhere Herodotus described Artabazus' army of forty thousand men, saying, "He led these, *having been* thoroughly *equipped.*" ἦγε κατηρτημένως (9.66). Galen used this word as a surgical term for "setting bones."[1] The writer of one of the papyri mentioned certain garments "which thy brother Pausanias went to the expense of *having made* [prepared] and given to thee." ἃ ἐδωρήσατο σοι Παυσανίας ὁ ἀδελφός σου πρὸ πολλοῦ ἐκ φιλοτιμίας αὐτοῦ κατηρτισμένα (*P. Oxy.,* VIII, 1153.16).

Although the word is scarce in the Septuagint, it does occur in several passages of the Psalms, some of which are important Messianic sections. In one the psalmist said, "Out of the mouth of babes and sucklings *thou didst perfect* praise, because of thine enemies" (Ps. 8:3; KJ Ps. 8:2). ἐκ στόματος νηπίων καὶ θηλαζόντων καταρτίσω αἶνον. In another the psalmist praised God, "who *preparest* my feet like those of a hind" (Ps. 17:34; KJ Ps. 18:33). ὁ καταρτιζόμενος τοὺς πόδας μου ὡς ἐλάφου. One of the Messianic psalms reads, "Sacrifice and offering thou didst not desire, but ears *thou didst prepare* for me" (Ps. 39:7; KJ Ps. 40:6). θυσίαν καὶ προσφορὰν οὐκ ἠθέλησας, ὠτία δὲ κατηρτίσω μοι. The New Testament interprets this as the body which was prepared for the Lord Jesus Christ

---
[1] Galen, Op. 19, p. 461, quoted in J. B. Lightfoot, *Notes on Epistles of St. Paul from Unpublished Commentaries,* p. 47.

(Heb. 10:5–7). In another of the Messianic psalms the Lord assured David that "his seed shall endure forever, and his throne as the sun before me, and as the moon *established* forever" (Ps. 88:38; KJ Ps. 89:36–37). καὶ ὡς ἡ σελήνη κατηρτισμένη εἰς τὸν αἰῶνα. In all of these examples one can perceive the root idea of "fitting together."

In the New Testament the Lord Jesus saw that James and John, the sons of Zebedee, "were in the boat, *mending* [restoring] their nets" (Mark 1:19). ἐν τῷ πλοίῳ καταρτίζοντας τὰ δίκτυα. The same meaning, transposed to a metaphorical sense, is in Paul's exhortation, "Brethren, if a man should even be overtaken in some trespass, ye who are spiritual, *restore* such a man in the spirit of meekness" (Gal. 6:1). ὑμεῖς οἱ πνευματικοὶ καταρτίζετε τὸν τοιοῦτον. We are praying, Paul wrote the Thessalonians, "that we may see your face and *may complete* that which is lacking in your faith" (I Thess. 3:10). καὶ καταρτίσαι τὰ ὑστερήματα τῆς πίστεως ὑμῶν. Speaking of a divine creative act, the writer to the Hebrews said, "By faith we understand that the ages *were created* [prepared] by the word of God" (Heb. 11:3). Πίστει νοοῦμεν κατηρτίσθαι τοὺς αἰῶνας ῥήματι θεοῦ. The Apostle Peter comforted his readers with the assurance that "the God of all grace, who called you unto his eternal glory in Christ, after ye have suffered a while, shall himself *restore* [perfect], establish, strengthen, settle you" (I Pet. 5:10). ὀλίγον παθόντας αὐτὸς καταρτίσει, στηρίξει, σθενώσει, θεμελιώσει.

τελειόω

Astyages said of the boy Cyrus, "But *he accomplished* in truth all the things which kings have done." ὁ δὲ πάντα ὅσα περ οἱ ἀληθέι λόγῳ βασιλέες ἐτελέωσε ποιήσας (Herodotus 1.120). King Darius offered to reward two of his followers with anything that they wanted, "and the desire of both *having been achieved,* these went their ways to the places of their choice." τελεωθέντων δὲ ἀμφοτέροισι, οὗτοι μὲν κατὰ τὰ εἵλοντο ἐτράποντο (Herodotus 5.12). Thucydides described the sailing of the Athenian fleet: "And when they had sung the paean and *had completed* the libations, they cast off." παιανίσαντες δὲ καὶ τελεώσαντες τὰς σπονδὰς ἀνήγοντο (6.32.2). Aristotle, in a long discussion on the perfection of the act of sight, wrote "For the act of seeing seems to be perfect at any moment of its duration; for it requires nothing to happen later in order *to perfect* its specific quality." δοκεῖ γὰρ ἡ μὲν ὅρασις καθ᾽ ὁντινοῦν χρόνον τελεία εἶναι· οὐ γάρ ἐστιν ἐνδεὴς οὐδενός, ὃ εἰς ὕστερον γενόμενον τελειώσει αὐτῆς τὸ εἶδος (*Nicomachean Ethics* 10.4.1). In the papyri the word is often used in a legal sense, as in the phrase, *"to execute* the deed in the proper way." τελειῶσαι τὸν χρηματισμὸν ὡς καθήκει (*P. Oxy.,* III, 483.20).

In the Septuagint David sang to the Lord, "With the *perfect* man thou

I COMPLETE

wilt *show thyself to be perfect*" (II Sam. 22:26). μετὰ ἀνδρὸς τελείου τελειωθήσῃ. Chronicles records, "All the work was prepared from the day the foundation was laid until Solomon *completed* the house of the Lord" (II Chron. 8:16). ἡτοιμάσθη πᾶσα ἡ ἐργασία ἀφ᾽ ἧς ἡμέρας ἐθεμελιώθη ἕως οὗ ἐτελείωσεν Σαλωμων τὸν οἶκον κυρίου. When Sanballat and Geshem tried to persuade Nehemiah to cease work on the wall of Jerusalem, Nehemiah answered them, "I am doing a great work, and I cannot come down lest the work cease; whenever *I finish* it, I will come down to you" (II Esdras 16:3; KJ Neh. 6:3). ὡς ἂν τελειώσω αὐτό, καταβήσομαι πρὸς ὑμᾶς. Later on, after the wall had been finished, Nehemiah said that the enemies of Israel were afraid because "they knew that it was from our God that this work *was perfected*" (II Esdras 16:16; KJ Neh. 6:16). ἔγνωσαν ὅτι παρὰ τοῦ θεοῦ ἡμῶν ἐγενήθη τελειωθῆναι τὸ ἔργον τοῦτο.

In the great high-priestly prayer the Lord Jesus said to the Father, "I glorified thee upon the earth, *having finished* the work which thou gavest me to do" (John 17:4). ἐγώ σε ἐδόξασα ἐπὶ τῆς γῆς, τὸ ἔργον τελειώσας ὃ δέδωκας μοι ἵνα ποιήσω. In the same sense Paul, knowing that bonds and afflictions were awaiting him, said, "But I do not hold my life of any account dear to myself, that *I may finish* my course and the ministry which I received from the Lord Jesus" (Acts 20:24). ὡς τελειώσω τὸν δρόμον μου. Sometimes this word is used in the clear meaning of "to make perfect," always with the sense of bringing something to completion or maturity. One of tne blessings of heaven is that believers will come "to the spirits of righteous men *made perfect*" (Heb. 12:23). πνεύμασι δικαίων τετελειωμένων. Even the Lord Jesus had to come to this perfection, as the writer to the Hebrews said, "For it was fitting for him, on account of whom are all things and through whom are all things, in leading many sons unto glory, *to make perfect* the author of their salvation through sufferings" (Heb. 2:10). πολλοὺς υἱοὺς εἰς δόξαν ἀγαγόντα τὸν ἀρχηγὸν τῆς σωτηρίας αὐτῶν διὰ παθημάτων τελειῶσαι. The great flaw in the law was that it could not bring men to such perfection: the law *"could* never *make perfect* the ones who draw near" (Heb. 10:1). οὐδέποτε δύναται τοὺς προσερχομένους τελειῶσαι. The believer, however, is brought to perfection by faith, not by the law; yet this faith must be one that is manifested by works, for James speaks concerning Abraham, "Thou seest that the faith worked together with his works, and out of the works the faith *was made perfect*" (James 2:22). καὶ ἐκ τῶν ἔργων ἡ πίστις ἐτελειώθη.

SUMMARY

Although both of these words may mean "I complete," there are sharp distinctions between them. The root meaning of καταρτίζω is "I fit together," a meaning that lends itself to the meanings "I restore, mend, reconcile, prepare." The word τελειόω means "I bring to maturity" or "completion," with such derived meanings as "I finish, accomplish, perfect."

4. I Deceive: ἀπατάω, παραλογίζομαι, πλανάω

These words express *I deceive,* but each has its own shade of meaning. The word ἀπατάω means *I trick* or *I cheat;* παραλογίζομαι extends this meaning to *I defraud;* the word πλανάω denotes *I lead astray, I cause to err,* or, in the passive, *I wander, I am misled.*

ἀπατάω

Agamemnon stated that even Zeus could be deceived: "But even him Hera, although just a woman, *tricked* [beguiled] in her craftiness on the day that Alcmene was to bring forth the mighty Heracles." ἀλλ' ἄρα καὶ τὸν Ἥρη θῆλυς ἐοῦσα δολοφροσύνης ἀπάτησεν (*Iliad* 19.97). When Tecmessa heard of the danger to Ajax, she cried out, "For I know too well that my lord *has cheated* me." ἔγνωκα γὰρ δὴ φωτὸς ἠπατημένη (Sophocles *Ajax* 807). Electra addressed the body of Aegisthus, saying, "But this was thy great *deception,* not having known." ὁ δ' ἠπάτα σε πλεῖστον οὐκ ἐγνωκότα (Euripides *Electra* 938).

In the Septuagint the first example is in the account of the temptation. Eve replied to the Lord, "The serpent *tricked* me, and I ate" (Gen. 3:13). ὁ ὄφις ἠπάτησέν με, καὶ ἔφαγον. The Lords of the Philistines ordered Delilah to ensnare Samson, saying, "*Trick* [entice] him, and see in what his great strength is, and in what we may prevail over him" (Judg. 16:5). ἀπάτησον αὐτὸν καὶ ἰδὲ ἐν τίνι ἡ ἰσχὺς αὐτοῦ ἡ μεγάλη. When David had let Abner go, Joab said to David, "Dost thou not know the evil of Abner the son of Ner, that he came *to trick* thee and to know thy going out and thy going in?" (II Sam. 3:25). ἦ οὐκ οἶδας τὴν κακίαν Αβεννηρ υἱοῦ Νηρ, ὅτι ἀπατῆσαί σε παρεγένετο καὶ γνῶναι τὴν ἔξοδόν σου. The psalmist could say, "In the day of my affliction I sought God with my hands in the night before him, and *I was* not *deceived"* (Ps. 76:3; KJ Ps. 77:2). ἐν ἡμέρᾳ θλίψεώς μου τὸν θεὸν ἐξεζήτησα, ταῖς χερσίν μου νυκτὸς ἐναντίον αὐτοῦ, καὶ οὐκ ἠπατήθην.

When Paul wrote to the believers, he warned them, "Let no one *deceive* [trick] you with empty words" (Eph. 5:6). μηδεὶς ὑμᾶς ἀπατάτω κενοῖς λόγοις. Referring to the temptation, Paul said, "And Adam *was* not *deceived* [tricked], but the woman, *being deceived,* has fallen into transgression" (I Tim. 2:14). καὶ Ἀδαμ οὐκ ἠπατήθη, ἡ δὲ γυνὴ ἐξαπατηθεῖσα ἐν παραβάσει γέγονεν. James warned his readers, "If any man thinks that he is religious, bridling not his own tongue but *deceiving* his own heart, this man's religion is vain" (James 1:26). εἴ τις δοκεῖ θρησκὸς εἶναι, μὴ χαλιναγωγῶν γλῶσσαν ἑαυτοῦ ἀλλὰ ἀπατῶν καρδίαν ἑαυτοῦ, τούτου μάταιος ἡ θρησκεία.

παραλογίζομαι

Aristotle speaks of the way in which wrong acts are aggravated by the injustice which underlies them. "Wherefore even the most trifling are sometimes the greatest, as in the charge which Callistratus brought against Melanopus, that *he had defrauded* the temple-builders of three consecrated half-obols." διὸ καὶ τὰ ἐλάχιστα μέγιστα, οἷον ὁ Μελανώπου Καλλίστρατος κατηγόρει, ὅτι παρελογίσατο τρία ἡμιωβέλια ἱερὰ τοὺς ναοποιούς (*Rhetoric* 1.14.1). Concerning exaggeration in a law court, Aristotle said, "There is no probable syllogism; for the hearer *is deceived* as to whether he is guilty or not, although neither has been proved." παραλογίζεται γὰρ ὁ ἀκροατὴς ὅτι ἐποίησεν ἢ οὐκ ἐποίησεν, οὐ δεδειγμένου (*Rhetoric* 2.24.4). An inscription mentioned one who "has spent unjustly and *has fraudulently counted* it." δεπάνας ἀδίκους καὶ παραλογισθείσας (*OGIS,* 665.16).

After Jacob had worked seven years for Rachel, Laban gave him Leah, and Jacob protested, "What is this that thou hast done unto me? Did I not slave for thee for Rachel? Why then *didst thou defraud* me?" (Gen. 29:25). οὐ περὶ Ραχηλ ἐδούλευσα παρὰ σοί; καὶ ἵνα τί παρελογίσω με; Because the men of Gibeon had said that they were from a far distance, Joshua had promised to let them live, but he soon found out that they were close neighbors. Then he said to them, "Why *did you deceive* me saying, We are far distant from thee, but ye are the nearest neighbor to us?" (Josh. 9:22). διὰ τί παρελογίσασθέ με λέγοντες Μακρὰν ἀπὸ σοῦ ἐσμεν σφόδρα; When Michal, the daughter of Saul, had helped David to escape from her father, Saul said to her, "Why *didst thou* thus *deceive* me and send away my enemy, and he escaped?" (I Sam. 19:17). ἵνα τί οὕτως παρελογίσω με καὶ ἐξαπέστειλας τὸν ἐχθρόν μου καὶ διεσώθη; Saul consulted the witch of Endor before his last battle, but when she saw Samuel, she cried out to Saul, "Why *didst thou deceive* me? Thou indeed art Saul" (I Sam. 28:12). ἵνα τί παρελογίσω με; καὶ σὺ εἶ Σαουλ.

This word occurs only twice in the New Testament. Paul warned the Colossians, saying, "I say this, that no one *may defraud* you with persuasive words" (Col. 2:4). τοῦτο λέγω ἵνα μηδεὶς ὑμᾶς παραλογίζηται ἐν πιθανολογίᾳ. James exhorted his readers, "But be ye doers of the word, and not hearers only, *defrauding* yourselves" (James 1:22). γίνεσθε δὲ ποιηταὶ λόγου, καὶ μὴ ἀκροαταὶ μόνον παραλογιζόμενοι ἑαυτούς.

I DECEIVE

πλανάω

Homer described a careless chariot-racer: "Another man, trusting in his horses and chariot, carelessly wheels wide to this side and to that, and his horses *wander* over the course, neither does he keep them in hand." ἀφραδέως ἐπὶ πολλὸν ἑλίσσεται ἔνθα καὶ ἔνθα, ἵπποι δὲ πλανόωνται ἀνὰ δρόμον, οὐδὲ κατίσχει (*Iliad* 23.321). When Herodotus recounted Darius' campaign against the Scythians, he said that the Scythians which were left behind "resolved that they should no longer *lead* the Persians *astray,* but attack them whenever they were foraging for grain." ἔδοξε πλανᾶν μὲν μηκέτι Πέρσας, σῖτα δὲ ἑκάστοτε ἀναιρεομένοισι ἐπιτίθεσθαι (4.128). Antigone, seeing a woman riding on a pony, wonders if it could be her sister, Ismene. "Is it, or is it not? Or *does* my opinion *deceive* me? I even think so, but I cannot be sure." ἆρ᾽ ἔστιν; ἆρ᾽ οὐκ ἔστιν; ἢ γνώμη πλανᾷ; (Sophocles *Oedipus at Colonus* 316). In his discussion of speeches and epic poems Aristotle said, "For that which is undefined *leads astray.*" τὸ γὰρ ἀόριστον πλανᾷ (*Rhetoric* 3.14.6). In one of the papyri a minor complains that his mother has defrauded him and speaks of her as one "who is wronging me much and who *has deceived* me." πολλά με ἀδικοῦσα ἔτι καὶ πλανήσασά με (*P. Oxy.,* VI., 898.8).

When Joseph went to look for his brothers and their sheep, "a man found him *wandering* in the plain" (Gen. 37:15). εὗρεν αὐτὸν ἄνθρωπος πλανώμενον ἐν τῷ πεδίῳ. Moses wrote in the statutes of the law, "But if thou shouldst meet the ox of thine enemy or his ass *going astray,* thou shalt turn back and restore it to him" (Exod. 23:4). ἐὰν δὲ συναντήσῃς τῷ βοὶ τοῦ ἐχθροῦ σου ἢ τῷ ὑποζυγίῳ αὐτοῦ πλανωμένοις, ἀποστρέψας ἀποδώσεις αὐτῷ. Later Moses warned the Israelites concerning the sun, moon, and all the host of heaven: "Thou mayest not *be led astray* and worship them and serve them" (Deut. 4:19). μὴ . . . πλανηθεὶς προσκυνήσῃς αὐτοῖς καὶ λατρεύσῃς αὐτοῖς. The prophet Isaiah said, "All we like sheep *went astray*" (Isa. 53:6). πάντες ὡς πρόβατα ἐπλανήθημεν. When the son of the Shunammite woman had died, she came to Elisha and said, "Did I ask a son of my lord? Did I not say, *Do* not *deceive* me?" (II Kings 4:28) μὴ ᾐτησάμην υἱὸν παρὰ τοῦ κυρίου μου; οὐκ εἶπα Οὐ πλανήσεις μετ᾽ ἐμοῦ;

In the New Testament the Lord Jesus warned His disciples, "Beware that no man *lead* you *astray*. For many shall come in my name, saying, I am the Messiah, and they *shall lead* many *astray*"(Matt. 24:4–5). βλέπετε μή τις ὑμᾶς πλανήσῃ. πολλοὶ γὰρ ἐλεύσονται ἐπὶ τῷ ὀνόματί μου λέγοντες· ἐγώ εἰμι ὁ χριστός, καὶ πολλοὺς πλανήσουσιν. When the Lord taught, the people were divided in their opinions concerning Him. Some maintained that He was a good man, but others said, "No, but *he*

A TREASURY OF NEW TESTAMENT SYNONYMS

misleads the multitude" (John 7:12). οὔ, ἀλλὰ πλανᾷ τὸν ὄχλον. The Apostle Paul warned Timothy, "But evil men and swindlers shall become worse and worse, *leading astray* and *being led astray*" (II Tim. 3:13). πονηροὶ δὲ ἄνθρωποι καὶ γόητες προκόψουσιν ἐπὶ τὸ χεῖρον, πλανῶντες καὶ πλανώμενοι. Peter also spoke of the false teachers who, "having forsaken the right way, *went astray*"(II Pet. 2:15). καταλείποντες εὐθεῖαν ὁδὸν ἐπλανήθησαν.

SUMMARY

The words which portray deception have distinct shades of meaning. The word ἀπατάω means "I trick" or "I cheat"; the word παραλογίζομαι, "I defraud"; πλανάω, "I lead astray" or "I mislead."

5. I Establish: βεβαιόω, θεμελιόω, ῥιζόομαι, στηρίζω

All four of these words in some contexts may mean *I establish*, but from widely divergent root meanings. The word βεβαιόω means *I make firm, I confirm,* or *I strengthen.* θεμελιόω denotes *I lay a foundation.* The word ῥιζόομαι denotes *I cause to take root.* The basic meaning of the word στηρίζω is *I support,* but it may mean *I set, stand firm, fix,* or *strengthen.*

βεβαιόω

Thucydides related that "the stories of former times, handed down by hearing, but very rarely *confirmed* by fact, ceased to be incredible." τά τε πρότερον ἀκοῇ μὲν λεγόμενα, ἔργῳ δὲ σπανιώτερον βεβαιούμενα οὐκ ἄπιστα κατέστη (1.23.3). In another place, upon describing the speech of the Corinthians in which they argued against a submission that their fathers would have spurned, he observed, for "they liberated Hellas, but we, rather than *making* this liberty *secure,* are allowing a city to be established as a tyrant in our midst." οἱ τὴν Ἑλλάδα ἠλευθέρωσαν· ἡμεῖς δὲ οὐδ᾽ ἡμῖν αὐτοῖς βεβαιοῦμεν αὐτό, τύραννον δὲ ἐῶμεν ἐγκαθεστάναι πόλιν (1.122.3). When Thucydides related Nicias' warning to the Athenians, he had Nicias say, "So we must consider these things and determine not to run into danger while the city is still amid the waves, and grasp after another kingdom before we have secured the one we have." ὥστε χρὴ σκοπεῖν τινα αὐτὰ καὶ μὴ μετεώρῳ τῇ πόλει ἀξιοῦν κινδυνεύειν καὶ ἀρχῆς ἄλλης ὀρέγεσθαι πρὶν ἣν ἔχομεν βεβαιωσώμεθα (6.10.5). In the *Gorgias,* Plato recalled the words of Socrates in a debate, "Do not fail to answer me this, Callicles, so that if you agree with me, *I may confirm myself* with you by the consent of so competent a man." μὴ φθόνει μοι ἀποκρίνασθαι τοῦτο, Καλλίκλεις, ἵν᾽, ἐάν μοι ὁμολογήσῃς, βεβαιώσωμαι ἤδη παρὰ σοῦ (489A). An inscription is recorded of a certain magistrate "But he *fulfilled* his promise by making the sacrifice to the gods." ἐβεβαίωσεν δὲ τὴν ἐπαγγελίαν παραστήσας μὲν τοῖς ἐντεμενίοις θεοῖς τὴν θυσίαν (*Priene* 123.9).

In the Septuagint the psalmist thus praises God: "But on account of my innocence thou hast upheld me and *hast established* me before thee forever" (Ps. 40:13; KJ Ps. 41:12). ἐμοῦ δὲ διὰ τὴν ἀκακίαν ἀντελάβου, καὶ ἐβεβαίωσάς με ἐνώπιόν σου εἰς τὸν αἰῶνα. In the longest Psalm the writer prays, "My soul drooped with heaviness; *strengthen* me with thy words" (Ps. 118:28; KJ Ps. 119:28). ἔσταξεν ἡ ψυχή μου ἀπὸ ἀκηδίας· βεβαίωσόν με ἐν τοῖς λόγοις σου.

When Paul wrote to the Romans, he declared solemnly, "For I say that Christ has been made a minister of the circumcision in behalf of the truth of God, in order *to confirm* the promises made to the fathers" (Rom. 15:8). λέγω γὰρ Χριστὸν διάκονον γεγενῆσθαι περιτομῆς ὑπὲρ ἀληθείας θεοῦ, εἰς τὸ βεβαιῶσαι τὰς ἐπαγγελίας τῶν πατέρων. To the Corinthians Paul wrote, "But the one who *is establishing* us with you in Christ, and has anointed us, is God" (II Cor. 1:21). ὁ δὲ βεβαιῶν ἡμᾶς σὺν ὑμῖν εἰς Χριστὸν καὶ χρίσας ἡμᾶς θεός. Paul exhorted the Colossians to keep walking in Christ, *"being rooted* and built up in him and *being made firm* in the faith even as ye were taught" (Col. 2:7). ἐρριζωμένοι καὶ ἐποικοδομούμενοι ἐν αὐτῷ καὶ βεβαιούμενοι τῇ πίστει καθὼς ἐδιδάχθητε. The writer to the Hebrews asked the rhetorical question "How shall we escape, if we neglect so great a salvation? which at the first having been spoken through the Lord, *was confirmed* unto us by the ones who had heard." πῶς ἡμεῖς ἐκφευξόμεθα τηλικαύτης ἀμελήσαντες σωτηρίας; ἥτις ἀρχὴν λαβοῦσα λαλεῖσθαι διὰ τοῦ κυρίου, ὑπὸ τῶν ἀκουσάντων εἰς ἡμᾶς ἐβεβαιώθη.

θεμελιόω

Xenophon described how Cyrus had laid siege to the city of Babylon: "First he began to build towers by the river, *having laid his foundation* with the trunks of date-palms not less than one hundred feet long—for they grow even taller than that." καὶ πρῶτον μὲν πυργοὺς ἐπὶ τῷ ποταμῷ ᾠκοδόμει φοίνιξι θεμελιώσας οὐ μεῖον ἢ πλεθριαίοις—εἰσὶ γὰρ καὶ μείζονες ἢ τοσοῦτοι τὸ μῆκος (*Cyropaedia* 7.5.11). An inscription dated 36–35 B.C. reads, "He managed *to found* the assembly." προεστάτησεν τοῦ θεμελιωθῆναι τὴν σύνοδον (*Syll.*, 732.15).

After Joshua had destroyed the city of Jericho, he swore an oath before the Lord: "Cursed be the man who shall rebuild that city; with his firstborn *he shall lay the foundation* of it and with his youngest son shall set up its gates" (Josh. 6:26). ἐν τῷ πρωτοτόκῳ αὐτοῦ θεμελιώσει αὐτήν. In the record of the building of Solomon's temple, the Septuagint says, "In the fourth year *he laid the foundation* of the house of the Lord" (I Kings 6:1; KJ I Kings 6:37). ἐν τῷ ἔτει τῷ τετάρτῳ ἐθεμελίωσεν τὸν οἶκον κυρίου. The psalmist exclaimed, "When I behold the heavens, the works of thy fingers, the moon and stars, which *thou hast established,* what is

I ESTABLISH

man?" (Ps. 8:4; KJ Ps. 8:3). σελήνην καὶ ἀστέρας, ἃ σὺ ἐθεμελίωσας. Another psalm says of God, *"Thou didst found* the earth, and it continues" (Ps. 118:90; KJ Ps. 119:90). ἐθεμελίωσας τὴν γῆν, καὶ διαμένει. Isaiah the prophet said, "And what shall the kings of the nations answer? That the Lord *founded* Zion, and through him the poor of the people shall be saved" (Isa. 14:32). ὅτι κύριος ἐθεμελίωσεν Σιων.

In the Sermon on the Mount the Lord Jesus spoke of a wise man who built his house on the rock, "and the rain came down, and the rivers came, and the winds blew, and they beat upon that house, and it did not fall; for *it was founded* upon the rock" (Matt. 7:25). καὶ προέπεσαν τῇ οἰκίᾳ ἐκείνῃ, καὶ οὐκ ἔπεσεν· τεθεμελίωτο γὰρ ἐπὶ τὴν πέτραν. The Apostle Paul wrote to the Colossians, speaking of their position in Christ: "If indeed ye continue in the faith, *having been founded* and steadfast" (Col. 1:23). εἴ γε ἐπιμένετε τῇ πίστει τεθεμελιωμένοι καὶ ἑδραῖοι. Peter promised suffering believers, "But the God of all grace, who called you unto his eternal glory in Christ, after ye have suffered a little while, shall himself restore, *support,* strengthen, *establish* you" (I Pet. 5:10). ὁ δὲ θεὸς πάσης χάριτος, ὁ καλέσας ὑμᾶς εἰς τὴν αἰώνιον αὐτοῦ δόξαν ἐν Χριστῷ, ὀλίγον παθόντας αὐτὸς καταρτίσει, στηρίξει, σθενώσει, θεμελιώσει.

ῥιζόομαι

Homer, describing the palace of Alcinous, said, "But there his fruitful vineyard *is planted."* ἔνθα δέ οἱ πολύκαρπος ἀλωὴ ἐρρίζωται (*Odyssey* 7.122). Herodotus concluded one of his narratives by saying, "Thus Pisistratus first won Athens, and thus he lost his sovereign power, which *was* not yet *firmly rooted."* οὕτω μὲν Πεισίστρατος ἔσχε τὸ πρῶτον Ἀθήνας, καὶ τὴν τυραννίδα οὔκω κάρτα ἐρριζωμένην ἔχων ἀπέβαλε (1.60). Xenophon related one of the questions which Ischomachus put to Socrates: "But if you placed the whole cutting upright, toward the heaven, do you think that it *would take root* better?" πότερα δὲ ὅλον τὸ κλῆμα ὀρθὸν τιθεὶς πρὸς τὸν οὐρανὸν βλέπον ἡγῇ μᾶλλον ἂν ῥιζοῦσθαι αὐτό; (*Oeconomicus* 19.9).

In the Septuagint Isaiah warns the princes of the earth, "For they shall never sow, nor shall they plant, nor shall their root *be rooted* in the ground" (Isa. 40:24). οὐ γὰρ μὴ σπείρωσιν οὐδὲ μὴ φυτεύσωσιν, οὐδὲ μὴ ῥιζωθῇ εἰς τὴν γῆν ἡ ῥίζα αὐτῶν. When Jeremiah was very troubled over the prosperity of the wicked, he said to the Lord, "Thou didst plant them, and they *were rooted;* they sprouted and produced fruit" (Jer. 12:2). ἐφύτευσας αὐτοὺς καὶ ἐρριζώθησαν. The son of Sirach said, "The calamity of the arrogant is no healing, for a plant of evil *has taken root* in him." φυτὸν γὰρ πονηρίας ἐρρίζωκεν ἐν αὐτῷ (Ecclesiasticus 3:28).

A TREASURY OF NEW TESTAMENT SYNONYMS

In the New Testament this word occurs only twice. Its use in Colossians 2:7 has already been discussed under βεβαιόω. When Paul prayed for the believers, he earnestly sought "that Christ may dwell in your hearts through faith, *being rooted* and *founded* in love" (Eph. 3:17). κατοικῆσαι τὸν Χριστὸν διὰ τῆς πίστεως ἐν ταῖς καρδίαις ὑμῶν, ἐν ἀγάπη ἐρριζωμένοι καὶ τεθεμελιωμένοι. Thus Paul brings together in one petition the images of rooting a plant and founding a building.

στηρίζω

Homer mentioned rainbows "which the son of Cronos *set* in the clouds." ἅς τε Κρονίων ἐν νέφεϊ στήριξε (*Iliad* 11.28). In Achilles' contest with the river, Homer said that the stream "beat upon his shield and thrust him backward, nor was he able *to stand firm* upon his feet." οὐδὲ πόδεσσιν εἶχε στηρίξασθαι (*Iliad* 21.242). Euripides described how Dionysus put Pentheus on the top of a bent pine tree and let the trunk gently rise: "straight up into the heights of air *it soared.*" ὀρθὴ δ' ἐς ὀρθὸν αἰθέρ' ἐστηρίζετο (*The Bacchanals* 1073). Aratus described the constellation of the Ram, Aries, as "weak and starless as on a moonlit night, but still thou canst trace him out by the belt of Andromeda; for he *is fixed* a little under her." ζώνῃ δ' ἂν ὅμως ἐπιτεκμήραιο Ἀνδρομέδης· ὀλίγον γὰρ ὑπ' αὐτὴν ἐστήρικται (*Phaenomina* 230). The belief in "fixed" stars and "fixed" constellations was common in ancient times.

After Jacob had stolen the blessing from Esau, Isaac said to Esau, "Since I made him thy lord and made all his brethren his servants and *supported* him with grain and wine, what shall I do for thee, son?" (Gen. 27:37). εἰ κύριον αὐτὸν ἐποίησά σου καὶ πάντας τοὺς ἀδελφοὺς αὐτοῦ ἐποίησα αὐτοῦ οἰκέτας, σίτῳ καὶ οἴνῳ ἐστήρισα αὐτόν. When Jacob fled from Esau, he rested at Bethel; "And he dreamed, and behold! a ladder *set* upon the earth, the top of which reached unto heaven" (Gen. 28:12). καὶ ἐνυπνιάσθη, καὶ ἰδοὺ κλίμαξ ἐστηριγμένη ἐν τῇ γῇ. In the battle with Amalek when Moses held up his hands, Israel won, "but Moses' hands were heavy; and they took a stone and put it under him, and he sat upon it, and Aaron and Hur *supported* his hands, one on the one side and one on the other" (Exod. 17:12). καὶ Ααρων καὶ Ωρ ἐστήριζον τὰς χεῖρας αὐτοῦ. David prayed, "Restore to me the joy of thy salvation and *support* me with an authoritative Spirit" (Ps. 50:14; KJ Ps. 51:12). καὶ πνεύματι ἡγεμονικῷ στήρισόν με.

In the account of the rich man and Lazarus, Abraham said to the rich man, "And besides all these things, between us and you a great gulf *has been fixed*" (Luke 16:26). καὶ ἐν πᾶσι τούτοις μεταξὺ ἡμῶν καὶ ὑμῶν χάσμα μέγα ἐστήρικται. At the start of the third missionary journey Paul

I ESTABLISH

went through "the Galatian and Phrygian region, *strengthening* all the disciples" (Acts 18:23). τὴν Γαλατικὴν χώραν καὶ Φρυγίαν, στηρίζων πάντας τοὺς μαθητάς. When Paul concluded his letter to the Romans, he said, "But to the one who is able *to establish* you according to my Gospel and the preaching of Jesus Christ" (16:25). τῷ δὲ δυναμένῳ ὑμᾶς στηρίξαι κατὰ τὸ εὐαγγέλιόν μου. Paul assured the Thessalonians, "But the Lord is faithful, who shall *establish* you and guard you from the evil one" (II Thess. 3:3). πιστὸς δέ ἐστιν ὁ κύριος, ὃς στηρίξει ὑμᾶς.

SUMMARY

Each of these words may mean "I establish," but their differences may best be seen from their cognate nouns: βέβαιος means "firm," and hence βεβαιόω "I make firm" or "I strengthen." θεμέλιος means "foundation," and thus θεμελιόω means "I lay a foundation." ῥίζα is the word for "root"; ῥιζόομαι, "I cause to take root." The word στῆριγξ means a "support"; στηρίζω therefore means "I support," "stand firm," "fix," "set," or "strengthen."

6. I Fill: πίμπλημι, πληρόω

I fill is the common meaning of both of these words: πίμπλημι indicates the simple filling of a vessel or a building; πληρόω, usually, a filling which meets a specific lack or need.

πίμπλημι

When Hermes paid a visit to Calypso, "the goddess set before him a table *filled* with ambrosia." θεὰ παρέθηκε τράπεζαν ἀμβροσίης πλήσασα (Homer *Odyssey* 5.93). Odysseus posed as a beggar when he returned to his home, and although Antinous repulsed him, "all the rest gave gifts and *filled* the bag with bread and pieces of meat." ἄλλοι πάντες δίδοσαν, πλῆσαν δ᾽ ἄρα πήρην σίτου καὶ κρειῶν (Homer *Odyssey* 17.411). An example of the verb used in the middle voice occurs when Homer relates that Odysseus, *"having filled for himself* the cup with wine, pledged Achilles." πλησάμενος δ᾽ οἴνοιο δέπας δείδεκτ᾽ Ἀχιλῆα (Homer *Iliad* 9.224). Describing the Babylonians and their boats, Herodotus writes, *"Having filled* every boat with reeds, they send it floating down the river *filled* with cargo." καλάμης πλήσαντες πᾶν τὸ πλοῖον τοῦτο ἀπιεῖσι κατὰ τὸν ποταμὸν φέρεσθαι, φορτίων πλήσαντες (1.194). In one of the papyri the writer commands, *"Fill* the vessel with green mustard." πλῆσον κεράμιον σινάπις χλωροῦ (*P. Lond.*, 453.6).

In the days of Noah "the earth *was filled* with iniquity" (Gen. 6:11). ἐπλήσθη ἡ γῆ ἀδικίας. After Abraham had sent away Hagar and Ishmael into the desert, Hager prayed, "and she saw a well of spring water and went and *filled* the vessel with water" (Gen. 21:19). καὶ εἶδεν φρέαρ ὕδατος ζῶντος καὶ ἐπορεύθη καὶ ἔπλησεν τὸν ἀσκὸν ὕδατος. Doing their best to oppose Isaac, "the Philistines stopped up and *filled* them [the wells which Abraham had dug] with earth" (Gen. 26:15). ἐνέφραξαν αὐτὰ οἱ Φυλιστιμ καὶ ἔπλησαν αὐτὰ γῆς. When Joseph's brethren came to him in Egypt, Joseph commanded his steward, *"Fill* the bags of these men with grain" (Gen. 44:1). πλήσατε τοὺς μαρσίππους τῶν ἀνθρώπων βρωμάτων. The Lord commanded Moses to pronounce another judgment on the Egyptians and promised, "The houses of the Egyptians *shall be filled* with flies" (Exod. 8:17; KJ Exod. 8:21). πλησθήσονται αἱ οἰκίαι τῶν Αἰγυπτίων τῆς κυνομυίης. After Moses had finished preparing the entire

I FILL

tabernacle for the Lord, "the cloud covered the tabernacle of the testimony, and the tabernacle *was filled* with the glory of the Lord" (Exod. 40:34). καὶ δόξης κυρίου ἐπλήσθη ἡ σκηνή.

The same idea of simple filling may be found in the New Testament. When Peter let down his nets at the bidding of the Lord, he caught such a great number of fish that he called to his partners to help him. "And they came and *filled* both the boats so that they began to sink" (Luke 5:7). καὶ ἦλθαν, καὶ ἔπλησαν ἀμφότερα τὰ πλοῖα. The word is also used in relation to the inward life of man. After the Lord Jesus had healed the paralytic, the people were amazed, "and they *were filled* with great fear, saying, We saw strange things today" (Luke 5:26). καὶ ἐπλήσθησαν φόβου λέγοντες ὅτι εἴδομεν παράδοξα σήμερον. On the day of Pentecost the disciples were all together, "and they *were* all *filled* with the Holy Spirit" (Acts 2:4). καὶ ἐπλήσθησαν πάντες πνεύματος ἁγίου. Later when Peter and John were arrested and brought before the Sanhedrin, "then Peter, *having been filled* with the Holy Spirit, said to them . . ." (Acts 4:8). τότε Πέτρος πλησθεὶς πνεύματος ἁγίου εἶπεν πρὸς αὐτούς. In the same way when Paul faced the false prophet Elymas, Scripture says, "But Saul, who is also called Paul, *having been filled* with the Holy Spirit, fixed his gaze on him" (Acts 13:9). Σαῦλος δέ, ὁ καὶ Παῦλος, πλησθεὶς πνεύματος ἁγίου. The use of this word is at least evidence that the apostles were in a Spirit-filled condition which was adequate for the circumstances which they had to face.

πληρόω

Herodotus related Oroetes' attempted deception, saying, "But when Oroetes learned that an inspection was to be expected, he *filled* eight chests with stones, except only a shallow layer at the top; then he put gold on the surface of the stones." ὁ δὲ Ὀροίτης μαθὼν τὸν κατάσκοπον ἐόντα προσδόκιμον ἐποίεε τοιάδε· λάρνακας ὀκτὼ πληρώσας λίθων (3.123). This filling was "needed" for the purpose of his deception. In another context Herodotus reported that when king Minos had need of them the Carians *"were filling* [manning] the ships for him." ἐπλήρουν οἱ τὰς νέας (1.171). A servant in Euripides' *Ion* relates, "And as the tent *was filled,* having been adorned with garlands, they *filled* their souls with plenteous meat." ὡς δ' ἐπληρώθη στέγη, στεφάνοισι κοσμηθέντες εὐόχθου βορᾶς ψυχὴν ἐπλήρουν (line 1170). The need for food is clear, but the use for the tent has a neutral sense. Thucydides, describing the character of the Athenians, said, "But if it so happens that they try a thing and fail, they form new hopes of other things instead and thus *fill up* the need." ἢν δ' ἄρα του καὶ πείρᾳ σφαλῶσιν, ἀντελπίσαντες ἄλλα ἐπλήρωσαν τὴν χρείαν (Thucydides 1.70.7). In the papyri the word frequently occurs with the meaning "to pay." One writer said, "You worry me about the money that you owe to Agathodaemon; *I have paid* him in full." ἐνοχλεῖς μοι ὅτι ὀφείλεις Ἀγαθὸς Δαίμονι χαλκόν· πεπλήρωσα [-κα] αὐτόν (*P. Oxy.*, XII, 1489. 5).

In the Septuagint the newly created earth "needed" inhabitants; hence God created sea creatures, "and God blessed them saying, Increase and multiply and *fill* the waters in the seas" (Gen. 1:22). λέγων Αὐξάνεσθε καὶ πληθύνεσθε καὶ πληρώσατε τὰ ὕδατα. In blessing man, God said, "*Fill* the earth and subdue it" (Gen. 1:28). πληρώσατε τὴν γῆν καὶ κατακυριεύσατε αὐτῆς. In order to build the temple, King Solomon brought Hiram down from Tyre. "He was a worker in brass, *having been filled* with art and understanding and knowledge to do all kinds of work in brass" (I Kings 7:14). τέκτων χαλκοῦ καὶ πεπληρωμένος τῆς τέχνης καὶ συνέσεως καὶ ἐπιγνώσεως. When the poor widow appealed to Elisha, he met her need by instructing her to take her pot of oil and empty vessels, and "Then go in and shut the door on thee and thy sons and pour out into these vessels and set aside that which *was filled*" (II Kings 4:4). καὶ ἀποχεεῖς εἰς τὰ σκεύη ταῦτα καὶ τὸ πληρωθὲν ἀρεῖς. In the face of death the psalmist sang to God, "Thou *wilt fill* me with joy with thy presence" (Ps. 15:11; KJ Ps. 16:11). πληρώσεις με εὐφροσύνης μετὰ τοῦ προσώπου σου. Although there are many other occurrences of this word in the Septuagint, particularly those that read "the word of the Lord *was fulfilled* (I Kings 2:27), they do not contribute to a comparison of these two words.

In the parables of the kingdom our Lord spoke of the dragnet, "which, when it *was filled,* they drew up on the beach and sat down and gathered the good into vessels, but cast the bad away" (Matt. 13:48). ἦν ὅτε ἐπληρώθη ἀναβιβάσαντες ἐπὶ τὸν αἰγιαλόν. There is an urgent need for a consummation of the present age. The wicked must not escape the consequences of their wrongdoing, and the righteous must receive their rewards. The present age often fails to accomplish either. One of the signs at Pentecost was the rushing mighty wind: "and it *filled* all the house where they were sitting" (Acts 2:2). καὶ ἐπλήρωσεν ὅλον τὸν οἶκον. Both the disciples and the multitude (2:6) needed this confirming sign. Later on, Peter challenged Ananias, the hypocrite, by saying, "Why hath Satan *filled* thy heart to lie to the Holy Spirit?" (Acts 5:2). τί ἐπλήρωσεν ὁ σατανᾶς τὴν καρδίαν σου; The spiritual lack in Ananias' heart was quickly filled by Satan. When the apostles were arrested and brought before the Sanhedrin, the high priest charged, "Behold, ye *have filled* Jerusalem with your teaching" (Acts 5:28). ἰδοὺ πεπληρώκατε τὴν Ἰερουσαλὴμ τῆς διδαχῆς ὑμῶν. The apostles certainly met the need for evangelism. In the storm center of trial and struggle Paul could say, "*I have been filled* with comfort"

I KNOW

(II Cor. 7:4). πεπλήρωμαι τῇ παρακλήσει. Paul prayed for the Philippians that they would be without offence unto the day of Christ, *"having been filled* with the fruit of righteousness which is through Jesus Christ" (Phil. 1:11). πεπληρωμένοι καρπὸν δικαιοσύνης. In the same epistle Paul gave that divine promise, "But my God *shall fill* [supply] all your need according to his riches in glory in Christ Jesus" (Phil. 4:19). ὁ δὲ θεός μου πληρώσει πᾶσαν χρείαν ὑμῶν.

SUMMARY

These words are difficult to distinguish. Both πίμπλημι and πληρόω are used with the simple meaning "I fill." πληρόω, however, frequently has a connotation of a need or lack which requires the filling.

7. I Know: γινώσκω, οἶδα, ἐπίσταμαι

Sometimes each of these words is used with the simple meaning *I know* without an intended distinction from the other words, but often there is a sharp distinction. The word γινώσκω signifies *I know by experience* or *I discern,* referring to acquired knowledge. In contrast, οἶδα means *I know* with the connotation of absolute, possessed knowledge such as God has, but often it refers to a person who is gifted or talented in a certain skill. The word ἐπίσταμαι implies *I know as a fact,* often with the connotation of scientific knowledge or skill in art or a trade.

γινώσκω

Pandarus, seeing Diomedes, the son of Tydeus, afar off, recognizes him by his armor, which he knows from experience to be that of Diomedes: "To the wise-hearted son of Tydeus do I liken him in all things, *knowing* him by his shield and his crested helmet." Τυδεΐδη μιν ἔγωγε δαΐφρονι πάντα ἐΐσκω, ἀσπίδι γιγνώσκων αὐλώπιδί τε τρυφαλείῃ (Homer *Iliad* 5.182). The Trojans, warns Polydamus, may come to "know" Achilles through experiencing Achilles' military prowess: "But if on the morrow he shall come out in armor and light on us still abiding here, many a one *shall learn to know* him well." εἰ δ᾿ ἄμμε κιχήδεται ἐνθάδ᾿ ἐόντας αὔριον ὁρμηθεὶς σὺν τεύχεδιν, εὖ νύ τις αὐτὸν γνώσεται (Homer *Iliad* 18.270). Although Odysseus had hoped to find a number of faithful servants when he returned home, he could find only two, and to them he said, "But *I know* that by you two alone of all my servants is my coming desired, but of the rest I have not heard one praying that I might come back again to my home." γιγνώσκω δ᾿ ὡς σφῶϊν ἐελδομένοισιν ἱκάνω οἴοισι δμώων (Homer *Odyssey* 21.209). He had learned by experience that he could depend on these two servants alone. Sophocles uses this word almost in the sense of "I understand" when the goddess Athena answers Odysseus' question about the slaughtered animals. "*I know,* Odysseus, and came forth long ago to meet thee and to aid thee in this chase." ἔγνων, Ὀδυσσεῦ, καὶ πάλαι φύλαξ ἔβην τῇ σῇ πρόθυμος εἰς ὁδὸν κυναγίᾳ (*Ajax* 36). An example of a very common idiom is found in the papyri: "I wish thee *to know* that I had no hope that thou wouldst come up unto the metrop-

I KNOW

olis." γεινώσκειν σαι θέλω, ὅτι οὐχ ἥλπιζον, ὅτι ἀναβένις εἰς τὴν μητρόπολιν.[1]

In the first use of this word in the Septuagint the Lord gave Adam permission to eat from any of the trees of the garden and then added, "But from the tree *to know* good and evil, ye shall not eat from it" (Gen 2:17). ἀπὸ δὲ τοῦ ξύλου τοῦ γινώσκειν καλὸν καὶ πονηρόν, οὐ φάγεσθε ἀπ᾽ αὐτοῦ. This knowledge is the experimental knowledge of good and evil. One of the most illuminating contrasts between this word and οἶδα appears in the statement of the serpent: "For God *knew* that in the day in which ye eat from it, your eyes would be opened, and ye would be like gods *knowing* good and evil" (Gen. 3:5). ᾔδει γὰρ ὁ θεὸς ὅτι ἐν ᾗ ἂν ἡμέρᾳ φάγητε ἀπ᾽ αὐτοῦ, διανοιχθήσονται ὑμῶν οἱ ὀφθαλμοί, καὶ ἔσεσθε ὡς θεοὶ γινώσκοντες καλὸν καὶ πονηρόν. Thus the absolute knowledge which God possesses is sharply distinguished from the knowledge the sinning pair will soon acquire. When Noah sent forth the dove from the ark, the Scripture recorded, "Towards evening the dove returned to him, and it had a dry olive leaf in its mouth, and Noah *knew* that the water had abated from the earth" (Gen. 8:11). καὶ ἔγνω Νωε ὅτι κεκόπακεν τὸ ὕδωρ ἀπὸ τῆς γῆς. He knew because the dove had brought him evidence. In accordance with the Hebrew practice of repeating words for emphasis, the Septuagint sometimes uses both these words together with no distinction: when David replied to Jonathan's optimism, he said, "Thy father *knoweth very well* that I have found favor in thy sight" (I Sam. 20:3). Γινώσκων οἶδεν ὁ πατήρ σου ὅτι εὕρηκα χάριν ἐν ὀφθαλμοῖς σου. Usually, however, the word γινώσκω implies a learning from experience, as when the psalmist said, "*I know*, O Lord, that thy judgments are righteous" (Ps. 118:75; KJ Ps. 119:75). ἔγνων, κύριε, ὅτι δικαιοσύνη τὰ κρίματά σου. The prophet Isaiah asked a rhetorical question: "Who *knew* the mind of the Lord?" (Isa. 40:13) τίς ἔγνω νοῦν κυρίου; No man can claim true experimental knowledge of the mind of God.

In the New Testament this same connotation is the usual one. When the Lord Jesus asked His disciples how many loaves were available, Scripture records, "And when *they knew*, they say, Five and two fish" (Mark 6:38). καὶ γνόντες λέγουσιν· πέντε, καὶ δύο ἰχθύας. The idea is "when they found out." The same meaning is present in the Lord Jesus' teaching, "But when thou art doing alms, *let* not thy left hand *know* [find out] what thy right hand is doing" (Matt. 6:3). σοῦ δὲ ποιοῦντος ἐλεημοσύνην μὴ γνώτω ἡ ἀριστερά σου τί ποιεῖ ἡ δεξιά σου. When the disciples wanted

---

[1] *Agyptische Urkunden aus den koniglichen Museen zu Berlin: Griechische Urkunden*, I, 27, 4, quoted in Moulton and Milligan, p. 127.

to know whether the Lord would then restore the kingdom to Israel, He answered them, "It is not for you *to know* the times or seasons, which the Father put in His own authority" (Acts 1:7). οὐχ ὑμῶν ἐστιν γνῶναι χρόνους ἢ καιροὺς οὓς ὁ πατὴρ ἔθετο ἐν τῇ ἰδίᾳ ἐξουσίᾳ. Peter objected when the Lord Jesus began to wash his feet, but the Lord answered him, "That which I am doing *thou knowest* not now, but *thou shalt come to know* after these things" (John 13:7). ὃ ἐγὼ ποιῶ σὺ οὐκ οἶδας ἄρτι, γνώσῃ δὲ μετὰ ταῦτα. "Knowledge as absolute and complete (οὐκ οἶδας) is contrasted with the knowledge which is gained by slow experience (γνώσῃ 'thou shalt learn' or 'understand')" (Westcott, *John,* p. 191). In the same way when the Lord inquired of Peter for the third time whether he loved Him, Peter broke forth to say, "Lord, *thou knowest* all things; *thou knowest* that I am affectionate toward thee" (John 21:17). κύριε, πάντα σὺ οἶδας, σὺ γινώσκεις ὅτι φιλῶ σε. Peter confesses the absolute knowledge of the Lord and then restricts that knowledge to the specific knowledge of Peter's own heart attitude, of which Jesus had experience. The Apostle Paul, writing to those who had experienced the grace of Christ, also uses γινώσκω in this characteristic sense: "For *ye know* the grace of our Lord Jesus Christ, that, although he was rich, yet for your sakes he became poor" (II Cor. 8:9). γινώσκετε γὰρ τὴν χάριν τοῦ κυρίου ἡμῶν Ἰησοῦ Χριστοῦ.

οἶδα

Homer has Hera exclaim to Zeus, "Indeed, even a man will try to accomplish his purpose for another man, who is but mortal and *knows* not the wisdom that is mine." ὅς περ θνητός τ' ἐστὶ καὶ οὐ τόσα μήδεα οἶδε (*Iliad* 18.363). This usage clearly portrays the absolute knowledge of the gods, but Homer used the word in a different sense when he said, "These with their seven ships were led by Philoctetes, *who was knowing* well archery." τῶν δὲ Φιλοκτήτης ἦρχεν τόξων εὖ εἰδὼς ἑπτὰ νεῶν (*Iliad* 2.718). This usage has the connotation of being "gifted" or "skillful" in archery. When the chorus cried out against Aegisthus for murdering Agamemnon, Aegisthus showed his arrogance toward the chorus by saying, "*Know thou* that thou shalt pay to me the penalty to requite thy folly." ἴσθι μοι δώσων ἄποινα τῆσδε μωρίας χάριν (Aeschylus *Agamemnon* 1670). Sophocles has Athena, the goddess of wisdom, refer to her wisdom when she directs a rhetorical question to Odysseus: "Tell me what is the purpose of thy eager search, and learn from *one who knows.*" σπουδὴν ἔθου τήνδ᾽, ὡς παρ᾽ εἰδυίας μάθῃς (*Ajax* 13). Although in the papyri the usage of Hellenistic Greek became more and more careless, many papyri writers continued to use οἶδα in the sense of thorough, accurate knowledge. One writer said, "I ask you therefore not to do otherwise; but *I know* that you will do everything well." ἐρωτῶ οὖν σε μὴ ἄλλως ποιῆσαι, οἶδα δὲ ὅτι πάντα καλῶς ποιήσεις (*P. Oxy.*, IV, 745.8).

When the Lord God caused the garden to grow in Eden, He made "the tree of life in the midst of the paradise and the tree *to know* what was to *be known* of good and evil" (Gen. 2:9). καὶ τὸ ξύλον τοῦ εἰδέναι γνωστὸν καλοῦ καὶ πονηροῦ. Perhaps this refers to a full knowledge of what was to be experienced. When the Lord expressed His confidence in Abraham, He said, "For *I know* that he will command his children and his household after him, and they shall keep the ways of the Lord to do righteousness and judgment" (Gen. 18:19). ᾔδειν γὰρ ὅτι συντάξει τοῖς υἱοῖς αὐτοῦ καὶ τῷ οἴκῳ αὐτοῦ μετ' αὐτόν. Here again this word refers to the absolute knowledge which God possesses. It is also used, in the negative, to express man's knowledge of God when the Old Testament refers to the sons of Eli, saying, "And the sons of Eli, the priest, were wicked men, not *knowing* the Lord" (I Sam. 2:12). καὶ οἱ υἱοὶ Ηλι τοῦ ἱερέως υἱοὶ λοιμοὶ οὐκ εἰδότες τὸν κύριον. When the servants of King Saul sought to give his troubled mind relief, they said to him, "Let indeed thy servants before thee give orders, and let them seek for our lord a man who *knows* [is skillful in] playing on a harp" (I Sam. 16:16). εἰπάτωσαν δὴ οἱ δοῦλοί σου ἐνώπιόν σου καὶ ζητησάτωσαν τῷ κυρίῳ ἡμῶν ἄνδρα εἰδότα ψάλλειν ἐν κινύρᾳ. But the usual sense is that of complete knowledge such as God has. Jonathan assured David, "The Lord God of Israel *knows* that I will, as occasion offers, during the three days sound out my father" (I Sam. 20:12). Κύριος ὁ θεὸς Ισραηλ οἶδεν ὅτι ἀνακρινῶ τὸν πατέρα μου ὡς ἂν ὁ καιρὸς τρισσῶς. When Job came to a full self-realization, he said, "But who will declare to me the things which *I did* not *know,* things great and wonderful which *I did* not *understand*" (Job 42:3). τίς δὲ ἀναγγελεῖ μοι ἃ οὐκ ᾔδειν, μεγάλα καὶ θαυμαστὰ ἃ οὐκ ἠπιστάμην; Such absolute knowledge was not within Job's power.

The first use of this word in the New Testament followed our Lord's rebuke of praying with vain repetitions: "Therefore be ye not like unto them; for God your Father *knows* the things of which ye have need before ye ask him" (Matt. 6:8). μὴ οὖν ὁμοιωθῆτε αὐτοῖς· οἶδεν γὰρ ὁ θεὸς ὁ πατὴρ ὑμῶν ὧν χρείαν ἔχετε πρὸ τοῦ ὑμᾶς αἰτῆσαι αὐτόν. Although the demons do not have omniscience, they do have full knowledge (certain, though not absolute), for when Christ was casting out demons, "he was not permitting the demons to be speaking, because they *knew* him" (Mark 1:34). οὐκ ἤφιεν λαλεῖν τὰ δαιμόνια, ὅτι ᾔδεισαν αὐτόν. These words are used with fine distinctions in meaning after the Lord has given the parable of the sower. "And he says to them, *Know* ye not this parable? and how *shall ye come to know* all parables?" (Mark 4:13). καὶ λέγει αὐτοῖς· οὐκ οἴδατε τὴν παραβολὴν ταύτην, καὶ πῶς πάσας τὰς παραβολὰς γνώσεσθε; The meaning is that if they do not have "insight" or "full comprehension" into this parable, how will they "find out" or "learn by experience" the meaning of other parables? The Apostle Paul also used these two words in the same context, in saying to the Galatians, "But then, not *knowing* God, ye were enslaved to those who by nature were not gods; but now, *having come to know* God, or rather *having been known* by God, how turn ye again to the weak and beggarly elements?" (Gal. 4:8–9). Ἀλλὰ τότε μὲν οὐκ εἰδότες θεὸν ἐδουλεύσατε τοῖς φύσει μὴ οὖσιν θεοῖς· νῦν δὲ γνόντες θεόν, μᾶλλον δὲ γνωσθέντες ὑπὸ θεοῦ. Especially valuable are the comments of Lightfoot on this text: "While οἶδα 'I know' refers to the knowledge of facts absolutely, γινώσκω 'I recognize,' being relative, gives prominence either to the *attainment* or the *manifestation* of the knowledge. Thus γινώσκειν will be used in preference to εἰδέναι; (1) where there is reference to some earlier state of ignorance, or to some prior facts on which the knowledge is based; (2) where the ideas of 'thoroughness, familiarity,' or of 'approbation,' are involved: these ideas arising out of the stress which γινώσκειν lays on the *process* of reception" (*Galatians,* p. 171).

A similar distinction may be found in Paul's statement "So that from now on *we know* no man according to the flesh, and if *we have known* Christ according to the flesh, now, however, *we know* him thus no longer" (II Cor. 5:16). Ὥστε ἡμεῖς ἀπὸ τοῦ νῦν οὐδένα οἴδαμεν κατὰ σάρκα· εἰ καὶ ἐγνώκαμεν κατὰ σάρκα Χριστόν, ἀλλὰ νῦν οὐκέτι γινώσκομεν. The New Testament revelation gave believers full knowledge of the Lord Jesus Christ; even though they had "known him by experience" during His earthly ministry, this experience was now no longer adequate. Scholars are divided on the interpretation of Ephesians 5:5. Some think that the two words for "I know" represent a "Hebraism," so that the passage should read, "For this thing *ye surely know,* that no fornicator, nor unclean person, not covetous person, who is an idolater, has any inheritance in the kingdom of Christ and God" (Eph. 5:5). τοῦτο γὰρ ἴστε γινώσκοντες, ὅτι πᾶς πόρνος ἢ ἀκάθαρτος ἢ πλεονέκτης. This was the view of the translators of the American Standard Edition of 1901. Others, however, hold that these same words should mean: "For *ye know* this *by your experience*" (Moulton and Milligan, p. 440). Either of these interpretations may be correct. It is characteristic of the Apostle John to stress the certainty of the believer's knowledge. In his first epistle he said, "And ye have an anointing from the Holy One, and *ye know* all things. I did not write to you because *ye know* not the truth, but because *ye know* it" (2:20–21). καὶ ὑμεῖς χρῖσμα ἔχετε ἀπὸ τοῦ ἁγίου, καὶ οἴδατε πάντες. οὐκ ἔγραψα ὑμῖν ὅτι οὐκ οἴδατε τὴν

I KNOW

ἀλήθειαν, ἀλλ' ὅτι οἴδατε αὐτήν. Such statements are common in his writings. For additional light on this *knowledge* consult Westcott, *The Epistles of St. John*, p. 74.

ἐπίσταμαι

In narrating one of the battles of the *Iliad* Homer wrote, "And Meriones slew Phereclus, son of Harmonides, the smith, who *knew* [was skillful] to make with his hands all kinds of intricate things." Μηριόνης δὲ Φέρεκλον ἐνήρατο, τέκτονος υἱὸν Ἁρμονίδεω, ὃς χερσὶν ἐπίστατο δαίδαλα πάντα τεύχειν (5.60). This designation of a specific skill or talent is common in classical Greek. In the *Odyssey,* Homer writes that certain women were skillful weavers, "for Athena gave to them above others *to know* [have skill in] fair handiwork." πέρι γάρ σφισι δῶκεν Ἀθήνη ἔργα τ' ἐπίστασθαι περικαλλέα (7.111). Often this word signifies "to know as a fact." Herodotus recounted the speech of Xerxes in which he said, "Now that Cyrus and Cambyses and Darius my father conquered and added to our realm the nations, no one needs to tell you, for you well *know* it *as a fact.*" Δαρεῖος κατεργάσαντο καὶ προεκτήσαντο ἔθνεα, ἐπισταμένοισι εὖ οὐκ ἄν τις λέγοι (7.8). Aristotle limited this word to "scientific knowledge" (*Metaphysics* 1.2.10). In the papyri one writer said, "Because *you know for a fact* how I esteem and love you." ἐπιστάμενος πῶς σε τίθεμαι κὲ φιλῶ (*P. Tebt.*, II, 408.3).

When Joseph brought his brethren in before Pharaoh, Pharaoh welcomed them to Egypt and added, "But if *thou knowest* any able men among them, appoint them overseers over my cattle" (Gen. 47:5; KJ 47:6). εἰ δὲ ἐπίστῃ ὅτι εἰσὶν ἐν αὐτοῖς ἄνδρες δυνατοί, κατάστησον αὐτοὺς ἄρχοντας τῶν ἐμῶν κτηνῶν. This is a matter of emphasis; the knowledge came from experience, but obviously Pharaoh meant "If thou knowest for a fact." He did not want incompetent administrators. Before Moses consented to lead the Israelites out of Egypt, he made a number of excuses, among them that he could not speak well. "And the anger of the Lord was kindled against Moses, and He said, Behold, is not thy brother Aaron the Levite? *I know* that he can speak very well for thee" (Exod. 4:14). Οὐκ ἰδοὺ Ααρων ὁ ἀδελφός σου ὁ Λευίτης; ἐπίσταμαι ὅτι λαλῶν λαλήσει αὐτός σοι. The accuracy of the Lord's knowledge could not be questioned. As Moses warned the Israelites of the judgment for disobedience which would befall them, he said, "A nation which *thou knowest* not will eat the fruits of thy land" (Deut. 28:33). φάγεται ἔθνος, ὃ οὐκ ἐπίστασαι. When Job answered the charges of Zophar, he retorted, "For *I know* as many things as *ye* also *know* and am not inferior to you in understanding" (Job 13:2). καὶ οἶδα ὅσα καὶ ὑμεῖς ἐπίστασθε. Job's full knowledge matched the accurate knowledge of his three friends. The same contrast exists in Job 42:3, which has already been discussed.

In the New Testament there is a striking contrast between two of these words. When the seven sons of Sceva attempted to cast out a demon by using the name of Jesus as a talisman, the demon answered them, "Jesus *I know* [from experience], and Paul *I know* [accurately], but who are ye?" (Acts 19:15). τὸν μὲν Ἰησοῦν γινώσκω καὶ τὸν Παῦλον ἐπίσταμαι· ὑμεῖς δὲ τίνες ἐστέ; The demon had personal experience of the Lord Jesus (perhaps during His earthly ministry), and he had accurate enough knowledge of Paul to know that these exorcists did not have his power to cast out demons. During his trial before Felix, Paul said, "Because *I know* that for many years thou wast a judge to this nation, cheerfully I make my defence" (Acts 24:10). ἐκ πολλῶν ἐτῶν ὄντα σε κριτὴν τῷ ἔθνει τούτῳ ἐπιστάμενος εὐθύμως τὰ περὶ ἐμαυτοῦ ἀπολογοῦμαι. Paul said the only good thing that he could honestly say about Felix: that he had much experience as a judge of the Jews! At a later trial before Festus and King Agrippa, Paul said, "For the king *knows* concerning these things, to whom I am speaking boldly, for I am persuaded that none of these things are escaping his notice" (Acts 26:26). ἐπίσταται γὰρ περὶ τούτων ὁ βασιλεύς, πρὸς ὃν καὶ παρρησιαζόμενος λαλῶ. When Paul wrote to Timothy, he warned him about a false teacher who had repudiated the doctrine and words of the Lord Jesus Christ and described the teacher by saying, "He has been puffed up, *knowing* nothing, but being sick concerning questionings and fights about words" (I Tim. 6:4). τετύφωται, μηδὲν ἐπιστάμενος, ἀλλὰ νοσῶν. Because the false teacher had rejected the words of the Lord Jesus, he had no accurate understanding of the truth. James warned his readers not to presume on a long life and future profit when "*ye know* not what your life will be on the morrow" (James 4:14). οὐκ ἐπίστασθε τῆς αὔριον ποία ἡ ζωὴ ὑμῶν. No man has accurate knowledge of the future; the believer must walk by faith, not by sight.

SUMMARY

The word γινώσκω means "I know by experience" or "I discern," with the implication of acquired knowledge. On the other hand the word οἶδα denotes "I know" in the full, absolute sense which befits an expert in a certain skill, or even God Himself. The word ἐπίσταμαι designates "I know as a fact" or "I know accurately," with the connotation of scientific or technical knowledge often present.

8. I Send: πέμπω, ἀποστέλλω

The word πέμπω is the general term which means *I send*. It can be used in a wide variety of contexts. A more limited term is the word ἀποστέλλω, which usually means *I send officially*.

πέμπω

When Telemachus and Peisistratus stop at the palace of Menelaus, Eteoneus says to Menelaus, "Shall we unyoke for them their swift horses, or *shall we send* them on their way to another who shall entertain them?" ἦ σφωιν καταλύσομεν ὠκέας, ἵππους, ἦ ἄλλον πέμπωμεν ἱκανέμεν, ὅς κε φιλήσῃ (Homer *Odyssey* 4.29). This use in the simple sense of "I send" can be contrasted with an official sending, as when Homer stated, "But Hector *sent* to the city two heralds with all speed." Ἕκτωρ δὲ προτὶ ἄστυ δύω κήρυκας ἔπεμπε (*Iliad* 3.116). It is also used for what the gods send, for Homer said of Zeus, "Wherefore content yourselves with whatever evil thing *he sends* on each one." τῶ ἔχεθ' ὅττι κεν ὔμμι κακὸν πέμπῃσιν ἑκάστῳ (*Iliad* 15.109). Most of the time it seems to be used with no official sense at all. Herodotus mentioned two brothers "who put on their sister the best adornment which they had and *sent* her to draw water, having a vessel upon her head." σκευάσαντες τὴν ἀδελφεὴν ὡς εἶχον ἄριστα, ἐπ' ὕδωρ ἔπεμπον ἄγγος ἐπὶ τῇ κεφαλῇ ἔχουσαν (5.12). The writer of one papyrus ordered, "But get the kid from Aristion and *send* it to us." κόμισαι δὲ καὶ τὸν ἔριφον παρὰ Ἀριστίωνος καὶ πέμψον ἡμῖν (*P. Hib.*, I, 54.19).

When Rebekah heard of the threats of Esau against Jacob, "she *sent* and called Jacob, her younger son, and said to him, Behold, Esau thy brother threatens to kill thee" (Gen. 27:42). πέμψασα ἐκάλεσεν Ιακωβ τὸν υἱὸν αὐτῆς τὸν νεώτερον καὶ εἶπεν αὐτῷ. Before King Artaxerxes would release Nehemiah from being his cupbearer, Nehemiah pleaded with him, "if thy servant shall find favor in thy sight, that *thou wouldst send* me unto Judah, unto the city of the sepulchres of my fathers, and I shall rebuild it" (II Esdras 12:5; KJ Neh. 2:5). εἰ ἀγαθυνθήσεται ὁ παῖς σου ἐνώπιόν σου ὥστε πέμψαι αὐτὸν εἰς Ιουδα. The book of Wisdom uses both of these words together. The writer prays to God for wisdom, saying, "*Send* her forth out of the holy heavens, and from the throne of thy glory *send* her." ἐξαπόστειλον αὐτὴν ἐξ ἁγίων οὐρανῶν καὶ ἀπὸ θρόνου δόξης σου πέμψον αὐτήν (9:10). Although there is no significant difference between the words in this passage, in a passage in II Maccabees there is a distinction: "But after many years, when it pleased God, Nehemiah, *having been sent* by the king of Persia, *sent* for the fire the descendants of the priests who had hidden it." ὅτε ἔδοξεν τῷ θεῷ, ἀποσταλεὶς Νεεμιας ὑπὸ τοῦ βασιλέως τῆς Περσίδος τοὺς ἐκγόνους τῶν ἱερέων τῶν ἀποκρυψάντων ἔπεμψεν ἐπὶ τὸ πῦρ (II Maccabees 1:20). The king of Persia could send by official commission, but Nehemiah, not having such regal authority, could not.

In the New Testament this same flexibility of usage is found. The Scripture states concerning John the Baptist, "But when John had heard in the prison the works of Christ, *he sent* to him through his disciples and said to him, Art thou the One who is coming?" (Matt. 11:2–3). ὁ δὲ Ἰωάννης ἀκούσας ἐν τῷ δεσμωτηρίῳ τὰ ἔργα τοῦ Χριστοῦ, πέμψας διὰ τῶν μαθητῶν αὐτοῦ εἶπεν αὐτῷ. This unofficial question ought to be contrasted with the official question sent to John himself: "And this is the testimony of John, when the Jews *sent* to him from Jerusalem priests and Levites. . . . Therefore they said to him, Who art thou? that we may give an answer to the ones *who sent* us" (John 1:19, 22). ὅτε ἀπέστειλαν πρὸς αὐτὸν οἱ Ἰουδαῖοι. . . . εἶπαν οὖν αὐτῷ· τίς εἶ; ἵνα ἀπόκρισιν δῶμεν τοῖς πέμψασιν ἡμᾶς. The Lord Jesus also used this word in the sense of "to send officially" when He said, "A slave is not greater than his master, nor is an *apostle* greater than the one *who sent* him" (John 13:16). οὐδὲ ἀπόστολος μείζων τοῦ πέμψαντος αὐτόν. Those who welcome the man of sin will not escape punishment, for Scripture says, "And on account of this God *sends* them an in-working of error that they should believe the lie" (II Thess. 2:11). καὶ διὰ τοῦτο πέμπει αὐτοῖς ὁ θεὸς ἐνέργειαν πλάνης. During the period of tribulation, when evil men finally succeed in slaying the two witnesses for the Lord, "the ones who dwell upon the earth rejoice over them and make merry, and *they shall send* gifts to one another" (Rev. 11:10). οἱ κατοικοῦντες ἐπὶ τῆς γῆς χαίρουσιν ἐπ' αὐτοῖς καὶ εὐφραίνονται, καὶ δῶρα πέμψουσιν ἀλλήλοις.

ἀποστέλλω

This word means "I send with a commission" or "I send officially"; thus it is often found in a military context. Herodotus wrote of the invasion of Egypt, "But those of them *who were sent* to war against the Ammonians, those set forth and journeyed from Thebes with guides." οἱ δ' αὐτῶν ἐπ' Ἀμμωνίους ἀποσταλέντες στρατεύεσθαι (3.26). Demaratus, giving advice to Xerxes on the conquest of the Greeks, said, "Thus *you should send* three hundred ships of your fleet to the Laconian country." εἰ τῆς ναυτικῆς

I SEND

στρατιῆς νέας τριηκοσίας ἀποστείλειας ἐπὶ τὴν Λάκαιναν χώρην (7.235). Sometimes a variety of words are used with the meaning "to send officially." When Croesus was ready to attack Persia, "Having decided this, he immediately made a trial of the oracles, both of those in Greece and of the one in Libya, *having sent* messengers separately to Delphi, to Abae in Phocia, and to Dodona; but others *were being sent* to Amphiaraus and Trophonius, and others to Branchidae in the Milesian country. These now are the Greek oracles to which Croesus *sent* for divination; but he *sent* others to inquire from Ammon in Libya." διαπέμψας ἄλλους ἄλλῃ, τοὺς μὲν ἐς Δελφοὺς ἰέναι, τοὺς δὲ ἐς Ἄβας τὰς Φωκέων, τοὺς δὲ ἐς Δωδώνην· οἱ δὲ τινὲς ἐπέμποντο παρά τε Ἀμφιάρεων καὶ παρὰ Τροφώνιον, οἱ δὲ τῆς Μιλησίης ἐς Βραγχίδας. ταῦτα μέν νυν τὰ Ἑλληνικὰ μαντήια ἐς τὰ ἀπέπεμψε μαντευσόμενος Κροῖσος· Λιβύης δὲ παρὰ Ἄμμωνα ἀπέστελλε ἄλλους χρησομένους (1.46). Thus three different forms of πέμπω are combined with ἀποστέλλω—all with the meaning "I send officially." Philoctetes uses ἀποστέλλω to represent the action of the gods in his despairing indictment: "Nothing evil has ever perished. But the gods care for them well; they rejoice in turning back from Hades the villains, but always *sending forth* the righteous and the good." ἀλλ᾽ εὖ περιστέλλουσιν αὐτὰ δαίμονες, καί πως τὰ μὲν πανοῦργα καὶ παλιντριβῆ χαίρουσ᾽ ἀναστρέφοντες ἐξ Ἀιδου, τὰ δὲ δίκαια καὶ τὰ χρήστ᾽ ἀποστέλλουσ᾽ ἀεί (Sophocles *Philoctetes* 450). The papyri record an oath by a shipowner who swore "that I will proceed with the officers *sent* for this purpose." ἀπαντῆσαι ἅμα τοῖς εἰς τοῦτον ἀποσταλῖσι ὀφφικιαλίοις (*P. Oxy.,* I 87.18).

In the account of the flood, while the waters were diminishing, Noah opened the ark and *"sent forth* a raven," and later on "he *sent forth* a dove" (Gen. 8:7–8). ἀπέστειλεν τὸν κόρακα. . . . ἀπέστειλεν τὴν περιστεράν. The birds "had a commission" to find dry land! When Abraham stayed in Gerar, he presented Sarah as his sister. "But Abimelech, the king of the Gerarites, *sent* and took Sarah" (Gen. 20:2). ἀπέστειλεν δὲ Ἀβιμελεχ βασιλεὺς Γεραρων καὶ ἔλαβεν τὴν Σαρραν. In his charge to his servant, Abraham assures him that God "himself *will send* his angel before thee, and thou shalt take a wife for my son Isaac from there" (Gen. 24:7). αὐτὸς ἀποστελεῖ τὸν ἄγγελον αὐτοῦ ἔμπροσθέν σου. When the Lord commissioned Moses to deliver Israel, He said, "And now come, *I will send* thee to Pharaoh, king of Egypt, and thou shalt lead my people, the children of Israel, out of Egypt" (Exod. 3:10). καὶ νῦν δεῦρο ἀποστείλω σε πρὸς Φαραω βασιλέα Αἰγύπτου. The psalmist said of God, *"He sent* redemption for his people; he commanded his covenant forever" (Ps. 110:9; KJ Ps. 111:9). λύτρωσιν ἀπέστειλεν τῷ λαῷ αὐτοῦ.

A TREASURY OF NEW TESTAMENT SYNONYMS

The New Testament sets forth the commissioning of the twelve apostles in these words: "These twelve Jesus *sent forth,* having charged them" (Matt. 10:5). τούτους τοὺς δώδεκα ἀπέστειλεν ὁ Ἰησοῦς παραγγείλας αὐτοῖς. In one of Jesus' encounters with the demonic hosts, the man who had the legion of demons "was beseeching him much that *he would* not *send* them outside the country" (Mark 5:10). παρεκάλει αὐτὸν πολλὰ ἵνα μὴ αὐτὰ ἀποστείλῃ ἔξω τῆς χώρας. Apparently the demons were fearful of an official consignment to the infernal regions. There is further evidence that both words are used in the sense of "I send officially." In the upper room the Lord Jesus said to the disciples, "Peace be unto you; even as the Father *has sent* me, I also *am sending* you" (John 20:21). εἰρήνη ὑμῖν· καθὼς ἀπέσταγκέν με ὁ πατήρ, κἀγὼ πέμπω ὑμᾶς. When Paul addressed the Jews in Rome, he concluded with the challenge "Therefore let it be known unto you that this salvation of God *was sent* to the Gentiles, and they will hear it" (Acts 28:28). γνωστὸν οὖν ἔστω ὑμῖν ὅτι τοῖς ἔθνεσιν ἀπεστάλη τοῦτο τὸ σωτήριον τοῦ θεοῦ. The Apostle Peter spoke of those "who preached the Gospel unto you through the Holy Spirit who *was sent* from heaven" (I Pet. 1:12). τῶν εὐαγγελισαμένων ὑμᾶς ἐν πνεύματι ἁγίῳ ἀποσταλέντι ἀπ' οὐρανοῦ. Clearly the Holy Spirit of God was sent under a divine commission.

SUMMARY

The word ἀποστέλλω denotes "I send with a commission" or "I send officially." πέμπω is a general term for "I send." In some contexts it certainly means "I send officially," but by no means always; the context must decide.

9. I Struggle: ἀγωνίζομαι, κοπιάω

The word ἀγωνίζομαι means *I strive* or *I struggle*. The root meaning is to contend in the athletic games. On the other hand κοπιάω specifies *I toil, I struggle,* or *I become weary,* with a strong connotation of labor, pain, and faintness.

ἀγωνίζομαι

Although this word has a wide application, the classical meaning of contending in athletic games is most common. In Herodotus the Eleans told the Egyptians that "it was lawful for all the Greeks, whether from Elis or elsewhere, *to contend in the games."* τῶν ἄλλων Ἑλλήνων ὁμοίως τῷ βουλομένῳ ἐξεῖναι ἀγωνίζεσθαι (2.160). But when Herodotus related the battles between the Pterians and Croesus, he said, "And both the armies *contended* thus." καὶ τὰ μὲν στρατόπεδα ἀμφότερα οὕτω ἠγωνίσατο (1.76). In a much milder sense Xenophon used the word to refer to a public debate. When Socrates urged Charmides to seek public office, "A private conversation is a different thing," he said, "O Socrates, from *debating* before the multitude." Οὐ ταὐτόν ἐστιν, ἔφη, ὦ Σώκρατες, ἰδίᾳ τε διαλέγεσθαι καὶ ἐν τῷ πλήθει ἀγωνίζεσθαι (Xenophon *Memorabilia* 3.7.4). In an inscription a Greek soldier is commended for his military defense of the realm, *"striving* in behalf of the common salvation." ἀγωνιζόμενος ὑπὲρ τῆς κοινῆς σωτηρίας (*Syll.,* 213.33).

After Theodotion, in his version of Daniel, recorded the trap laid for Daniel through the decree of King Darius, he added, "Then when the king heard this matter, he was exceedingly grieved for it and *strove hard* for Daniel to deliver him and *continued striving* until evening to deliver him" (Dan. 6:15; KJ Dan. 6:14). πολὺ ἐλυπήθη ἐπ᾽ αὐτῷ καὶ περὶ τοῦ Δανιηλ ἠγωνίσατο τοῦ ἐξελέσθαι αὐτὸν καὶ ἕως ἑσπέρας ἦν ἀγωνιζόμενος τοῦ ἐξελέσθαι αὐτόν. The son of Sirach exhorted his readers, *"Strive thou* for the truth unto death, and the Lord God will fight in behalf of thee." ἕως θανάτου ἀγώνισαι περὶ τῆς ἀληθείας, καὶ κύριος ὁ θεὸς πολεμήσει ὑπὲρ σοῦ (Ecclesiasticus 4:28). Jewish history exhibits another use of this word: "And Alcimus *strove* for the highpriesthood." καὶ ἠγωνίσατο Ἄλκιμος περὶ τῆς ἀρχιερωσύνης (I Maccabees 7:21).

Paul repeatedly used the metaphor of the athletic games. To the

A TREASURY OF NEW TESTAMENT SYNONYMS

Corinthians he wrote, "But every one who *contends in the games* is self-controlled in all things. Therefore those on the one hand do it to receive a corruptible crown, but on the other hand we an incorruptible" (I Cor. 9:25). πᾶς δὲ ὁ ἀγωνιζόμενος πάντα ἐγκρατεύεται. When the disciples asked the Lord Jesus whether there are only few that are saved, He answered them, *"Strive ye* to enter in through the narrow door, because many, I say to you, shall seek to enter in and shall not be able" (Luke 13:24). ἀγωνίζεσθε εἰσελθεῖν διὰ τῆς στενῆς θύρας. Implicit in our Lord's exhortation is the urgency and struggle characteristic of an athletic contest. Arndt and Gingrich translate this phrase very strikingly: "strain every nerve to enter" (Arndt and Gingrich, p. 15). Sometimes this word implies military action. During the trial of the Lord Jesus before Pilate, He said, "My kingdom is not of this world; if my kingdom were of this world, my servants *would fight,* that I should not be delivered up to the Jews" (John 18:36). εἰ ἐκ τοῦ κόσμου τούτου ἦν ἡ βασιλεία ἡ ἐμή, οἱ ὑπηρέται ἂν οἱ ἐμοὶ ἠγωνίζοντο. When the Apostle Paul wrote to the Colossians, he sent greetings to them from one of his most faithful helpers, Epaphras, "who is always *striving* in your behalf in his prayers, that ye may stand perfect and fully assured in all the will of God" (Col. 4:12). πάντοτε ἀγωνιζόμενος ὑπὲρ ὑμῶν ἐν ταῖς προσευχαῖς. This is a touching portrayal of a dedicated man wrestling in prayer for the Colossians. At the end of his life Paul could write to Timothy, *"I have fought* the good fight, I have finished the course, I have kept the faith" (II Tim. 4:7). τὸν καλὸν ἀγῶνα ἠγώνισμαι, τὸν δρόμον τετέλεκα, τὴν πίστιν τετήρηκα. The earnestness of Paul's labors for the Lord Jesus is well expressed by this word.

κοπιάω

The first-known classical use of this word is in the comedies of Aristophanes. One passage from *The Birds* reads, "Laughter and youth and the milk of the birds we'll supply; we'll never forsake you, but rather we'll *weary* you with good things." ὥστε παρέσται κοπιᾶν ὑμῖν (line 734). Another use of the word in the papyri exhibits the sense of "to work hard." The writer mentioned those who were "cheerful concerning their works and *were working hard* with pleasure." ἱλαροὺς περὶ τὰς πράξεις καὶ μεθ' ἡδονῆς κοπιῶντας (W. Kroll, *Vettii Valentis Anthologiarum Libri,* p. 266, 6).

In the Septuagint Moses warns the Israelites about the treachery of Amalek, "How he rose up against thee in the way and smote thy rear, the ones *who were faint* behind thee, and thou wast hungry and *wast faint*" (Deut. 25:18). πῶς ἀντέστη σοι ἐν τῇ ὁδῷ καὶ ἔκοψέν σου τὴν οὐραγίαν,

I STRUGGLE

τοὺς κοπιῶντας ὀπίσω σου, σὺ δὲ ἐπείνας καὶ ἐκοπίας. When the Philistines returned the ark of the Lord, they set it in a cart pulled by two cows. "And the cows traveled the straight road to the road leading to Bethshemesh; they went on in one track, and though *they were weary,* they turned not aside to the right hand, nor to the left" (I Sam. 6:12). καὶ κατεύθυναν αἱ βόες ἐν τῇ ὁδῷ εἰς ὁδὸν Βαιθσαμυς, ἐν τρίβῳ ἑνὶ ἐπορεύοντο καὶ ἐκοπίων καὶ οὐ μεθίσταντο δεξιὰ οὐδὲ ἀριστερά. In one of Israel's many battles with the Philistines, King Saul forbade them to eat. "And they smote on that day those of the aliens [Philistines] at Michmash, and the people *were* exceedingly *faint,* and the people turned upon the spoils" (I Sam. 14:31). καὶ ἐπάταξεν ἐν τῇ ἡμέρᾳ ἐκείνῃ ἐκ τῶν ἀλλοφύλων ἐν Μαχεμας, καὶ ἐκοπίασεν ὁ λαὸς σφόδρα. The book of Isaiah has one of the most distinctive passages in which this word occurs. He proclaimed that the Everlasting God *"shall* not *become weary."* οὐδὲ κοπιάσει. Then he prophesied that "the young men *shall become weary."* κοπιάσουσιν νεανίσκοι. Finally he gave the great promise "But the ones who wait upon God shall have new strength; they shall put forth fresh feathers like eagles; they shall run and not *become wearied;* they shall march on and shall not faint" (Isa. 40:28, 30, 31). οἱ δὲ ὑπομένοντες τὸν θεὸν ἀλλάξουσιν ἰσχύν, πτεροφυήσουσιν ὡς ἀετοί, δραμοῦνται καὶ οὐ κοπιάσουσιν.

After a long journey, Jesus and His disciples came to Jacob's well. "Therefore Jesus, *having been wearied* from the journey, was sitting thus at the spring" (John 4:6). ὁ οὖν Ἰησοῦς κεκοπιακὼς ἐκ τῆς ὁδοιπορίας ἐκαθέζετο οὕτως ἐπὶ τῇ πηγῇ. The Lord Jesus did experience the bodily weariness common to man. He seeks to relieve men of the weariness brought on by those toils and burdens they need not bear: "Come unto me, all ye *who are toiling* and have been heavily burdened, and I will give you rest" (Matt. 11:28). Δεῦτε πρός με πάντες οἱ κοπιῶντες καὶ πεφορτισμένοι. Although the Apostle Paul had been a persecutor, God's grace was not wasted on him, for he said, "But *I toiled* more abundantly than they all" (I Cor. 15:10). ἀλλὰ περισσότερον αὐτῶν πάντων ἐκοπίασα. When Paul wrote to the changeable Galatians, he said, "I am afraid of you, lest *I have labored* upon you in vain" (Gal. 4:11). φοβοῦμαι ὑμᾶς μή πως εἰκῆ κεκοπίακα εἰς ὑμᾶς. On another occasion he exhorted the Philippians "to be holding forth the word of life, that I may have glory in the day of Christ, that I did not run in vain nor *labor* in vain" (Phil. 2:16). ὅτι οὐκ εἰς κενὸν ἔδραμον οὐδὲ εἰς κενὸν ἐκοπίασα. In one important passage the apostle used both of these words together. After warning Timothy of the dangers and labors ahead of him, Paul said, "For unto this purpose *we are laboring* and *struggling,* because we have hoped upon the living God" (I Tim. 4:10). εἰς τοῦτο γὰρ κοπιῶμεν καὶ ἀγωνιζόμεθα, ὅτι ἠλπίκαμεν ἐπὶ θεῷ ζῶντι. Here the distinction between "toiling to exhaustion" and "straining as an athlete." Paul was confident of his reward.

SUMMARY

The word ἀγωνίζομαι expresses the basic idea of "I contend in the athletic games," although it commonly indicates simply "I strive" or "I struggle." The word κοπιάω means "I toil," "I become weary," or "I struggle," with the root meaning of "hard work" perhaps resulting in pain and faintness.

10. I Teach: διδάσκω, νουθετέω, σωφρονίζω

The usual word for *I teach* is διδάσκω. The word νουθετέω means *I admonish* or *I instruct;* σωφρονίζω, *I bring to one's senses, I make sober-minded,* or *I encourage.*

διδάσκω

Before the chariot race, Nestor encouraged his son, "Antilochus, even though thou art young, still Zeus and Poseidon loved thee and *taught* thee all styles of horsemanship." φίλησαν Ζεύς τε Ποσειδάων τε, καὶ ἱπποσύνας ἐδίδαξαν παντοίας (Homer *Iliad* 23.307). Of Menelaus Homer wrote, "For Artemis herself *taught* him to smite all wild animals." δίδαξε γὰρ Ἄρτεμις αὐτὴ βάλλειν ἄγρια πάντα (*Iliad* 5.51). Thucydides quoted Pericles, "For he who decides on a policy and does not *explain* it clearly to others is the same as though he never had a conception of it." ὅ τε γὰρ γνοὺς καὶ μὴ σαφῶς διδάξας ἐν ἴσῳ καὶ εἰ μὴ ἐνεθυμήθη (2.60.6).

In the Septuagint Moses exhorted the Israelites, "And now, O Israel, hear the righteous ordinances and judgments which *I teach* you to practise this day" (Deut. 4:10). καὶ νῦν, Ισραηλ, ἄκουε τῶν δικαιωμάτων καὶ τῶν κριμάτων, ὅσα ἐγὼ διδάσκω ὑμᾶς σήμερον ποιεῖν. The book of Judges states that the Lord left some of the pagan nations in Palestine for the sake of the children of Israel, "*to teach* them war" (3:2). τοῦ διδάξαι αὐτοὺς πόλεμον. The psalmist said of God, "He *is teaching* my hands to war" (Ps. 17:35; KJ Ps. 18:34). διδάσκων χεῖράς μου εἰς πόλεμον. The book of Proverbs says, "For *I am teaching* thee ways of wisdom" (4:11). ὁδοὺς γὰρ σοφίας διδάσκω σε.

This commonly denoted the activity of our Lord: "And he was going about in the whole of Galilee, *teaching* in their synagogues and preaching the Gospel of the kingdom" (Matt. 4:23). καὶ περιῆγεν ἐν ὅλῃ τῇ Γαλιλαίᾳ, διδάσκων ἐν ταῖς συναλωλαῖς αὐτῶν. That this activity is also the ministry of the Holy Spirit is clear from the Lord Jesus' promise, "But the Comforter, the Holy Spirit, whom the Father shall send in my name, that One *shall teach* you all things" (John 14:26). ἐκεῖνος ὑμᾶς διδάξει πάντα. Paul stated plainly to the Corinthians his reason for sending Timothy to them: Timothy "shall remind you of my ways which are in

A TREASURY OF NEW TESTAMENT SYNONYMS

Christ Jesus, even as *I am teaching* everywhere in every church" (I Cor. 4:14). καθὼς πανταχοῦ ἐν πάσῃ ἐκκλησίᾳ διδάσκω.

νουθετέω

"But this," wrote Herodotus of King Amasis' levity, "displeased his friends, who *admonished* him saying, O king, you have not guided yourself correctly." ἀχθεσθέντες δὲ τούτοισι οἱ φίλοι αὐτοῦ ἐνουθέτεον αὐτόν (2. 173). The suffering Prometheus retorted to the chorus's reproach, "It is easy for one who keeps his foot free from harm to counsel and *to admonish* one who is in misery." ἐλαφρὸν ὅστις πημάτων ἔξω πόδα ἔχει παραινεῖν νουθετεῖν τε τὸν κακῶς πράσσοντ᾽ (Aeschylus *Prometheus Bound* 266). After crying out against Clytemnaestra for murdering her father, Sophocles' Electra complains, "But in *instructing* thee it is useless." ἀλλ᾽ οὐ γὰρ οὐδὲ νουθετεῖν ἔξεστί σε (*Electra* 595).

The Lord told the young Samuel of the coming judgment on the house of Eli "because his sons spoke evil of God, and he [Eli] *did* not *admonish* them" (I Sam. 3:13). ὅτι κακολογοῦντες θεὸν υἱοὶ αὐτοῦ, καὶ οὐκ ἐνουθέτει αὐτούς. The verb νουθετέω occurs with some frequency in the book of Job. Eliphaz, for instance, trying to relate Job's suffering to past wrongdoing, said, "For if thou *didst admonish* many and didst strengthen weak hands . . ." (4:3). εἰ γὰρ σὺ ἐνουθέτησας πολλούς. Later Job complained, "But now they ridicule me; now those who are least *admonish* me, whose fathers I held in contempt" (30:1). ἐλάχιστοι νῦν νουθετοῦσίν με ἐν μέρει.

When Paul addressed the Ephesian elders, he urged them, "Wherefore watch ye, remembering that for three years night and day I did not cease *admonishing* each one with tears" (Acts 20:31). οὐκ ἐπαυσάμην μετὰ δακρύων νουθετῶν ἕνα ἕκαστον. In his first letter to the Corinthians, Paul explained, "I do not write these things to shame you, but to *admonish* you as my beloved children" (4:14). ἀλλ᾽ ὡς τέκνα μου ἀγαπητὰ νουθετῶν. Paul exhorted the Colossians, "Let the word of Christ dwell in you richly, in all wisdom *teaching* and *admonishing* yourselves with psalms, hymns, and spiritual songs" (Col. 3:16). ἐν πάσῃ σοφίᾳ διδάσκοντες καὶ νουθετοῦντες ἑαυτούς, ψαλμοῖς ὕμνοις ᾠδαῖς πνευματικαῖς. To the Thessalonians Paul wrote, "But we exhort you, brethren, *admonish* the disorderly, encourage the fainthearted, support the weak" (I Thess. 5:14). παρακαλοῦμεν δὲ ὑμᾶς, ἀδελφοί, νουθετεῖτε τοὺς ἀτάκτους. In this last passage the word is very close to the meaning "warn."

σωφρονίζω

Thucydides recounted the speech of Hermocrates, in which he said, "But because of these things he wishes that the Syracusans may be humbled,

I TEACH

indeed, in order that we *may be made sober-minded* [brought to our senses]. διὰ δὲ αὐτὰ τὰς Συρακούσας κακωθῆναι μέν, ἵνα σωφρονισθῶμεν, βούλεται (6.78.2). Euripides' Hecuba said to Cassandra, after her daughter's wild speech, "Thy misfortunes, child, *have* not *brought thee to thy senses,* but thou art still raving." οὐδέ σ᾽ αἱ τύχαι, τέκνον, σεσωφρονήκασ᾽ (*Daughters of Troy* 350). Xenophon attributed to Socrates the following observation concerning an apparently common method of handling servants: "But now let us see how masters treat such servants. Do they not starve them to keep them *sober-minded,* lock up their goods to keep them from stealing?" ἆρα οὐ τὴν μὲν λαγνείαν αὐτῶν τῷ λιμῷ σωφρονίζουσι; (*Memorabilia* 2.1.16).

Although this verb does not occur in the Septuagint, a noun form does occur. The book of Wisdom speaks of the fruits of wisdom, "For she teaches *soberness* and understanding, righteousness and courage." σωφροσύνην γὰρ καὶ φρόνησιν ἐκδιδάσκει (8:7). In an unusual papyrus the emperor said to Appianus, who had insulted him, "We are also accustomed *to bring to their senses* those who are mad or beside themselves." ἰώθαμεν καὶ ἡμεῖς μαινομένους καὶ ἀπονενοημένους σωφρινίζειν (*P. Oxy.,* I, 33.4.11).

In the New Testament this word occurs in only one passage. When Paul wrote to Titus, he told him to exhort the older women "that they may *encourage* [bring to their senses] the younger women that they love their husbands, that they love their children, that they may be *sober-minded,* pure, workers at home" (Titus 2:4–5). ἵνα σωφρονίζωσιν τὰς νέας φιλάνδρους εἶναι, φιλοτέκνους, σώφρονας, ἁγνάς, οἰκουργούς. The word almost has the sense of "to instruct" in this context.

SUMMARY

The word διδάσκω is the general term "I teach." The word νουθετέω means "I admonish" or "instruct." Etymologically it means "I put in mind" from τίθημι and νοῦς; it implies a moral earnestness. σωφρονίζω means "I bring to one's senses," "I make sober-minded," or "I encourage." It comes from σῶς and φρονέω, "I make sound-minded."

11. I Think About: φροντίζω, μεριμνάω

Both of these words mean *I think about*—φροντίζω without, and μεριμνάω usually with, anxiety.

φροντίζω

Herodotus relates that Cleisthenes, when he wanted to expel Adrastus, "*was trying to think of* some plan which might rid him of Adrastus." ἐφρόντιζε μηχανὴν τῇ αὐτὸς ὁ Ἄδρηστος ἀπαλλάξεται (5.67). Herodotus elsewhere relates that the Persians levied tribute as far north as the Caucasian mountains, "which," he added, "is as far as the Persian rule reaches, but the country north of the Caucasus *takes no thought for* the Persians." τὰ δὲ πρὸς βορέην ἄνεμον τοῦ Καυκάσιος Περσέων οὐδὲν ἔτι φροντίζει (3.97). In Aeschylus' *Prometheus Bound* Hermes advised Prometheus, "Consider thou warily and *reflect,* and never deem stubbornness better than wise counsel." σὺ δὲ πάπταινε καὶ φρόντιζε (line 1037). In one of the papyri the writer urged, "*Be careful* to send someone immediately to take it." φρόντισον εὐθέως πέμψαι τὸν ληψόμενον αὐτόν (*P. Ryl.,* II, 78.26).

The Septuagint translators used this word when the future king Saul was seeking his father's asses and could not find them. "Saul said to his servant who was with him, Come, let us return, lest my father, forgetting the asses, *be concerned* for us" (I Sam. 9:5). Δεῦρο καὶ ἀναστρέψωμεν, μὴ ἀνεὶς ὁ πατήρ μου τὰς ὄνους φροντίζῃ περὶ ἡμῶν. In view of Saul's commanding stature, the meaning is probably "concern" rather than "anxiety." Job stated concerning his relation to God, "On account of this I gave serious attention to Him; and being chastened, *I thought of* Him" (Job 23:15). διὰ τοῦτο ἐπ᾽ αὐτῷ ἐσπούδακα· νουθετούμενος δὲ ἐφρόντισα αὐτοῦ. When the psalmist encouraged himself in the help and presence of God, he said, "But I am poor and needy; [yet] the Lord *will care for* me" (Ps. 39:18; KJ Ps. 40:17). ἐγὼ δὲ πτωχός εἰμι καὶ πένης· κύριος φροντιεῖ μου. In praise of a virtuous woman Proverbs says, "Her husband, when long abroad, *is* not *concerned for* those at home" (31:21). οὐ φροντίζει τῶν ἐν οἴκῳ ὁ ἀνὴρ αὐτῆς. Ignatius urged Polycarp, "*Care for* unity, for there is nothing better." τῆς ἑνώσεως φρόντιζε, ἧς οὐδὲν ἄμεινον (*Ignatius to Polycarp* 1.2).

I THINK ABOUT

In the New Testament this word occurs only once. When Paul wrote to Titus on the island of Crete, he urged him, "This is a faithful saying, and concerning these things I wish that thou affirm confidently, in order that those who have believed God *may be careful* to keep maintaining good works" (Titus 3:8). ἵνα φροντίζωσιν καλῶν ἔργων προΐστασθαι οἱ πεπιστευκότες θεῷ. There is no idea of anxiety here, but rather the idea that believers should take careful thought to maintain good works. The life of the believer must always agree with his testimony for the Lord.

μεριμνάω

Xenophon recalled some of Socrates' teaching: "But he said that the one who *was anxious* about these things would be in danger even of losing his senses, nothing better than Anaxagoras, the greatest thinker, lost his senses upon leading forth the machines of the gods." κινδυνεῦσαι δ᾽ ἂν ἔφη καὶ παραφρονῆσαι τὸν ταῦτα μεριμνῶντα οὐδὲν ἧττον ἢ Ἀναξαγόρας παρεφρόνησεν ὁ μέγιστον φρονήσας ἐπὶ τῷ τὰς τῶν θεῶν μηχανὰς ἐξηγεῖσθαι (*Memorabilia* 4.7.6). Oedipus asks a herdman, "What kind of work *was* thy *care* or what was thy business?" ἔργον μεριμνῶν ποῖον ἢ βίον τίνα; (Sophocles *Oedipus Rex* 1124). In one of the papyri the writer tries to be reassuring: "But I am now writing in haste to prevent *your being anxious,* for I will see to it that you are not worried." νῦν δὲ μετὰ σπουδῆς γράφω ὅπως μὴ μεριμνῇς, ἐγὼ γάρ σε ἄσκυλτον ποιήσω (*P. Tebt.*, II, 315.9).

When Pharaoh heard that the children of Israel wished to leave the land of Egypt, he commanded, "Let the works of these men be made heavy, and *let them be concerned about* these things, and *let them* not *be concerned about* vain words" (Exod. 5:9). βαρυνέσθω τὰ ἔργα τῶν ἀνθρώπων τούτων, καὶ μεριμνάτωσαν ταῦτα καὶ μὴ μεριμνάτωσαν ἐν λόγοις κενοῖς. God gave to David great promises after David had expressed the desire to build a temple for God. The Lord promised him, "And I will appoint a place for my people Israel, and I will plant them, and they shall dwell by themselves, and *they shall* no longer *be anxious,* and no son of wickedness shall afflict them, as from the beginning" (II Sam. 7:10). καὶ καταφυτεύσω αὐτόν, καὶ κατασκηνώσει καθ᾽ ἑαυτὸν καὶ οὐ μεριμνήσει οὐκέτι. The psalmist said, "For I will declare my lawlessness and *will be anxious* over my sin" (Ps. 37:19; KJ Ps. 38:18). ὅτι τὴν ἀνομίαν μου ἐγὼ ἀναγγελῶ καὶ μεριμνήσω ὑπὲρ τῆς ἁμαρτίας μου. After God had prophesied judgment on the sins of Israel, He added in a curious Septuagint translation, "And I will cause my wrath upon thee to cease, and my jealousy shall depart from thee, and I shall rest and *shall* no longer *be anxious*" (Ezek. 16:42). ἐξαρθήσεται ὁ ζῆλός μου ἐκ σοῦ, καὶ ἀναπαύσομαι καὶ οὐ μὴ μεριμνήσω οὐκέτι. Perhaps the Septuagint rendering of this phrase is a simple translation error; the Hebrew word rendered "to cease from being anxious" means literally "to cease from being angry."

In the New Testament the Lord Jesus exhorted His followers, "On account of this I say to you, *Stop being anxious* for your life, what ye shall eat, or what ye shall drink" (Matt. 6:25). μὴ μεριμνᾶτε τῇ ψυχῇ ὑμῶν τί φάγητε. Immediately afterwards our Lord asked, "Which of you *by being anxious* can add one cubit unto his stature?" (Matt. 6:27). τίς δὲ ἐξ ὑμῶν μεριμνῶν δύναται προσθεῖναι ἐπὶ τὴν ἡλικίαν αὐτοῦ πῆχυν ἕνα; When Paul exhorted the Corinthians to unity, he wrote "that there should be no schism in the body, but that the members *should have* the same *concern* for one another" (I Cor. 12:25). ἀλλὰ τὸ αὐτὸ ὑπὲρ ἀλλήλων μεριμνῶσιν τὰ μέλη. Paul promised the church at Philippi that he would send Timothy to them, "For I have no man likeminded, who *will* truly *be concerned* for your state" (Phil. 2:20). οὐδένα γὰρ ἔχω ἰσόψυχον, ὅστις γνησίως τὰ περὶ ὑμῶν μεριμνήσει. In a familiar exhortation Paul said: "*Be anxious* for nothing, but in everything by prayer and supplication with thanksgiving let your requests be made known to God" (Phil. 4:6). μηδὲν μεριμνᾶτε, ἀλλ᾽ ἐν παντὶ τῇ προσευχῇ καὶ τῇ δεήσει. These last two passages show that this word may be used without the sense of worldly anxiety (Phil. 2:20) or with it (Phil. 4:6). Only the context can determine the exact connotation.

SUMMARY

Both of these verbs may be used in a neutral sense with the meaning "I am concerned about." However, φροντίζω may mean "I am careful" without great anxiety, whereas μεριμνάω may mean "I am anxious" with the connotation of a considerable amount of worldly care.

12. I Watch: τηρέω, φυλάσσω, φρουρέω, γρηγορέω, ἀγρυπνέω, νήφω

Each of these verbs indicates some kind of watching. The first three denote *I guard,* often with a military connotation: τηρέω, the most general term, may mean *I guard, watch, observe,* or *keep safely,* with no necessity of a military sense; on the other hand φυλάσσω usually means *I guard from outside attack* and φρουρέω often means *I guard by occupying with troops* or *I guard by putting in prison.* Each of these three words has a cognate noun which means *guard* or *guard post:* τηρός, φύλαξ, φρούριον. The last three words mean *I stay awake* or *alert:* γρηγορέω and ἀγρυπνέω, very close synonyms, both mean *I stay awake* or *I keep watch;* νήφω means *I am sober* or *I am self-controlled.*

τηρέω

Thucydides relates a speech of Hermocrates in which he warned of "the Athenians, who have military power greater than that of any of the other Hellenic states and are now at hand with a few ships *to watch closely* for our mistakes." οἱ δύναμιν ἔχοντες μεγίστην τῶν Ἑλλήνων τάς τε ἁμαρτίας ἡμῶν τηροῦσιν ὀλίγαις ναυσὶ παρόντες (4.60). In another passage Thucydides tells how the ephors trapped an enemy in a temple: "and *watching* until he was inside and cutting off his retreat, they walled up the doors, and invested the place and starved him to death." καὶ τὰς θύρας ἔνδον ὄντα τηρήσαντες αὐτὸν καὶ ἀπολαβόντες ἔσω ἀπῳκοδόμησαν (1.134). The chorus of clouds in Aristophanes chants, "We who always *guard* you." αἵτινες τηροῦμεν ὑμᾶς (*The Clouds* 579). Aristotle, discussing concord and discord, says, "But while each one desires these things for himself, he spies on his neighbor to prevent him from doing the same; for unless *they keep watch* over one another, the common interests are ruined." ἑαυτῷ δ᾽ ἕκαστος βουλόμενος ταῦτα τὸν πέλας ἐξετάζει καὶ κωλύει· μὴ γὰρ τηρούντων τὸ κοινὸν ἀπόλλυται (*Ethics* 9.6.4). In one of the papyri the writer said, "*I am keeping* for the trial the money that I have collected." σεσύλληχα δὲ κέρματα τηρῶ αὐτὰ εἰς τὴν δίκην (*P. Oxy.,* VIII, 1160.16).

The Septuagint translators gave the word an unusual meaning in the "Protevangelium." The Lord told the serpent concerning the coming Deliverer, "*He shall watch for* [*i.e.* to wound] thy head, and thou *shalt watch for* his heel" (Gen. 3:15). αὐτός σου τηρήσει κεφαλήν, καὶ σὺ τηρήσεις αὐτοῦ πτέρναν. Proverbs says, "My son, forget not my rules, but *let* thy heart *keep* my words" (3:1). τὰ δὲ ῥήματά μου τηρείτω σὴ καρδία. Twice Proverbs uses τηρέω and φυλάσσω together. In one place Proverbs says, "Good counsel *will guard* thee, and holy understanding *will keep* thee" (2:11). βουλὴ καλὴ φυλάξει σε, ἔννοια δὲ ὁσία τηρήσει σε. The counsel will guard from external foes, and the understanding will keep safe within. With a somewhat different meaning Proverbs says, "He who *guards* his own mouth *keeps* his own life" (13:3). ὃς φυλάσσει τὸ ἑαυτοῦ στόμα, τηρεῖ τὴν ἑαυτοῦ ψυχήν. Thus it is by no means necessary for φυλάσσω to mean "I guard from external attack."

In the New Testament τηρέω has a variety of meanings. After the magistrates had beaten Paul and Silas at Philippi, "they cast them into prison, charging the jailor *to guard* them securely" (Acts 16:23). ἔβαλον εἰς φυλακήν, παραγγείλαντες τῷ δεσμοφύλακι ἀσφαλῶς τηρεῖν αὐτούς. Paul exhorted Timothy, "*Keep* thyself pure" (I Tim. 5:22). σεαυτὸν ἁγνὸν τήρει. Peter assured believers that they have come "unto an inheritance incorruptible and undefiled and unfading, *having been reserved* in heaven for you" (I Pet. 1:4). εἰς κληρονομίαν ἄφθαρτον καὶ ἀμίαντον καὶ ἀμάραντον, τετηρημένην ἐν οὐρανοῖς εἰς ὑμᾶς. After the soldiers had finished crucifying the Lord Jesus, "sitting down, they *were watching* him there" (Matt. 27:36). καθήμενοι ἐτήρουν αὐτὸν ἐκεῖ.

φυλάσσω

When Hector called together the rulers of the Trojans, he sent Dolon to spy out the camp of the Greeks to see whether they were "planning flight among themselves, not wishing *to watch* the night through, being worn out with weariness." οὐδ᾽ ἐθέλουσι νύκτα φυλασσέμεναι, καμάτῳ ἀδηκότες αἰνῷ (Homer, *Iliad* 10.312). Plainly Hector wished to know whether the Greek camp was guarded against outside attack before he started such an attack. Athena commanded Odysseus to sail by night as well as by day, "and one of the immortals, who *guards* and delivers thee, will send a fair breeze in thy wake." πέμψει δέ τοι οὖρον ὄπισθεν ἀθανάτων ὅς τίς σε φυλάσσει τε ῥύεταί τε (Homer *Odyssey* 15. 35). In Aeschylus' *The Seven Against Thebes* the chorus chants, "Thou too, O Ares (woe! woe!), *guard* the city that bears the name of Cadmus." σύ τ᾽, Ἄρης, φεῦ, φεῦ, πόλιν ἐπώνυμον Κάδμου φύλαξον (line 136). When Astyages wished to slay Cyrus at his birth, he sent for his daughter, "and when she came, he *kept* her *guarded*, desiring to slay whatever child was born from her." ἀπικο-

I WATCH

μένην δὲ ἐφύλασσε βουλόμενος τὸ γενόμενον ἐξ αὐτῆς διαφθεῖραι (1.108). All of these examples suggest a guarding from outside attack or interference.

In the Septuagint account of creation "the Lord God took the man whom he had made and placed him in the paradise to work it and *to guard it*" (Gen. 2:15). καὶ ἔθετο αὐτὸν ἐν τῷ παραδείσῳ ἐργάζεσθαι αὐτὸν καὶ φυλάσσειν. After the fall of man, the Lord cast out Adam "and placed the Cherubim and the whirling, flaming sword *to guard* the way of the tree of life" (Gen. 3:24). καὶ τὴν φλογίνην ῥομφαίαν τὴν στρεφομένην φυλάσσειν τὴν ὁδὸν τοῦ ξύλου τῆς ζωῆς. When Jacob was bargaining for his wages, he said to Laban, "If thou wilt do this thing for me, I will again shepherd thy sheep and *keep guard*" (Gen. 30:31). πάλιν ποιμανῶ τὰ πρόβατά σου καὶ φυλάξω. At the giving of the law on Mount Sinai the Lord said to Moses, "Now if ye shall hear my voice and *keep* my covenant, ye shall be my own people" (Exod. 19:5). νῦν ἐὰν ἀκοῇ ἀκούσητε τῆς ἐμῆς φωνῆς καὶ φυλάξητε τὴν διαθήκην μου. Here the sense of the word is "I observe."

In the New Testament φυλάσσω may have this same meaning. When the Lord Jesus pointed out the commandments to the rich young man, he said to Jesus, "All these things *I observed;* what do I lack yet?" (Matt. 19:20). ταῦτα πάντα ἐφύλαξα· τί ἔτι ὑστερῶ; But the meaning "I guard from outside attack" is also common in the New Testament. In the night in which the Lord was born, Luke tells us, "there were shepherds in the same country abiding in the field and *keeping watch* [literally guarding guards] by night over their flock" (Luke 2:8). ποιμένες ἦσαν ἐν τῇ χώρᾳ τῇ αὐτῇ ἀγραυλοῦντες καὶ φυλάσσοντες φυλακὰς τῆς νυκτός. When Paul made his defense before the Jews in Jerusalem, he testified, "When the blood of Stephen, thy witness, was shed, I myself was also standing by and consenting and *guarding* the garments of those who were slaying him" (Acts 22:20). καὶ αὐτὸς ἤμην ἐφεστὼς καὶ συνευδοκῶν καὶ φυλάσσων τὰ ἱμάτια τῶν ἀναιρούντων αὐτόν. In his second epistle to the Thessalonians Paul declared, "But the Lord is faithful, who shall establish you and *guard* you from the evil one" (3:3). πιστὸς δέ ἐστιν ὁ κύριος, ὃς στηρίξει ὑμᾶς καὶ φυλάξει ἀπὸ τοῦ. The verb φυλάσσω may also mean "to guard as a prisoner": when he was finally brought to Rome, "Paul was permitted to remain by himself with the soldier who *was guarding* him" (Acts 28:16). ἐπετράπη τῷ Παύλῳ μένειν καθ' ἑαυτὸν σὺν τῷ φυλάσσοντι αὐτὸν στρατιώτῃ. The sense, then, "to guard from outside attack" is not always present in φυλάσσω; but, as Milligan points out, when this verb is used in preference to its synonyms, the distinction intended is that of guarding against an outside enemy or attack (*Thessalonians,* p. 111).

A TREASURY OF NEW TESTAMENT SYNONYMS

φρουρέω

In his description of Egypt, Herodotus said, "But still in my time the *guards* of the Persians are throughout these areas as also in the time of Psammetichus; for also Persians *are standing guard* at Elephantine and at Daphnae." Περσέων κατὰ ταὐτὰ αἱ φυλακαὶ ἔχουσι ὡς καὶ ἐπὶ Ψαμμητίχου ἦσαν· καὶ γὰρ ἐν Ἐλεφαντίνῃ Πέρσαι φρουρέουσι καὶ ἐν Δάφνῃσι (2.30). When Herodotus mentioned the wages that King Darius paid to his troops, he said, "But a hundred and forty of these [talents] were expended on the horsemen who *were guarding* the country of Cilicia." τούτων δὲ τεσσεράκοντα καὶ ἑκατὸν ἐς τὴν φρουρέουσαν ἵππον τὴν Κιλικίην χώρην ἀναισιμοῦτο (3.90). Thucydides related that "one hundred ships *were guarding* Attica, Euboea, and Salamis." Ἀττικὴν καὶ Εὔβοιαν καὶ Σαλαμῖνα ἑκατὸν ἐφύλασσον (3.17.2). Then he added, "The hoplites *were guarding* [laying siege to] Potidaea for wages of two drachmas a day." Ποτίδαιαν δίδραχμοι ὁπλῖται ἐφρούρουν (3.17.3). Aeschylus has the god Apollo say, "For marriage between man and woman, appointed by fate, is greater than an oath and *is being guarded* by Justice." εὐνὴ γὰρ ἀνδρὶ καὶ γυναικὶ μόρσιμος ὅρκου 'στι μείζων τῇ δίκῃ φρουρουμένη (*Eumenides.* 218). One of the papyri says, "At Kerkeosiris, which *is* not *garrisoned* and is not located on the great river." Κερκεοσίρεως τῆς μὴ φρουρουμένης μηδ' οὔσης ἐπὶ τοῦ μεγάλου ποταμοῦ (*P. Tebt.,* I, 92.2). Thus φρουρέω is often used like φυλάσσω with the meaning "to guard from outside attack"; but it is usually used with the specific meaning "to guard with troops" or "to garrison."

In the Septuagint King Darius is pictured as lending help to the Jews. "And to all who *were guarding* the city he wrote to give them lands and wages." καὶ πᾶσι τοῖς φρουροῦσι τὴν πόλιν (I Esdras 4:56). The book of Wisdom speaks concerning the judgments on the Egyptians during the plagues, "So then, whoever the person might be, falling down there, he *was kept under guard,* being shut up in prison not barred with iron." ἐφρουρεῖτο εἰς τὴν ἀσίδηρον εἱρκτὴν κατακλεισθείς (17:15; KJ 17:16). I Maccabees, describing the invasion of Ptolemy, records, "But as he was entering the cities of Ptolemais, he was setting his forces *for a garrison* in each city." ἀπέτασσε τὰς δυνάμεις φρουρὰν ἐν ἑκάστῃ πόλει (11:3).

These same uses appear in the New Testament. Paul describing the persecution he faced after his conversion, wrote, "In Damascus the ethnarch under Aretas, the king, *was guarding* [garrisoning] the city of the Damascenes in order to take me" (II Cor. 11:32). ἐν Δαμασκῷ ὁ ἐθνάρχης Ἀρέτα τοῦ βασιλέως ἐφρούρει τὴν πόλιν. The same meaning, but with a happier context, may be seen in the promise to the Philippians, "And the peace of God, which surpasses all understanding, *shall guard* [garrison] your hearts and your minds in Christ Jesus" (Phil. 4:7). ἡ εἰρήνη τοῦ θεοῦ ἡ ὑπερέχουσα πάντα νοῦν φρουρήσει τὰς καρδίας ὑμῶν. Paul used the harsher meaning "to guard as a prisoner" when he wrote to the Galatians, "But before faith came, we *were held in custody* [guarded as prisoners] under the law, being shut up unto the about-to-be-revealed faith" (Gal. 3:23). πρὸ τοῦ δὲ ἐλθεῖν τὴν πίστιν ὑπὸ νόμον ἐφρουρούμεθα συγκλειόμενοι εἰς τὴν μέλλουσαν πίστιν ἀποκαλυφθῆναι. Thus the use of troops either as a protection or as a restriction is implied.

γρηγορέω

This is a late Greek word originating from a perfect tense form of ἐγείρω. In one of the minor works of Aristotle this word occurs several times: "But how can this be, seeing that we find many animals which have no breath, and again (accurately) we find that plants neither sleep nor *wake*? For *awakening* means nothing apart from the conditions of sensation, and sleeping means nothing but the weakening of this." ὅτι τὰ φυτὰ οὔτε ὑπνώττουσιν οὔτε γρηγοροῦσιν. τὸ γὰρ γρηγορεῖν οὐδέν ἐστιν εἰ μὴ ἀπὸ διαθέσεως τῆς αἰσθήσεως (*On Plants*, 1.2.2).

In the Septuagint Nehemiah charged his faithful helpers, "The gates of Jerusalem shall not be opened until sunrise, and while they *are* still *watching,* let the doors be shut and bolted, and appoint *watches* of the inhabitants in Jerusalem" (II Esdras 17:3; KJ Neh. 7:3). οὐκ ἀνοιγήσονται πύλαι Ιερουσαλημ ἕως ἅμα τῷ ἡλίῳ, καὶ ἔτι αὐτῶν γρηγορούντων κλειέσθωσαν αἱ θύραι καὶ σφηνούσθωσαν· καὶ στῆσον προφύλακας οἰκούντων ἐν Ιερουσαλημ. Jeremiah pronounced a warning against the Jews who turned away from the law of God: "A leopard *has watched* [lain in wait] against their cities" (Jer. 5:6). πάρδαλις ἐγρηγόρησεν ἐπὶ τὰς πόλεις αὐτῶν. In Theodotion's version of Daniel's prayer, Daniel says, "And the Lord *watched* and brought upon us these things" (Dan. 9:14). καὶ ἐγρηγόρησεν κύριος καὶ ἐπήγαγεν αὐτὰ ἐφ' ἡμᾶς. But in the Septuagint a form of the word ἀγρυπνέω is used. "And the Lord God *watched* over the evil things" (Dan. 9:14). καὶ ἠγρύπνησε κύριος ὁ θεὸς ἐπὶ τὰ κακά. Theodotion obviously felt that these words were very close synonyms. When Jonathan was warned of a night attack, I Maccabees says, "But as soon as the sun set, Jonathan commanded his men *to watch* and to be in arms that they might be ready for battle all through the night, and he sent forth *guards* in a circle around the camp." ὡς δὲ ἔδυ ὁ ἥλιος ἐπέταξεν Ιωναθαν τοῖς παρ' αὐτοῦ γρηγορεῖν καὶ εἶναι ἐπὶ τοῖς ὅπλοις ἑτοιμάζεσθαι εἰς πόλεμον δι' ὅλης τῆς νυκτὸς καὶ ἐξέβαλεν προφύλακας κύκλῳ τῆς παρεμβολῆς (12:27).

A TREASURY OF NEW TESTAMENT SYNONYMS

The Lord Jesus concluded the parable of the fig tree, saying, *"Watch ye* therefore, because ye know not in what day your Lord comes. But know ye this, that if the master of the house had known in what *watch* the thief would come, he *would have watched"* (Matt. 24:42-43). γρηγορεῖτε οὖν, ὅτι οὐκ οἴδατε ποίᾳ ἡμέρᾳ ὁ κύριος ὑμῶν ἔρχεται. Ἐκεῖνο δὲ γινώσκετε ὅτι εἰ ᾔδει ὁ οἰκοδεσπότης ποίᾳ φυλακῇ ὁ κλέπτης ἔρχεται, ἐγρηγόρησεν ἄν. In the garden the Lord said to Peter, James, and John, "My soul is exceedingly grieved, even unto death; abide ye here and *watch* with me" (Matt. 26:38). περίλυπός ἐστιν ἡ ψυχή μου ἕως θανάτου· μείνατε ὧδε καὶ γρηγορεῖτε μετ᾽ ἐμοῦ. The Apostle Paul exhorted the Corinthians, *"Watch ye,* stand fast in the faith, act like men, be strong" (I Cor. 16:13). γρηγορεῖτε, στήκετε ἐν τῇ πίστει, ἀνδρίζεσθε, κραταιοῦσθε. Paul urged the Thessalonians, "Therefore then let us not sleep, as the rest, but *let us watch* and *be sober"*(I Thes. 5:6). ἄρα οὖν μὴ καθεύδωμεν ὡς οἱ λοιποί, ἀλλὰ γρηγορῶμεν καὶ νήφωμεν. Here the meaning seems to be to stay alert both by avoiding sleep and by avoiding strong drink.

ἀγρυπνέω

Xenophon reported that Pheraulas said, "But you shall be convinced that what I say is true, for not one of those who are rich is made *sleepless* for joy, but of those who lose something you will not see anyone who is able to sleep for grief." γνώσει δ᾽ ὅτι ἐγὼ ἀληθῆ λέγω· τῶν μὲν γὰρ πλουτούντων οὐδεὶς ἀναλκάζεται ὑφ᾽ ἡδονῆς ἀγρυπνεῖν, τῶν δὲ ἀποβαλλόντων τι ὄψει οὐδένα δυνάμενον καθεύδειν ὑπὸ λύπης (*Cyropaedia* 8.3.42). A papyrus mentions one who "is being kept *sleepless* and is being punished." ἀγρυπνεῖται καὶ κολάζεται (*P. Ryl.*, II, 62.9).

In the Septuagint David fasted and prayed when the child of Bathsheba was smitten, but after it died, he began to eat. "And his servants said to him, What is this thing which thou didst do? On account of the child while it was yet living, thou didst fast and weep and *didst keep* thyself *awake"*(II Sam. 12:21). Τί τὸ ῥῆμα τοῦτο, ὃ ἐποίησας; ἕνεκα τοῦ παιδαρίου ἔτι ζῶντος ἐνήστευες καὶ ἔκλαιες καὶ ἠγρύπνεις. The psalmist prayed out of his affliction, *"I spent sleepless nights* and became like a solitary bird on the roof" (Ps. 101:8; KJ Ps. 102:7). ἠγρύπνησα καὶ ἐγενήθην ὡσεὶ στρουθίον μονάζον ἐπὶ δώματι. Proverbs uses several of these words in a single verse: "Blessed is the man who will hearken to me, and the man who *will guard* my ways, *keeping watch* every day at my gates, *waiting* at the posts of my doors" (8:34). μακάριος ἀνήρ, ὃς εἰσακούσεταί μου, καὶ ἄνθρωπος, ὃς τὰς ἐμὰς ὁδοὺς φυλάξει ἀγρυπνῶν ἐπ᾽ ἐμαῖς θύραις καθ᾽ ἡμέραν τηρῶν σταθμοὺς ἐμῶν εἰσόδων.

I WATCH

When the Lord Jesus taught the parable of the fig tree in Mark, He exhorted the disciples, "Take heed, *watch ye,* for ye know not when the time is" (Mark 13:33). βλέπετε, ἀγρυπνεῖτε· οὐκ οἴδατε γὰρ πότε ὁ καιρός ἐστιν. But in the same context the Lord said, *"Watch* therefore, for ye know not when the lord of the house comes" (Mark 13:35). γρηγορεῖτε οὖν· οὐκ οἴδατε γὰρ πότε ὁ κύριος τῆς οἰκίας ἔρχεται. Thus it would be difficult to draw a distinction between these two words. Paul exhorted believers to be "praying at every season in the Spirit, and *watching* unto it with all perseverance and supplication" (Eph. 6:18). προσευχόμενοι ἐν παντὶ καιρῷ ἐν πνεύματι, καὶ εἰς αὐτὸ ἀγρυπνοῦντες ἐν πάσῃ προσκαρτερήσει καὶ δεήσει. The writer to the Hebrews charged his readers, "Obey the ones who have the rule over you and submit to them, for they themselves *watch* in behalf of your souls as those who must give account" (Heb. 13:17). αὐτοὶ γὰρ ἀγρυπνοῦσιν ὑπὲρ τῶν ψυχῶν ὑμῶν. Paul used the noun form of this verb when he told the Corinthians that he was "in *watchings* many times" (II Cor. 11:27). ἐν ἀγρυπνίαις πολλάκις. In the context it means that Paul went without sleep many times.

νήφω

Plato has Alcibiades retort to Eryximachus, "Thou sayest well, but to pit a drunken man against *sober* words is hardly fair." καλῶς μὲν λέγεις, μεθύοντα δὲ ἄνδρα παρὰ νηφόντων λόγους παραβάλλειν μὴ οὐκ ἐξ ἴσου ᾖ (*Symposium* 214C). A more raucous exchange in Aristophanes has the second Athenian saying, "Rightly, when *we're sober,* we're not healthy, which I shall persuade the Athenians saying, We ought to send envoys always everywhere being drunk!" ὀρθῶς γ᾽, ὁτιὴ νήφοντες οὐχ ὑγιαίνομεν. ἢν τοὺς Ἀθηναίους ἐγὼ πείσω λέγων, μεθύοντες ἀεὶ πανταχοῦ πρεσβεύσομεν (*Lysistrata* 1228). One of the papyri has the statement, "But I will send to thee the very letter by Syrus in order that thou mayest read it, *being sober,* and mayest condemn thyself." αὐτὴν δέ σοι τὴν ἐπιστολὴν πέμψω διὰ Σύρον ἵνα αὐτὴν ἀναγνοῖς νήφων καὶ σαυτοῦ καταγνοῖς (*P. Oxy.,* VII, 1062.13).

Although this word does not occur at all in the Septuagint, there are a number of occurrences in the New Testament. Paul exhorted the Thessalonians, "Let us, who are of the day, *be sober"* (I Thess. 5:8). ἡμεῖς δὲ ἡμέρας ὄντες νήφωμεν. Paul in his second letter to Timothy urged him, "But *be thou sober* in all things, suffer hardship, do the work of an evangelist" (II Tim. 4:5). σὺ δὲ νῆφε ἐν πᾶσιν. Peter exhorted, *"Be sober, watch ye.* The devil, your adversary, as a roaring lion is walking about, seeking whom he may devour" (I Pet. 5:8). Νήψατε, γρηγορήσατε. ὁ ἀντίδικος ὑμῶν διάβολος ὡς λέων ὠρυόμενος περιπατεῖ.

A TREASURY OF NEW TESTAMENT SYNONYMS

SUMMARY

The word τηρέω is the most general of this group, meaning "I watch," "guard," "keep safely," or "observe." The word φυλάσσω usually denotes "I guard from outside attack"; very close in meaning is φρουρέω, denoting "I guard with troops," either by occupying a city or by putting a person in prison. The word γρηγορέω has the sense of mental alertness with the meaning "I watch" or "I keep awake." Another word which may have these same meanings is ἀγρυπνέω, which has the sense of avoiding sleep. The word νήφω means "I am sober," with the idea of being alert by avoiding strong drink.

Bibliography

A. GENERAL WORKS ON SYNONYMS OR SEMANTICS

Barr, James. *The Semantics of Biblical Language.* London: Oxford Univ. Press, 1961.

Bridges, Ronald, and Luther Weigle. *The Bible Word Book.* New York: Thomas Nelson, 1960.

Buck, Carl Darling. *A Dictionary of Selected Synonyms in the Principal Indo-European Languages.* Chicago: Univ. of Chicago Press, 1949.

Collins, Vere Henry. *The Choice of Words.* London: Longmans, 1952.

Fernald, James C. *Funk and Wagnalls Standard Handbook of Synonyms, Antonyms, and Prepositions.* New York: Funk and Wagnalls, 1947.

Girdlestone, Robert Baker. *Synonyms of the Old Testament.* Grand Rapids: Eerdmans, 1897 (Reprinted).

Lewis, Clives Staples. *Studies in Words.* Cambridge: Cambridge Univ. Press, 1961.

Linsky, Leonard, ed. *Semantics and the Philosophy of Language.* Urbana: Univ. of Illinois Press, 1952.

Nida, Eugene A. *Toward a Science of Translating.* Leiden: Brill, 1964.

Smith, Stephenson. *The Command of Words.* New York: Crowell, 1949.

Sondel, Bess. *The Humanity of Words.* New York: World, 1958.

Soule, Richard. *A Dictionary of English Synonyms.* Ed. Alfred Dwight Sheffield. New York: Bantam, 1960.

Stern, Gustaf. *Meaning and Change of Meaning.* Bloomington: Indiana Univ. Press, 1931.

Trench, Richard Chenevix. *Synonyms of the New Testament.* 1876; rpt. Grand Rapids: Eerdmans Publishing Company, n.d.

―――. *The Study of Words.* New York: Redfield, 1855.

Ullmann, Stephen. *Semantics: An Introduction to the Science of Meaning.* New York: Barnes and Noble, 1962.

Walpole, Hugh. *Semantics.* New York: Norton, 1941.

Webster. *Dictionary of Synonyms.* Springfield, Mass.: G. and C. Merriam, 1942.

A TREASURY OF NEW TESTAMENT SYNONYMS

B. Greek Lexicons

Abbott-Smith, G. *Manual Greek Lexicon of the New Testament.* Edinburgh: Clark, 1921.

Arndt, William F., and F. Wilbur Gingrich. *A Greek-English Lexicon of the New Testament and Other Early Christian Literature.* Chicago: Univ. of Chicago Press, 1957.

Autenrieth, Georg. *A Homeric Dictionary.* New York: American Book Company, 1904.

Berry, George Ricker. *A New Greek-English Lexicon to the New Testament.* Chicago: Wilcox and Follett, 1897.

Cremer, Hermann. *Biblico-Theological Lexicon of New Testament Greek.* Edinburgh: Clark, 1872.

Elliott, Leslie R. *A Comparative Lexicon of New Testament Greek.* Kansas City: Central Seminary Press, 1945.

Kittel, Gerhard. *Theological Dictionary of the New Testament.* 8 vols. Grand Rapids: Eerdmans, 1964.

Lampe, G. W. H. *A Patristic Greek Lexicon.* Oxford: Clarendon, 1961.

Liddell, Henry, and Robert Scott. *A Greek-English Lexicon.* 9th ed. Oxford: Clarendon, 1940.

Metzger, Bruce M. *Lexical Aids for Students of New Testament Greek.* Princeton, N.J.: the author, 1946.

Moulton, James Hope, and George Milligan. *The Vocabulary of the Greek New Testament.* Grand Rapids: Eerdmans, 1949.

Sophocles, Evangelinus Apostolides. *Greek Lexicon of the Roman and Byzantine Periods.* 2 vols. New York: Ungar, 1887.

Thayer, Joseph Henry. *A Greek-English Lexicon of the New Testament.* New York: American Book Company, 1889.

C. Other Reference Works

Alford, Henry. *The Greek Testament.* 4 vols. London: Rivingtons, 1874.

Hastings, James. *Dictionary of the Bible.* New York: Scribners, 1909.

Hatch, Edwin, and Henry Redpath. *A Concordance to the Septuagint.* 2 vols. Oxford: Clarendon, 1897.

International Standard Bible Encyclopaedia. Gen. ed. James Orr. 5 vols. Grand Rapids: Eerdmans, 1939.

Moulton, William Fiddian, and Alfred Shenington Geden. *A Concordance to the Greek Testament.* Edinburgh: Clark, 1953.

The New Schaff-Herzog Encyclopedia of Religious Knowledge. Gen. ed. Samuel M. Jackson. New York: Funk and Wagnalls, 1908.

Nicoll, W. Robertson, ed. *The Expositor's Greek Testament.* 5 vols. Grand Rapids: Eerdmans, 1951.
Robertson, Archibald Thomas. *Word Pictures in the New Testament.* 6 vols. Nashville: Broadman, 1930.
Vincent, Marvin R. *Word Studies in the New Testament.* 4 vols. Grand Rapids: Eerdmans, 1887.
Young, Robert. *Analytical Concordance to the Bible.* Grand Rapids: Eerdmans, 1951.
―――. *Dictionary of Bible Words and Synonyms.* London: Pickering and Inglis, 1883.

D. Related Monographs

Alexander, Archibald B. D. *The Ethics of St. Paul.* Glasgow: Maclehose, 1910.
Barclay, William. *A New Testament Wordbook.* London: SCM, 1955.
―――. *Flesh and Spirit.* Nashville: Abingdon, 1962.
―――. *More New Testament Words.* New York: Harper, 1958.
Barr, James. *Biblical Words For Time.* Naperville, Ill.: Allenson, 1962.
Blass, Friedrich Wilhelm, and Albert Debrunner. *A Greek Grammar of the New Testament.* Trans. Robert W. Funk. Chicago: Univ. of Chicago Press, 1961.
Broadus, John A. *Commentary on the Gospel of Matthew.* Philadelphia: American Baptist Publication Society, 1886.
Buck, Carl Darling. *Comparative Grammar of Greek and Latin.* Chicago: Univ. of Chicago Press, 1933.
Burton, Ernest De Witt. *The Epistle to the Galatians.* International Critical Commentary. New York: Scribner's, 1920.
Crosby, Henry, and John Schaeffer. *An Introduction to Greek.* New York: Allyn and Bacon, 1928.
Cullmann, Oscar. *Christ and Time.* Philadelphia, Westminster, 1950.
Daube, David. *The "Sudden" in the Scriptures.* Leiden: Brill, 1964.
Deissmann, Adolf. *Light From the Ancient East.* New York: Harper, 1922.
Ellis, E. Earle. *Paul's Use of the Old Testament.* Grand Rapids: Eerdmans, 1957.
Fobes, Francis H. *Philosophical Greek.* Chicago: Univ. of Chicago Press, 1957.
Fuller, Reginald H. *The Foundations of New Testament Christology.* New York: Scribner's, 1965.
Gale, Herbert M. *The Use of Analogy in the Letters of Paul.* Philadelphia: Westminster, 1964.

Hatch, Edwin. *Essays in Biblical Greek.* Oxford: Clarendon, 1889.

Hobbs, Herschel L. *Preaching Values from the Papyri.* Grand Rapids: Baker, 1964.

Hodge, Charles. *Commentary on the Epistle to the Romans.* Grand Rapids: Eerdmans, 1953.

Hort, Fenton J. A. *The Christian Ecclesia.* London: Macmillan, 1898.

———. *The First Epistle of St. Peter I.1—II.17.* New York: Macmillan, 1898.

Jeremias, Joachim. *The Central Message of the New Testament.* New York: Scribner's, 1965.

Leete, Frederick. *New Testament Windows.* New York: Funk and Wagnalls, 1939.

Lightfoot, Joseph Barber. *Dissertations on the Apostolic Age.* London: Macmillan, 1892.

———. *The Epistle of St. Paul to the Galatians.* 1865; rpt. Grand Rapids: Zondervan, n.d.

———. *Notes on Epistles of St. Paul from Unpublished Commentaries.* London: Macmillan, 1895.

———. *Saint Paul's Epistle to the Philippians.* London: Macmillan, 1898.

———. *Saint Paul's Epistles to the Colossians and to Philemon.* London: Macmillan, 1879.

Marsh, John. *The Fulness of Time.* New York: Harper, 1952.

Mickelsen, A. Berkeley. *Interpreting the Bible.* Grand Rapids: Eerdmans, 1963.

Milligan, George. *St. Paul's Epistles to the Thessalonians.* Grand Rapids: Eerdmans, 1908.

Moule, Charles Francis Digby. *An Idiom Book of New Testament Greek.* 2nd ed. Cambridge: Cambridge Univ. Press, 1959.

Pharr, Clyde. *Homeric Greek.* New York: Heath, 1920.

Ramsay, Sir William M. *A Historical Commentary on St. Paul's Epistle to the Galatians.* London: Hodder and Stoughton, 1899.

Ridderbos, Herman N. *The Epistle of Paul to the Churches of Galatia.* Grand Rapids: Eerdmans, 1953.

Robertson, Archibald Thomas. *A Grammar of the Greek New Testament in the Light of Historical Research.* Nashville: Broadman, 1934.

Sanday, William, and Arthur Headlam. *Commentary on the Epistle to the Romans.* International Critical Commentary. Edinburgh: Clark, 1902.

Schep, J. A. *The Nature of the Resurrection Body.* Grand Rapids: Eerdmans, 1964.

BIBLIOGRAPHY

Terry, Milton S. *Biblical Hermeneutics.* 1883; rpt. Grand Rapids: Zondervan Publishing House, n.d.

Webster, William. *The Syntax and Synonyms of the Greek Testament.* London: Rivingtons, 1864.

Westcott, Brooke Foss. *The Epistle to the Hebrews.* Grand Rapids: Eerdmans, 1889.

———. *The Epistles of St. John.* Grand Rapids: Eerdmans, 1883.

———. *The Gospel According to John.* Grand Rapids: Eerdmans, 1881.

Wuest, Kenneth S. *The Practical Use of the Greek New Testament.* Chicago: Moody, 1946.

———. *Studies in the Vocabulary of the Greek New Testament.* Grand Rapids: Eerdmans, 1945.

Zimmerli, Walther, and Joachim Jeremias. *The Servant of God.* London: SCM, 1957.

E. The Literary Sources

Aeschylus. *Works.* Loeb Classical Library. 2 vols. London: Heinemann, 1926–27.

The Apostolic Fathers. Loeb Classical Library. 2 vols. London: Heinemann, 1950–59.

Aratus. *Phaenomina.* Loeb Classical Library. London: Heinemann, 1955.

Aristophanes. *Works.* Loeb Classical Library. 3 vols. London: Heinemann, 1927.

Aristotle. *The "Art" of Rhetoric.* Loeb Classical Library. London: Heinemann, 1959.

———. *The Athenian Constitution, The Eudemian Ethics.* Loeb Classical Library. London: Heinemann, 1938.

———. *Minor Works.* Loeb Classical Library. London: Heinemann, 1936.

———. *The Nicomachean Ethics.* Loeb Classical Library. London: Heinemann, 1956.

Chrysostom. *Patrologiae Cursus Completus.* Series Graeca prior. Ed. J. P. Migne. Vol. 62. Parisiorum: D'Enfer, 1862.

Dionysius of Halicarnassus. *The Roman Antiquities.* Loeb Classical Library. 7 vols. London: Heinemann, 1948–50.

Euripides. *Works.* Loeb Classical Library. 4 vols. London: Heinemann, 1924–25.

Herodotus. *Histories.* Loeb Classical Library. 4 vols. London: Heinemann, 1960–63.

Homer. *The Iliad.* Loeb Classical Library. 2 vols. London: Heinemann, 1928–29.

———. *The Odyssey.* Loeb Classical Library. 2 vols. London: Heinemann, 1960.
Menander. *The Principal Fragments.* Loeb Classical Library. London: Heinemann, 1930.
Nestle, Eberhard, Edwin Nestle, and Kurt Aland. *Novum Testamentum Graece.* 25th ed. Stuttgart: Privileg. Wurtt. Bibelanstalt, 1963.
The Oxyrhynchus Papyri. Ed. Bernard P. Grenfell and Arthur S. Hunt. 13 vols. London: Egypt Exploration Fund, 1898.
Philo. *Works.* Loeb Classical Library. London: Heinemann, 1950.
Plato. *Cratylus, Parmenides.* Loeb Classical Library. London: Heinemann, 1939.
———. *Lysis, Symposium, Gorgias.* Loeb Classical Library. London: Heinemann, 1939.
———. *Phaedrus.* Loeb Classical Library. London: Heinemann, 1960.
———. *The Republic.* Ed. James Adam. 2nd edition. 2 vols. Cambridge: Cambridge Univ. Press, 1963.
———. *The Statesman, Philebus.* Loeb Classical Library. London: Heinemann, 1942.
Rahlfs, Alfred. *Septuaginta.* 2 vols. Stuttgart: Privilegierte Württembergische Bibelanstalt, 1935.
Sophocles. *Works.* Loeb Classical Library. 2 vols. London: Heinemann, 1924.
Thucydides. *History of the Peloponnesian War.* Loeb Classical Library. 4 vols. London: Heinemann, 1930–35.
Xenophon. *Cyropaedia.* Loeb Classical Library. 2 vols. London: Heinemann, 1943.
———. *Hellenica, Anabasis, Apology.* Loeb Classical Library. 3 vols. London: Heinemann, 1930.
———. *Memorabilia and Oeconomicus.* Loeb Classical Library. London: Heinemann, 1923.

F. English Translations

Else, Gerald F., trans. *Aristotle's Poetics: The Argument.* Cambridge, Mass.: Harvard Univ. Press, 1957.
Fitzgerald, Robert, trans. *Homer: The Odyssey.* New York: Doubleday, 1961.
Grene, David, and Richmond Lattimore, eds. *Aeschylus.* Chicago: Univ. of Chicago Press, 1959.
———. *Euripides.* 2 vols. Chicago: Univ. of Chicago Press, 1959.
———. *Sophocles.* Chicago: Univ. of Chicago Press, 1959.

BIBLIOGRAPHY

Jowett, Benjamin, trans. *The Dialogues of Plato.* 2 vols. New York: Random House, 1920.

———, trans. *Thucydides.* 2 vols. Oxford: Clarendon, 1900.

Lattimore, Richmond, trans. *Homer: The Iliad.* Chicago: Univ. of Chicago Press, 1951.

Rawlinson, George, trans. *Herodotus: The History of Herodotus.* 2 vols. London: Dent, 1910.

G. Periodicals

Adriani, Nico. "Some Principles of Bible Translation," *The Bible Translator,* 14 (Jan. 1963), 9–13.

Jones, Douglas. "ἀνάμνησις in the LXX and the Interpretation of I Cor. 11:25," *Journal of Theological Studies,* NS, 6 (Oct. 1955), 183–91.

Marshall, Alfred. "This Question of 'Synonyms,'" *The Bible Translator,* 10 (July 1959), 121–23.

Reumann, John. "'Stewards of God'—Pre-Christian Religious Application of οἰκονόμος in Greek," *Journal of Biblical Literature,* 77 (Dec. 1958), 339–49.

Stoessel, Horace. "Notes on Romans 12:1–2," *Interpretation,* 17 (April 1963), 161–75.

Toussaint, Stanley D. "A Method of Making a New Testament Word Study," *Bibliotheca Sacra,* 120 (Jan.–March 1963), 35–41.

Zuck, Roy B. "Greek Words for Teach," *Bibliotheca Sacra,* 122 (April–June 1965), 158–68.

Index of Greek Words

	page		page
ἀγαθός	14	κτήματα	24
ἀγρυπνέω	132	κυβεία	72
ἀγωνίζομαι	117	λόγος	78
ἀλείφω	83	μάχαιρα	69
ἀνάμνησις	37	μεθοδεία	72
ἀνάπαυσις	40	μεριμνάω	125
ἀπατάω	93	νήφω	133
ἀποκρίνομαι	86	νουθετέω	122
ἀποστέλλω	114	νοῦς	57
βάρος	1	ξένος	62
βεβαιόω	97	ὄγκος	3
βία	27	οἶδα	108
βροχή	35	οἰκονόμος	21
γινώσκω	106	ὄμβρος	35
γρηγορέω	131	παῖς θεοῦ	54
δαιμόνιον	7	πανουργία	73
δαίμων	6	παραλογίζομαι	94
διάβολος	5	παρεπίδημος	64
διδάσκω	121	πάροικος	63
δικαιοσύνη	46	πέμπω	113
δικαίωμα	43	πηγή	76
δικαίωσις	45	πίμπλημι	102
δόξα	9	πλανάω	95
δύναμις	28	πληρόω	103
ἐνέργεια	32	πνεῦμα	58
ἐξουσία	31	ποταμός	49
ἔπαινος	10	ῥῆμα	81
ἐπίσταμαι	111	ῥιζόομαι	99
ἐπίτροπος	20	ῥομφαία	70
ἐριθεία	67	στηρίζω	100
ἔρις	66	σωφρονίζω	122
θεμελιόω	98	τελειόω	90
ἰσχύς	30	τηρέω	127
καιρός	xiv	τιμή	12
καλός	16	ὑετός	34
καρδία	56	υἱὸς θεοῦ	52
κατάπαυσις	41	ὑπάρξεις	25
καταρτίζω	89	ὑπολαμβάνω	87
κοπιάω	118	ὑπόμνησις	38
κράτος	29	φορτίον	2

INDEX OF GREEK WORDS

φρέαρ 75
φροντίζω 124
φρουρέω 130
φυλάσσω 128

ψυχή 60
χείμαρρος 50
χρίω 84
χρόνος xiv